Valuation of Fixed Income Securities and Derivatives

Third Edition

Frank J. Fabozzi, CFA
Adjunct Professor of Finance
School of Management
Yale University

JOHN WILEY & SONS

To my wife Donna
and my son Francesco Alfonso

ISBN: 1-883249-25-2

Printed in the United States of America.

10 9 8 7 6 5 4 3 2

Table of Contents

Preface

Today's fixed income market includes securities with complex structures and derivative instruments resulting in a wide-range of risk/return relationships. The purpose of *Valuation of Fixed Income Securities and Derivatives* is to provide a framework for properly valuing any fixed income product. The valuation framework takes into account the term structure of interest rates and the value of any embedded options. The framework relies on state-of-the-art technology for valuing interest rate options. The two valuation methodologies described in this book are the binomial method and the Monte Carlo simulation method. Applications of these methodologies to valuing callable and putable bonds, step-up notes, range notes, mortgage-backed securities (particularly, collateralized mortgage obligations), asset-backed securities, inverse floating-rate securities, and convertible bonds are provided. The principles discussed in the book are also applied to value interest rate futures, options on fixed income securities, futures options, interest rate swaps, and interest rate caps and floors.

I am grateful to several individuals who have assisted me in various stages of this project. First, Bill McLellan was kind enough to read the entire third edition. He not only pointed out errors and inconsistencies in the illustrations, but also built spreadsheets to verify many of the calculations. While all remaining errors in this book are mine, there would have been a good number more had it not been for Bill's efforts.

Andrew Kalotay (Andrew Kalotay Associates), George Williams, and Martin Czigler provided helpful comments on Chapters 6 and 7. Andrew Kalotay associates furnished the software used to generate the illustrations in those two chapters. Yu Zhu and Mihir Bhattacharya commented on Chapter 11 and provided the information for one of the illustrations. Several of the illustrations in Chapter 8 are drawn from my work with Scott Richard (Miller, Anderson & Sherrerd). I am grateful to Phil Galdi (Merrill Lynch) for providing the data points for some of the illustrations in Chapter 2 and Tom Macirowski (Goldman Sachs) for furnishing the information on the credit term structure of interest rates reported in Chapter 2.

I have benefited from discussions with Cliff Asness (Goldman Sachs Asset Management), Anand Bhattacharya (Prudential Securities), Gifford Fong (Gifford Fong Associates), Frank Jones (The Guardian Life), Jan Mayle (TIPS), Franco Modigliani (MIT), and Scott Pinkus (Goldman Sachs).

Frank J. Fabozzi

Index of Advertisers

Chapter 1

Fundamental Valuation Principles

The objectives of this chapter are to:

1. explain what is meant by the cash flows of a financial asset;

2. discuss the process involved in valuing a fixed income security;

3. explain the situations in which determination of the cash flows of a fixed income security is complex;

4. review the provisions that allow the cash flows to be altered by either the issuer or the investor;

5. explain why a fixed income security should be viewed as a package of zero-coupon securities;

6. review risk measures associated with investing in fixed income securities; and,

7. explain the role of valuation in deriving risk measures.

Valuation is the process of determining the fair value of a financial asset. The process is also referred to as "valuing" or "pricing" a financial asset. The fundamental principle of valuation is that the value of any financial asset is the present value of the expected cash flows. This principle applies regardless of the financial asset. Consequently, it applies equally to common stock, preferred stock, a bond, a mortgage loan, and real estate.

ESTIMATING CASH FLOWS

Cash flow is simply the cash that is expected to be received at some time from an investment. In the case of a fixed income security, it does not make any difference whether the cash flow is interest income or repayment of principal. The cash flows of a security are the collection of each period's cash flow.

Holding aside the risk of default, the cash flows for only a few fixed income securities are simple to project. Noncallable Treasury securities have known cash flows. For a Treasury coupon security, the cash flows are the coupon interest payments every six months up to the maturity date and the principal payment at the maturity date. So, for example, the cash flows per $100 of par value for a 7% 10-year Treasury security are $3.5 (7%/2 × $100) every six months for the next 20 six-month periods and $100 20 six-month periods from now. Or, equivalently, the cash flows are $3.5 every six months for the next 19 six-month periods and $103.50 20 six-month periods from now.

The issuer of a bond agrees to repay the principal by the stated maturity date. The issuer can agree to repay the entire amount borrowed in one lump sum payment at the maturity date. That is, the issuer is not required to make any principal repayments prior to the maturity date. Such bonds are said to have a *bullet maturity*.

Fixed income securities backed by pools of loans (mortgage-backed securities and asset-backed securities) often have a schedule of principal repayments. Such fixed income securities are said to be *amortizing securities*. For many loans, the payments are structured so that when the last loan payment is made, the entire amount owed is fully paid off.

Another example of an amortizing feature is a bond that has a sinking fund provision. This provision for repayment of a bond may be designed to liquidate all of an issue by the maturity date, or it may be arranged to repay only a part of the total by the maturity date.

For any fixed income security in which neither the issuer/borrower nor the investor can alter the repayment of the principal before its contractual due date, the cash flows can easily be determined assuming that the issuer does not default. Difficulty in determining a security's cash flows arises under the following circumstances:

1. either the issuer or the investor has the option to change the contractual due date of the repayment of the principal;
2. the coupon payment is reset periodically based on some reference rate and there are restrictions on the new coupon rate (that is, there is a cap or a floor); or,
3. the investor has an option to convert the fixed income security to an equity issue.

Provisions for Altering Principal Repayment

Many non-Treasury securities include a provision in the indenture that grants the issuer or the security holder the right to change the scheduled date or dates when the principal repayment is due. Assuming that the issuer does not default, the investor knows that the amount borrowed will be repaid, but does not know when the principal repayments will be received. Because of this, the cash flows — which include principal repayment and coupon interest payments — are not known with certainty.

The four most common provisions in fixed income securities that allow for the altering of the principal repayment date are described below.

Call and Refunding Provisions in Bond Indentures

An important question in negotiating the terms of a new bond issue is whether the issuer shall have the right to redeem the bonds outstanding before the maturity date. Issuers generally want this right because they recognize that at some time in the future the general level of interest rates may fall sufficiently below the issue's coupon rate, so redeeming the issue and replacing it with another issue with a lower coupon rate would be attractive. This right is a disadvantage to the bondholder.

The right of the issuer to retire the issue prior to the stated maturity date is referred to as a *call option*. If an issuer exercises this right, the issuer is said to "call the bond." Thus, a call provision is an "embedded option" granted to the issuer. By an embedded option we mean an option that is part of the structure of a bond, as opposed to a bare option, which trades separately from an underlying security.

The price which the issuer must pay to retire the issue is referred to as the *call price*. Typically, there is not one call price but a call schedule which sets forth a call price based on when the issuer can exercise the call option.

When a bond is issued, typically the issuer may not call the bond for a number of years. That is, the issue is said to have a *deferred call*. The date at which the bond may first be called is referred to as the *first call date*. Not all issues have a deferred call. That is, an issue may be immediately callable.

Bonds can be called in whole (the entire issue) or in part (only a portion). When less than the entire issue is called, the specific bonds to be called are selected randomly or on a pro rata basis. When bonds are selected randomly, the serial number of the certificates called is published in *The Wall Street Journal* and major metropolitan dailies.

Call Schedule Generally, the call schedule is such that the call price at the first call date is a premium over the par value and scaled down to the par value over time. The date at which the issue is first callable at par value is referred to as the *first par call date*. For example, the Becton Dickinson & Co. 8.70s due 1/15/2025 was issued on 1/10/95. The first par call date is 1/15/2015. Thus, at issuance this corporate bond had a 10-year deferred call. The call schedule for this issue is as follows:

If redeemed during the 12 months beginning January 15:	Call price
2005	103.949
2006	103.554
2007	103.159
2008	102.764
2009	102.369
2010	101.975
2011	101.580
2012	101.185
2013	100.790
2014	100.395
2015 and thereafter	100.000

The $150 million Anheuser Busch Company 8⅝s due 12/1/2016 issued 11/20/1986 also had a 10-year deferred call and the following call schedule:

If redeemed during the 12 months beginning December 1:	Call price
1996	104.313
1997	103.881
1998	103.450
1999	103.019
2000	102.588
2001	102.156
2002	101.725
2003	101.294
2004	100.863
2005	100.431
2006 and thereafter	100.000

Not all issues have a call schedule in which the call price starts out as a premium over par. There are issues where the call price at the first call date and subsequent call dates is par value. In such cases, the first call date is the same as the first par call date. For example, the first par call date for the U.S. Treasury 12¾s due 11/15/2010 issued on 11/07/1980 is 11/15/2005 and this date is the first call date. The first call date for the $250 million J.C. Penney 9.45s due 7/15/2002 issued on 7/16/1990 is 7/15/2000 at which time the issue is callable at par value.

Regular versus Special Redemption Prices The call prices for the various issues cited above are called the *regular* or *general redemption prices*. There are also *special redemption prices* for debt redeemed through the sinking fund and through other provisions, and the proceeds from the confiscation of property through the right of eminent domain. The special redemption price is usually par value, but in the case of some utility issues it initially may be the public offering price, which is amortized down to par value (if a premium) over the life of the bonds.

Noncallable versus Nonrefundable Bonds If a bond issue does not have any protection against early call, then it is said to be a *currently callable issue*. But most new bond issues, even if currently callable, usually have some restrictions against certain types of early redemption. The most common restriction is that prohibiting the refunding of the bonds for a certain number of years. *Refunding* a bond issue means redeeming bonds with funds obtained through the sale of a new bond issue.

Many investors are confused by the terms noncallable and nonrefundable. Call protection is much more absolute than refunding protection. While there may be certain exceptions to absolute or complete call protection in some cases, it still provides greater assurance against premature and unwanted redemption than does refunding protection. Refunding prohibition merely prevents redemption only from certain sources of funds, namely the proceeds of other debt issues sold at a lower cost of money. The bondholder is only protected if interest rates decline, and the borrower can obtain lower-cost money to pay off the debt.

Beginning in early 1986 a number of industrial companies issued long-term debt with extended call protection, not refunding protection. A number are noncallable for the issue's life such as Dow Chemical Company's 8⅝s due in 2006 and Atlantic Richfield's 9⅞s due in 2016. The prospectuses for both issues expressly prohibit redemption prior to maturity. These noncallable-for-life issues are referred to as *bullet bonds*. Other issues carry 15 years of call protection, such as Eastman Kodak's 9.95s due 7/1/2018 and not callable prior to 7/1/2003.

Accelerated Sinking Fund Provisions in Bond Indentures

An indenture may require the issuer to retire a specified portion of an issue each year. This is referred to as a *sinking fund requirement*. The alleged purpose of the sinking fund provision is to reduce credit risk. This kind of provision for repayment of debt may be designed to liquidate all of a bond issue by the maturity date, or it may be arranged to pay only a part of the total by the end of the term. If only a part is paid, the remainder is called a *balloon maturity*.

The following two issues are examples of issues that will be paid off by the sinking fund requirement by the maturity date. The $150 million Ingersoll Rand 7.20s issue due 6/1/2025 and issued on 6/5/1995 has a sinking fund schedule that begins on 6/1/2006. Each year the issuer must retire $7.5 million. The $125 million May Department Store 9¾s issue due 2/15/2021 issued on 2/12/1991 has a sinking fund that begins 8/15/2001. Every six months (8/15 and 2/15) this issuer must retire $3.125 million.

Generally, the issuer may satisfy the sinking fund requirement by either (1) making a cash payment of the face amount of the bonds to be retired to the trustee, who then calls the bonds for redemption using a lottery, or (2) delivering to the trustee bonds purchased in the open market that have a total par value equal to the amount that must be retired. If the bonds are retired using the first method, interest payments stop at the redemption date.

Usually, the periodic payments required for sinking fund purposes will be the same for each period. A few indentures might permit variable periodic payments, where payments change according to certain prescribed conditions set forth in the indenture. Many indentures include a provision that grants the issuer the option to retire more than the amount stipulated for sinking fund retirement. This is referred to as an *accelerated sinking fund provision*. For example, the Anheuser Busch 8⅝s due 12/1/2016 whose call schedule was presented earlier has a sinking fund requirement of $7.5 million per annum beginning on 12/1/1997. The issuer is permitted to retire up to $15 million each year.

Usually the sinking fund call price is the par value if the bonds were originally sold at par. When issued at a price in excess of par, the call price generally starts at the issuance price and scales down to par as the issue approaches maturity.

There is a difference between the amortizing feature for a bond with a sinking fund provision, and the regularly scheduled principal repayment for a mortgage-backed and an asset-backed security. The owner of a mortgage-backed security and an asset-backed security knows that assuming no default that there will be principal repayments. In contrast, the owner of a bond with a sinking fund provision is not assured that his or her particular holding will be called to satisfy the sinking fund requirement.

Put Provision in Bond Indentures

An issue with a put provision included in the indenture grants the bondholder the right to sell the issue back to the issuer at a specified price on designated dates. The specified price is called the *put price*. Typically, a bond is putable at par if it is issued at or close to par value. For a zero-coupon bond, the put price is below par.

The advantage of the put provision to the bondholder is that if after the issue date market rates rise above the issue's coupon rate, the bondholder can force the issuer to redeem the bond at the put price and then reinvest the proceeds at the prevailing higher rate.

An example of a putable bond is the American Brands Inc. 9s due 6/15/1999 issued on 6/12/1989. This issue is putable at par value (the put price) beginning 6/15/1994. Another example is the Baker Hughes Inc. zero-coupon bond issued on 4/28/1993. This issue is putable on 5/5/1998 at 70.683 and 5/5/2003 at 84.073. The initial offering price for this issue was 58.088. As can be seen from the Baker Hughes Inc. issue, an issue can be putable and callable.

Prepayments

For amortizing securities that are backed by loans and have a schedule of principal repayments, individual borrowers typically have the option to pay off all or part of their loan prior to the scheduled date. Any principal repayment prior to the scheduled date is called a *prepayment*. The right of borrowers to prepay is called the *prepayment option*.

Basically, the prepayment option is the same as a call option. However, unlike a call option, there is not a call price that depends on when the borrower pays off the issue. Typically, the price at which a loan is prepaid is par value.

Note that in all but the put provision, the option to alter the principal repayment schedule rests with the issuer/borrower. The put provision allows the investor to alter the scheduled principal repayment date. Also it should be noted that the exercise of an option to change the cash flow will depend on the prevailing market interest rate relative to the interest rate paid by the borrower. Consequently, the valuation of securities with any of the embedded options described above must take into account future interest rates.

Floating-Rate Securities

The coupon rate on a bond need not be fixed over the issue's life. Floating-rate securities, sometimes called variable-rate securities, have coupon payments that reset periodically according to some reference rate. The typical coupon formula is:

Reference rate + Index spread

The *index spread* is the additional amount that the issuer agrees to pay above the reference rate. For example, suppose that the reference rate is the 1-month London interbank offered rate (LIBOR) and that the index spread is 100 basis points. Then the coupon formula is:

1-month LIBOR + 100 basis points

So, if 1-month LIBOR on the coupon reset date is 5%, the coupon rate is reset for that period at 6% (5% plus 100 basis points).

The index spread need not be a positive value. The index spread could be subtracted from the reference rate. For example, the reference rate could be the yield on a 5-year Treasury security and the coupon rate could reset every six months based on the following coupon formula:

5-year Treasury yield – 90 basis points

So, if the 5-year Treasury yield is 7% on the coupon reset date, the coupon rate is 6.1% (7% minus 90 basis points).

The reference rate for most floating-rate securities is an interest rate or an interest rate index. There are some issues where this is not the case. Instead, the reference rate is some financial index such as the return on the Standard & Poor's 500 or a nonfinancial index such as the price of a commodity. Through financial engineering, issuers have been able to structure floating-rate securities with almost any reference rate. In several countries, there are government bonds whose coupon formula is tied to an inflation index. In 1997 the U.S. government began issuing such bonds.

Caps and Floors

A floating-rate security may have a restriction on the maximum coupon rate that will be paid at a reset date. The maximum coupon rate is called a *cap*. For example, suppose for our hypothetical floating-rate security whose coupon rate formula is 1-month LIBOR plus 100 basis points, there is a cap of 11%. If 1-month LIBOR is 10.5% at a coupon reset date, then the coupon rate formula would give a value of 11.5%. However, the cap restricts the coupon rate to 11%. Thus, for our hypothetical security, once 1-month LIBOR exceeds 10%, the coupon rate is capped at 11%.

Because a cap restricts the coupon rate from increasing, a cap is an unattractive feature for the investor. In contrast, there could be a minimum coupon rate specified for a floating-rate security. The minimum coupon rate is called a *floor*. If the coupon formula produces a coupon rate that is below the floor, the floor is paid instead. Thus, a floor is an attractive feature for the investor.

Effectively, caps and floors are options. In the case of a cap, the security holder effectively sold an option to the issuer specifying that if the coupon reset rate based on the formula is above a specified rate, the security holder has to compensate the issuer by accepting the maximum coupon rate. For a floor, the issuer effectively sold an option to the security holder specifying that if the coupon reset rate based on the formula is below a specified rate, the issuer has to compensate the security holder by paying the minimum coupon rate. Thus, just as the provisions described earlier for altering the principal repayment can be viewed as embedded options, cap and floor provisions are also embedded options.

Inverse Floaters

Typically, the coupon formula on floating-rate securities is such that the coupon rate increases when the reference rate increases, and decreases when the reference rate decreases. There are issues whose coupon rate moves in the opposite direction from the change in the reference rate. Such issues are called *inverse floaters* or *reverse floaters*. A general formula for an inverse floater is:

$$K - L \times (\text{Reference rate})$$

For example, suppose that for a particular inverse floater K is 12% and L is 1. Then the coupon formula would be:

$$12\% - \text{Reference rate}$$

Suppose that the reference rate is 1-month LIBOR, then the coupon formula would be

12% − 1-month LIBOR

If in some month 1-month LIBOR at the coupon reset date is 5%, the coupon rate for the period is 7%. If in the next month 1-month LIBOR declines to 4.5%, the coupon rate increases to 7.5%.

Notice that if 1-month LIBOR exceeded 12%, then the coupon formula would produce a negative coupon rate. To prevent this, there is a floor imposed on the coupon rate. Typically, the floor is zero. There is a cap on the inverse floater. This occurs if 1-month LIBOR is zero. In that unlikely event, the maximum coupon rate is 12% for our hypothetical inverse floater. In general, it will be the value of K in the coupon formula for an inverse floater.

Range Notes

A range note is a floating-rate security whose coupon rate is equal to the reference rate as long as the reference rate is within a certain range at the reset date. If the reference rate is outside of the range, the coupon rate is zero for that period.

For example, a 3-year range note might specify that the reference rate is 1-year LIBOR and that the coupon rate resets every year. The coupon rate for the year will be 1-year LIBOR as long as 1-year LIBOR at the coupon reset date falls within the range as specified below:

	Year 1	Year 2	Year 3
Lower limit of range	4.5%	5.25%	6.00%
Upper limit of range	5.5%	6.75%	7.50%

If 1-year LIBOR is outside of the range, the coupon rate is zero. For example, if in Year 1 1-year LIBOR is 5% at the coupon reset date, the coupon rate for the year is 5%. However, if 1-year LIBOR is 6%, the coupon rate for the year is zero since 1-year LIBOR is greater than the upper limit for Year 1 of 5.5%.

Conversion or Exchange Provision

The conversion provision grants the security holder the right to convert the security into some financial asset or commodity either at any time during the life of the security or only at the maturity date. For example, a bond may be exchangeable into two ounces of gold at the maturity date. The more common type of conversion provision is one in which the investor has the right to convert the security into a predetermined number of shares of common stock of the issuer. A convertible security is therefore a security with an embedded call option to buy the common stock of the issuer. An *exchangeable security* grants the security holder the right to exchange the security for the common stock of a firm *other* than the issuer of the security.

Because there is uncertainty about the future value of the underlying stock into which the investor may convert, the cash flows of a convertible security are not known with certainty. Also, these securities are typically callable and some are putable which makes the estimation of a convertible security's cash flows even more complicated.

Cash Flows and Interest Rate Volatility

In our description of embedded options, a key factor that determines whether either the issuer of the security or the investor would exercise an option is the level of interest rates in the future relative to the security's coupon rate. Specifically, for a callable bond, if the prevailing market rate at which the issuer can refund an issue is sufficiently below the issue's coupon rate to justify the costs associated with refunding the issue, the issuer is likely to call the issue. Similarly, for a mortgage loan, if the refinancing rate available in the mortgage market is sufficiently below the loan's mortgage rate so that there will be savings by refinancing after considering the associated refinancing costs, then the homeowner has an incentive to refinance. For a putable bond, if the rate on comparable securities rises such that the value of the putable bond falls below the value at which it must be repurchased by the issuer, then the investor will put the issue.

What this means is that to properly estimate the cash flows of a fixed income security it is necessary to incorporate into the analysis how interest rates can change in the future and how such changes affect the cash flows. As we will see in later chapters, this is done in valuation models by introducing a parameter that reflects the volatility of interest rates.

DISCOUNTING THE CASH FLOWS

Once the cash flows for a fixed income security are estimated, the next step is to determine the appropriate interest rate at which to discount those cash flows. To determine the appropriate rate, the investor must address the following three questions:

1. What is the minimum interest rate the investor should require?
2. How much more than the minimum interest rate should the investor require?
3. Should the investor use the same interest rate for each estimated cash flow or a unique interest rate for the estimated cash flow of each period?

The minimum interest rate that an investor should require is the yield available in the marketplace on a default-free cash flow. In the U.S., this is the yield on a U.S. Treasury security. The premium over the yield on a Treasury security that the investor should require should reflect the risks associated with realizing the estimated cash flow. Below we address the third question.

Exhibit 1: Cash Flows for Three 10-Year Hypothetical Treasury Securities Per $100 of Par Value
(Each period is six months)

Period	12% coupon	8% coupon	0% coupon
1	$6	$4	$0
2	6	4	0
3	6	4	0
4	6	4	0
5	6	4	0
6	6	4	0
7	6	4	0
8	6	4	0
9	6	4	0
10	6	4	0
11	6	4	0
12	6	4	0
13	6	4	0
14	6	4	0
15	6	4	0
16	6	4	0
17	6	4	0
18	6	4	0
19	6	4	0
20	106	104	100

Traditional Valuation Approach

The traditional practice in valuation has been to discount every cash flow of a fixed income security by the same interest rate (or discount rate). For example, consider the three hypothetical 10-year Treasury securities shown in Exhibit 1: a 12% coupon bond, an 8% coupon bond, and a zero-coupon bond. The cash flows for each security are shown in the exhibit. Since the cash flows of all three securities are viewed as default free, the traditional practice is to use the same discount rate to calculate the present value of all three securities and the same discount rate for the cash flow for each period.

Contemporary Approach

The fundamental flaw of the traditional approach is that it views each security as the same package of cash flows. For example, consider a 10-year U.S. Treasury bond with an 8% coupon rate. The cash flows per $100 of par value would be 19 payments of $4 every six months and $104 20 six-month periods from now. The traditional practice would discount the cash flow for all 20 periods using the same interest rate.

The proper way to view the 10-year 8% coupon bond is as a package of zero-coupon instruments. Each period's cash flow should be considered a zero-coupon instrument whose maturity value is the amount of the cash flow and whose maturity date is the payment date of the cash flow. Thus, the 10-year 8% coupon bond should be viewed as 20 zero-coupon instruments. The reason that this is the proper way is because it does not allow a market participant to realize an arbitrage profit. This will be made clearer in the next chapter.

By viewing any financial asset in this way, a consistent valuation framework can be developed. For example, under the traditional approach to the valuation of fixed income securities, a 10-year zero-coupon bond would be viewed as the same financial asset as a 10-year 8% coupon bond. Viewing a financial asset as a package of zero-coupon instruments means that these two bonds would be viewed as different packages of zero-coupon instruments and valued accordingly.

The difference between the traditional valuation approach and the contemporary approach is depicted in Exhibit 2 which shows how the three bonds whose cash flows are depicted in Exhibit 1 should be valued. With the traditional approach, the minimum interest rate for all three securities is the yield on a 10-year U.S. Treasury security. With the contemporary approach the minimum yield for a cash flow is the theoretical rate that the U.S. Treasury would have to pay if it issued a zero-coupon bond with a maturity date equal to the maturity date of the estimated cash flow.

Exhibit 2: Comparison of Traditional Approach and Contemporary Approach in Valuing a Bond
(Each period is six months)

| | Discount (Interest) Rate | | Treasury Security (coupon) | | |
| | Traditional Approach | Contemporary Approach | | | |
Period	(Treasury rate)	(spot rate)	12%	8%	0%
1	10-year	1-period	$6	$40	$0
2	10-year	2-period	6	4	0
3	10-year	3-period	6	4	0
4	10-year	4-period	6	4	0
5	10-year	5-period	6	4	0
6	10-year	6-period	6	4	0
7	10-year	7-period	6	4	0
8	10-year	8-period	6	4	0
9	10-year	9-period	6	4	0
10	10-year	10-period	6	4	0
11	10-year	11-period	6	4	0
12	10-year	12-period	6	4	0
13	10-year	13-period	6	4	0
14	10-year	14-period	6	4	0
15	10-year	15-period	6	4	0
16	10-year	16-period	6	4	0
17	10-year	17-period	6	4	0
18	10-year	18-period	6	4	0
19	10-year	19-period	6	4	0
20	10-year	20-period	106	104	100

Therefore, to implement the contemporary approach it is necessary to determine the theoretical rate that the U.S. Treasury would have to pay to issue a zero-coupon instrument for each maturity. Another name used for the zero-coupon rate is the *spot rate*. As explained in the next chapter, the spot rate can be estimated from the Treasury yield curve.

RISK MEASURES

Investors are not only interested in determining the fair value of a fixed income security but also the identification of the risks inherent with investing in a security. There are several types of risk associated with investing in a security. One risk is credit or default risk. This risk can be gauged by the rating assigned by one or more of the four commercial rating companies — Standard & Poor's, Moody's Investors Service, Fitch Investors Service, and Duff & Phelps Credit Company.

Another key risk measure is the price sensitivity of a fixed income security to changes in interest rates. This measure is popularly referred to as *duration*. The duration of any fixed income security is measured by changing interest rates up and down by a small number of basis points and determining how the value of the security changes. To determine what the value of a security would be if interest rates change, it is necessary to have a valuation model. Thus duration is a by-product of a valuation model. If the valuation model used to value a fixed income security is poor, the resulting duration measure will also be a poor measure of the price sensitivity of a security to changes in interest rates.

A drawback of duration is that it is a measure of the price sensitivity of a security assuming the interest rate for all maturities change by the same number of basis points. But as explained earlier, each cash flow should be discounted at its own unique discount rate. Thus, a security's price may be highly sensitive to a change in interest rates that is not the same for all maturity levels. Using a valuation model that recognizes that each cash flow should be discounted at its own unique discount rate, the price sensitivity of a security to changes in interest rates that are not the same for each maturity can be determined.

OVERVIEW OF BOOK

The discussion in this chapter has provided a bird's eye view of the principles of the valuation of fixed income securities. The 15 chapters to follow provide more detailed information about the valuation process.

The valuation process begins with estimation of the theoretical Treasury spot rate or zero-coupon rate for each maturity. It is these rates that are the benchmark or minimum interest rates that should be used to discount a security's estimated cash flows. Chapter 2 describes this process and shows how the theoretical Treasury spot rates should be used in the valuation of any security.

The theoretical spot rates are related to forward rates. Forward rates are viewed as the market's consensus of future interest rates. In Chapter 3 we explain forward rates, how they can be determined, and their relationship to spot rates. Valuing a security using spot rates or forward rates will produce the same value for a security. As we noted, modeling of future interest rates is essential to valuing fixed income securities with embedded options because of the effect that future rates have on cash flows. Most valuation models model short-term rates. This is done by assuming that short rates follow a certain stochastic process. This more technical phase of the valuation process is described in the appendix to Chapter 3.

A byproduct of the valuation process is the price sensitivity of a fixed income security to interest rate changes. In Chapter 4 we describe two popular measures of duration, modified duration (or its sister measure, Macaulay duration) and effective duration. We note in that chapter that the former may be of limited value for security's with embedded options.

In Chapter 5, we explain how a fixed income security with an embedded option should be viewed conceptually. There we argue that the value of such securities will depend on the value of the embedded option. Consequently, it is important to understand the factors that affect the value of an option. These factors are described in Chapter 5.

There are two valuation methods that are commonly used to value fixed income securities with embedded options: binomial model and Monte Carlo model. A byproduct of these models is the option-adjusted spread (OAS). In Chapter 5 we explain what this measure is. It is important to note that the OAS is not a new technology for valuing securities. That is, it is not a valuation model as it is often referred to by market participants. Instead, it is a measure that is derived from one of the two valuation methods.

The two valuation models are explained and illustrated in Chapters 6, 7, and 8. In Chapter 6 the binomial model is explained and applied to the valuation of callable corporate and agency debenture securities. In Chapter 7, the binomial model is used to value other corporate and agency debentures with embedded options. The Monte Carlo model is the subject of Chapter 8. This model is commonly used to value mortgage-backed securities. For each model, the procedure for calculating the OAS and effective duration is explained.

In Chapter 9, we explain the principles for valuing asset-backed securities. The valuation of inverse floating-rate securities is provided in Chapter 10. In Chapter 11, we explain the state-of-the-art technology for valuing convertible securities.

Chapters 12, 13, 14, and 15 cover interest rate derivative contracts. These contracts include futures (Chapter 12), options (Chapter 13), swaps (Chapter 14), and caps and floors (Chapter 15). A basic description of each contract is provided. Then, a valuation framework is presented for each contract.

Throughout the book we emphasize the importance of the interest rate volatility assumption in the valuation of securities with embedded options. In the final chapter, Chapter 16, we explain how to estimate historical yield volatility.

KEY POINTS

1. *Valuation is the process of determining the fair value of a financial asset.*

2. *The fundamental principle of valuation is that the value of any financial asset is the present value of the expected cash flows.*

3. *The cash flow for some period is the cash that is expected to be received that period from an investment.*

4. *For any fixed income security in which neither the issuer nor the investor can alter the repayment of the principal before its contractual due date, the cash flows can easily be determined assuming that the issuer does not default.*

5. *The difficulty in determining the cash flows arises for securities where either the issuer or the investor can alter the cash flows.*

6. *An embedded option is an option that is part of the structure of a bond, as opposed to a bare option, which trades separately from an underlying security.*

7. *Many non-Treasury securities include an embedded option, a provision that grants the issuer or the investor the right to change the scheduled date or dates when the principal repayment is due.*

8. *The four most common provisions in fixed income securities that allow for the altering of the principal repayment are call and refunding provisions, accelerated sinking fund provisions, put provisions, and prepayment provisions in mortgage loans.*

9. *For all but the put provision, the option to alter the principal repayment schedule rests with the issuer/borrower.*

10. *The cash flows for a floating-rate security are not known because the future values of the reference rate are unknown.*

11. *The cash flows for a convertible security are unknown because the investor has the right to convert the security into some financial asset or commodity either at any time during the life of the security or only at the maturity date.*

12. *A key factor that determines whether either the borrower or the investor would exercise an option is the level of interest rates in the future relative to the security's coupon rate.*

13. *To estimate the cash flows of a fixed income security it is necessary to incorporate into the analysis how interest rates can change in the future and how such changes affect the security's cash flows.*

14. *The traditional practice in the valuation of a fixed income security has been to discount every period's cash flow by the same interest rate.*

15. *The fundamental flaw of the traditional approach is that it views each security as the same package of cash flows.*

16. *The contemporary approach values a bond as a package of cash flows, with each cash flow viewed as a zero-coupon instrument and each cash flow discounted at its own discount rate.*

17. *To implement the contemporary approach it is necessary to determine the theoretical spot rate that the U.S. Treasury would have to pay to issue a zero-coupon instrument for each maturity.*

18. *A key risk measure is the price sensitivity of a fixed income security to changes in interest rates, referred to as duration.*

19. *A valuation model is needed to determine what the value of a security would be if interest rates change and therefore to determine a security's duration.*

20. *A drawback of duration is that it is a measure of the price sensitivity of a security assuming the interest rate for all maturities changes by the same number of basis points.*

Chapter 2

Spot Rates and Their Role in Valuation

The objectives of this chapter are to:

1. *explain the difference between the Treasury yield curve and the Treasury spot rate curve;*

2. *discuss the different Treasury securities that can be used to construct the theoretical spot rate curve;*

3. *explain the various methodologies that can be used to construct the theoretical spot rate curve;*

4. *discuss the advantages and disadvantages of each methodology for constructing the theoretical spot rate curve;*

5. *explain what the discount function is and how it is determined;*

6. *demonstrate how the Treasury spot rate curve can be used to price any Treasury security;*

7. *show why, based on arbitrage arguments, the price of a Treasury security will not deviate significantly from its theoretical value based on spot rates;*

8. *explain the drawbacks of the traditional (or nominal) spread measure;*

9. *present a measure called the zero volatility spread that is superior to the nominal spread measure, and describe the circumstances under which the two measures will deviate; and,*

10. *explain how credit risk can be introduced into the term structure.*

As we emphasized in the previous chapter, the key to the valuation of any security is the estimation of its cash flows and the discounting of each cash flow by an appropriate rate. The starting point for the determination of the appropriate rate is the theoretical spot rate on default-free securities. Since Treasury securities are viewed as default-free securities, the theoretical spot rates on these securities are the benchmark rates.

TREASURY YIELD CURVE

The graphical depiction of the relationship between the yields on Treasury securities of different maturities is known as the *yield curve*. The Treasury yield curve is typically constructed from on-the-run Treasury issues — 3-month, 6-month, 1-year, 2-year, 3-year, 5-year, 10-year, and 30-year recently auctioned issues.

The first three issues are Treasury bills which are issued as discount securities. These securities are sold at auction at a price below their maturity value and pay no coupon interest. The investor realizes interest by the difference between the maturity value and the price paid. Thus, Treasury bills are zero-coupon securities. In contrast, the five issues that mature after one year are coupon securities. There are no securities issued by the U.S. Department of the Treasury with a maturity greater than one year that are discount or zero-coupon securities. Consequently, the Treasury yield curve is a combination of zero-coupon securities and coupon securities.

In the valuation of securities what is needed is the rate on zero-coupon default-free securities or, equivalently, the rate on zero-coupon Treasury securities. However, as just noted, there are no zero-coupon Treasury securities issued by the U.S. Department of the Treasury with a maturity greater than one year. Our goal is to construct a theoretical rate that the U.S. government would have to offer if it issued zero-coupon securities with a maturity greater than one year.

There are, in fact, zero-coupon Treasury securities with a maturity greater than one year that are created by government dealer firms. The process is depicted in Exhibit 1. These securities are called *stripped Treasury securities*. Prior to 1985, stripped Treasury securities were either created as trademark products by dealer firms such as TIGRs (a Merrill Lynch product) and CATs (a Salomon Brothers product) or Trust Receipts (TRs) not associated with any particular dealer firm. Today, all stripped Treasury securities are created by dealer firms under a Treasury Department program called STRIPS, which stands for Separate Trading of Registered Interest and Principal Securities.

We shall refer to the STRIPS as *Treasury strips* or simply *strips*. For a reason discussed below, it is common to distinguish between strips based on whether they are created from the coupon payments or the principal payments. The former are called *coupon strips* and the latter are called *principal strips*. On dealer sheets, the distinction is made.

Exhibit 1: Creating Treasury Strips
Dealer purchases $500 million par of a 6% 10-year Treasury

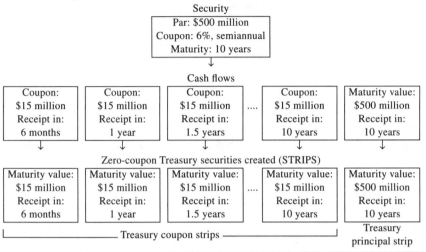

It would seem logical that the observed yield on strips could be used to construct an actual spot rate curve rather than go through the procedure we will describe. There are three problems with using the observed rates on strips. First, the liquidity of the strips market is not as great as that of the Treasury coupon market. Thus, the observed rates on strips reflect a premium for liquidity.

Second, the tax treatment of strips is different from that of Treasury coupon securities. Specifically, the accrued interest on strips is taxed even though no cash is received by the investor. Thus they are negative cash flow securities to taxable entities, and, as a result, their yield reflects this tax disadvantage.

Finally, there are maturity sectors where non-U.S. investors find it advantageous to trade off yield for tax advantages associated with a strip. Specifically, certain foreign tax authorities allow their citizens to treat the difference between the maturity value and the purchase price as a capital gain and tax this gain at a favorable tax rate. Some will grant this favorable treatment only when the strip is created from the principal rather than the coupon. For this reason, those who use Treasury strips to represent theoretical spot rates restrict the issues included to coupon strips.

CONSTRUCTING THE THEORETICAL SPOT RATE CURVE FOR TREASURIES

A default-free theoretical spot rate curve can be constructed from the yield on Treasury securities. The Treasury issues that are candidates for inclusion are:

1. on-the-run Treasury issues
2. on-the-run Treasury issues and selected off-the-run Treasury issues
3. all Treasury coupon securities and bills
4. Treasury coupon strips

Once the securities that are to be included in the construction of the theoretical spot rate curve are selected, the methodology for constructing the curve must be determined. The methodology depends on the securities included. If Treasury coupon strips are used, the procedure is simple since the observed yields are the spot rates. If the on-the-run Treasury issues with or without selected off-the-run Treasury issues are used, then a methodology called bootstrapping is used. When all Treasury coupon securities and bills are used, then elaborate statistical techniques are used.

On-the-Run Treasury Issues

The on-the-run Treasury issues are the most recently auctioned issues of a given maturity. These issues include the 3-month, 6-month, and 1-year Treasury bills, the 2-year, 3-year, 5-year, and 10-year Treasury notes, and the 30-year Treasury bond. Treasury bills are zero-coupon instruments; the notes and the bond are coupon securities.[1]

There is an observed yield for each of the on-the-run issues. For the coupon issues, these yields are not the yields used in the analysis when the issue is not trading at par. Instead, for each on-the-run coupon issue, the estimated yield necessary to make the issue trade at par is used. The resulting on-the-run yield curve is called the *par coupon curve*.

The goal is to construct a theoretical spot rate curve with 60 semiannual spot rates — 6-month rate to 30-year rate. Excluding the 3-month bill, there are only seven maturity points available when only on-the-run issues are used. The 53 missing maturity points are extrapolated from the surrounding maturity points on the par yield curve. The simplest extrapolation method, and the one most commonly used, is linear extrapolation. Specifically, given the yield on the par coupon curve at two maturity points, the following is calculated:

$$\frac{\text{Yield at higher maturity} - \text{Yield at lower maturity}}{\text{Number of semiannual periods between the two maturity points}}$$

Then, the yield for all intermediate semiannual maturity points is found by adding to the yield at the lower maturity the amount computed above.

For example, suppose that the yield from the par yield curve for the 3-year and 5-year on-the-run issues is 6% and 6.4%, respectively. There are four semiannual periods between these two maturity points. The extrapolated yield for the 3.5, 4.0, and 4.5 maturity points is found as follows. Calculate

$$\frac{6.4\% - 6.0\%}{4} = 0.10\%$$

---

[1] At one time, the Department of the Treasury issued 7-year notes, 15-year bonds, and 20-year bonds.

Then,

$$3.5\text{-year yield} = 6.00\% + 0.10\% = 6.10\%$$
$$4.0\text{-year yield} = 6.10\% + 0.10\% = 6.20\%$$
$$4.5\text{-year yield} = 6.20\% + 0.10\% = 6.30\%$$

There are two problems with using just the on-the-run issues. First, there is a large gap between some of the maturities points which may result in misleading yields for those maturity points when estimated using the linear extrapolation method. Specifically, the concern is with the large gap between the 5-year and 10-year maturity points and the 10-year and 30-year maturity points. The second problem is that the yields for the on-the-run issues themselves may be misleading because most are on special in the repo market. This means that the true yield is greater than the quoted (observed) yield.

Now let's look at how the par yield curve is converted into the theoretical spot rate curve. The methodology that is used is called *bootstrapping*. For simplicity, we will illustrate this methodology to calculate the theoretical spot rate curve for only 10 years. That is, 20 semiannual spot rates will be computed. Suppose that the par yield curve is the one shown in Exhibit 2.[2] Our focus is on the first three columns of this exhibit. Our goal is to explain how the values in the last two columns of the exhibit are derived.

The basic principle to obtain the theoretical spot rates is that the value of a Treasury coupon security should be equal to the value of the package of zero-coupon instruments that duplicates the coupon security's cash flows. Consider the 6-month Treasury bill in Exhibit 2. Since a Treasury bill is a zero-coupon instrument, its annualized yield of 3.00% is equal to the spot rate. Similarly, for the 1-year Treasury, the cited yield of 3.30% is the 1-year spot rate. Given these two spot rates, we can compute the spot rate for a theoretical 1.5-year zero-coupon Treasury. The price of a theoretical 1.5-year Treasury should equal the present value of the three cash flows from the 1.5-year coupon Treasury, where the yield used for discounting is the spot rate corresponding to the cash flow. Since all the coupon bonds are selling at par, the yield to maturity for each bond is the coupon rate. Using $100 as par, the cash flows for the 1.5-year coupon Treasury are:

$$
\begin{array}{lll}
0.5 \text{ year} & 0.035 \times \$100 \times 0.5 & = \quad \$1.75 \\
1.0 \text{ year} & 0.035 \times \$100 \times 0.5 & = \quad \$1.75 \\
1.5 \text{ year} & 0.035 \times \$100 \times 0.5 + 100 & = \$101.75
\end{array}
$$

The present value of the cash flows is then:

$$\frac{1.75}{(1+z_1)^1} + \frac{1.75}{(1+z_1)^2} + \frac{101.75}{(1+z_3)^3}$$

---

[2] Note that the intermediate points in this illustration were not calculated using the linear extrapolation procedure.

Exhibit 2: Par Coupon Curve for 10 Years

Period	Years	Yield to maturity (%)	Spot rate (%)	Discount function
1	0.5	3.00	3.0000	0.9852
2	1.0	3.30	3.3000	0.9678
3	1.5	3.50	3.5053	0.9492
4	2.0	3.90	3.9164	0.9254
5	2.5	4.40	4.4376	0.8961
6	3.0	4.70	4.7520	0.8686
7	3.5	4.90	4.9622	0.8424
8	4.0	5.00	5.0650	0.8187
9	4.5	5.10	5.1701	0.7948
10	5.0	5.20	5.2772	0.7707
11	5.5	5.30	5.3864	0.7465
12	6.0	5.40	5.4976	0.7222
13	6.5	5.50	5.6108	0.6979
14	7.0	5.55	5.6643	0.6764
15	7.5	5.60	5.7193	0.6551
16	8.0	5.65	5.7755	0.6341
17	8.5	5.70	5.8331	0.6134
18	9.0	5.80	5.9584	0.5895
19	9.5	5.90	6.0863	0.5658
20	10.0	6.00	6.2169	0.5421

where

z_1 = one-half the 6-month theoretical spot rate,
z_2 = one-half the 1-year theoretical spot rate, and
z_3 = one-half the 1.5-year theoretical spot rate.

Since the 6-month spot rate and 1-year spot rate are 3.00% and 3.30%, respectively, we know that:

$$z_1 = 0.0150 \quad \text{and} \quad z_2 = 0.0165$$

We can compute the present value of the 1.5-year coupon Treasury security as:

$$\frac{1.75}{(1+z_1)^1} + \frac{1.75}{(1+z_2)^2} + \frac{101.75}{(1+z_3)^3} = \frac{1.75}{(1.015)^1} + \frac{1.75}{(1.0165)^2} + \frac{101.75}{(1+z_3)^3}$$

Since the price of the 1.5-year coupon Treasury security is par, the following relationship must hold:

$$\frac{1.75}{(1.015)^1} + \frac{1.75}{(1.0165)^2} + \frac{101.75}{(1+z_3)^3} = 100$$

We can solve for the theoretical 1.5-year spot rate as follows:

$$1.7241 + 1.6936 + \frac{101.75}{(1+z_3)^3} = 100$$

$$\frac{101.75}{(1+z_3)^3} = 96.5822$$

$$(1+z_3)^3 = \frac{101.75}{96.5822}$$

$$z_3 = 0.0175265 = 1.7527\%$$

Doubling this yield we obtain the bond-equivalent yield of 3.5053%, which is the theoretical 1.5-year spot rate. That rate is the rate that the market would apply to a 1.5-year zero-coupon Treasury security if, in fact, such a security existed.

Given the theoretical 1.5-year spot rate, we can obtain the theoretical 2-year spot rate. The cash flows for the 2-year coupon Treasury in Exhibit 2 are:

0.5 years	$0.039 \times \$100 \times 0.5$	= $	1.95
1.0 years	$0.039 \times \$100 \times 0.5$	= $	1.95
1.5 years	$0.039 \times \$100 \times 0.5$	= $	1.95
2.0 years	$0.039 \times \$100 \times 0.5 + 100$	= $	101.95

The present value of the cash flows is then:

$$\frac{1.95}{(1+z_1)^1} + \frac{1.95}{(1+z_2)^2} + \frac{1.95}{(1+z_3)^3} + \frac{101.95}{(1+z_4)^4}$$

where z_4 = one-half the 2-year theoretical spot rate.

Since the 6-month spot rate, 1-year spot rate, and 1.5-year spot rate are 3.00%, 3.30%, and 3.5053%, respectively, then:

$$z_1 = 0.0150, z_2 = 0.0165, \text{ and } z_3 = 0.017527$$

Therefore, the present value of the 2-year coupon Treasury security is:

$$\frac{1.95}{(1.0150)^1} + \frac{1.95}{(1.0165)^2} + \frac{1.95}{(1.017527)^3} + \frac{101.95}{(1+z_4)^4}$$

Since the price of the 2-year coupon Treasury security is par, the following relationship must hold:

$$\frac{1.95}{(1.0150)^1} + \frac{1.95}{(1.0165)^2} + \frac{1.95}{(1.017527)^3} + \frac{101.95}{(1+z_4)^4} = 100$$

We can solve for the theoretical 2-year spot rate as follows:

$$\frac{101.95}{(1+z_4)^4} = 94.3407$$

$$(1+z_4)^4 = \frac{101.95}{94.3407}$$

$$z_4 = 0.019582 = 1.9582\%$$

Doubling this yield, we obtain the theoretical 2-year spot rate bond-equivalent yield of 3.9164%.

One can follow this approach sequentially to derive the theoretical 2.5-year spot rate from the calculated values of z_1, z_2, z_3, z_4 (the 6-month, 1-year, 1.5-year, and 2-year rates), and the price and coupon of the bond with a maturity of 2.5 years. Further, one could derive the theoretical spot rate for the remaining 15 half-yearly rates.

The spot rates obtained are shown in the next-to-the-last column of Exhibit 2. They represent the term structure of default-free spot rates for maturities up to ten years for the particular par coupon curve.

Exhibit 3 shows in table form and Exhibit 4 in graph form the theoretical spot rate curve estimated on August 13, 1996 by applying the bootstrapping methodology to on-the-run issues. Also shown in the two exhibits are the rates based on the coupon strips. Note the significant divergence between the coupon strips and the rates generated from bootstrapping after the 6-year maturity point.

On-the-Run Treasury Issues and Selected Off-the-Run Treasury Issues

As noted above, one of the problems with using just the on-the-run issues   is the large gaps between maturities, particularly after five years. To mitigate this problem, some dealers and vendors use selected off-the-run Treasury issues. Typically, the issues used are the 20-year issue and 25-year issue.[3] Given the par coupon curve including any off-the-run selected issues, the linear extrapolation method is used to fill in the gaps for the other maturities. The bootstrapping method is then used to construct the theoretical spot rate curve.

Exhibit 3 compares in table form the theoretical annual spot rates on August 13, 1996 using the bootstrapping methodology applied to (1) the on-run-issues and (2) the on-the-run issues plus the 20-year and 25-year off-the-run issues. The exhibit also includes the coupon strip rates. Exhibit 4 compares the first two curves to the coupon strips curve. Notice how much closer the theoretical spot rate curve comes to the coupon strips curve when the on-the-run issues are supplemented with the 20-year and 25-year off-the-run issues.

All Treasury Coupon Securities and Bills

Using only on-the-run issues, even when extended to include a few off-the-run issues, fails to recognize the information embodied in Treasury prices that are not included in the analysis. Thus, it is argued that it is more appropriate to use all

---

[3] See, for example, Philip H. Galdi and Shenglin Lu, *Analyzing Risk and Relative Value of Corporate and Government Securities*, Merrill Lynch & Co., Global Securities Research & Economics Group, Fixed Income Analytics, 1997, p. 11.

Treasury coupon securities and bills to construct the theoretical spot rate curve. Some practitioners do not use callable Treasury bonds. Moreover, a common practice is to filter the Treasury securities universe to eliminate securities that are on special in the repo market.

Exhibit 3: Comparison of Theoretical Annual Spot Rates Using Bootstrapping Methodology, Merrill Lynch Exponential Spline Methodology, and Coupon Strips on August 13, 1996

	Zero Curves (%)			
	Bootstrapping using on-the-run issues	Bootstrapping Using On-the-Run Issues + 20-Year and 25-Year Issues	Exponential Spline	Coupon Strip
1	5.62	5.62	5.69	5.60
2	5.98	5.98	6.00	5.98
3	6.17	6.17	6.18	6.17
4	6.27	6.27	6.29	6.27
5	6.36	6.36	6.37	6.35
6	6.42	6.42	6.44	6.42
7	6.47	6.47	6.51	6.51
8	6.53	6.53	6.58	6.60
9	6.59	6.59	6.65	6.68
10	6.66	6.66	6.71	6.74
11	6.66	6.68	6.77	6.79
12	6.67	6.72	6.83	6.84
13	6.68	6.75	6.89	6.90
14	6.69	6.78	6.94	6.94
15	6.71	6.82	6.98	6.98
16	6.72	6.86	7.02	7.03
17	6.73	6.89	7.06	7.06
18	6.75	6.94	7.09	7.07
19	6.77	6.98	7.12	7.10
20	6.78	7.02	7.14	7.11
21	6.80	7.04	7.16	7.13
22	6.82	7.04	7.16	7.14
23	6.84	7.05	7.16	7.14
24	6.86	7.05	7.15	7.13
25	6.88	7.06	7.12	7.10
26	6.90	7.01	7.08	7.06
27	6.92	6.96	7.02	6.98
28	6.95	6.91	6.95	6.95
29	6.98	6.86	6.85	6.88
30	7.00	6.81	6.74	6.85*

* 29.5 yrs

Source: The data points were provided by Philip H. Galdi, First Vice President at Merrill Lynch, and Shenglin Lu, Vice President at Merrill Lynch. These data were used to construct the spot rate curves in Exhibis 4 and 5 in this chapter and which appear in Philip H. Galdi and Shenglin Lu, *Analyzing Risk and Relative Value of Corporate and Government Securities*, Merrill Lynch & Co., Global Securities Research & Economics Group, Fixed Income Analytics, 1997. Copyright ©1997 Merrill Lynch, Pierce, Fenner & Smith Incorporated.

Exhibit 4: Comparison of Theoretical Spot Rates Using the Bootstrapping Methodology and Based on Coupon Strips (August 13, 1996)

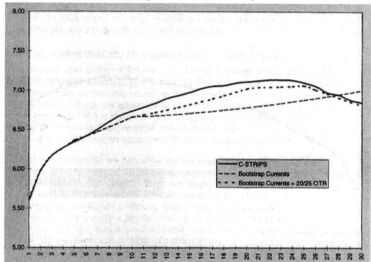

Source: Figure 7 in Philip H. Galdi and Shenglin Lu, *Analyzing Risk and Relative Value of Corporate and Government Securities*, Merrill Lynch & Co., Global Securities Research & Economics Group, Fixed Income Analytics, 1997, p. 11. Copyright ©1997 Merrill Lynch, Pierce, Fenner & Smith Incorporated.

When all coupon securities and bills are used, statistical methodologies must be employed to construct the theoretical spot rate curve rather than bootstrapping since there may be more than one yield for each maturity. Several statistical methodologies have been proposed to estimate the spot rate curve.[4] The most common methodology used is "exponential spline fitting."[5] The methodology produces forward rates (discussed in the next chapter) that are a smooth continuous function of time. The methodology has desirable asymptotic properties for long maturities, and exhibits both a sufficient flexibility to fit a wide variety of shapes of the spot rate curve, and a sufficient robustness to produce stable forward rate curves. An adjustment for the effect of taxes and for call features on U.S. Treasury bonds can be incorporated into the statistical model. A discussion of this statistical methodology is beyond the scope this book.

---

[4] Willard R Carleton and Ian Cooper, "Estimation and Uses of the Term Structure of Interest Rates," *Journal of Finance* (September 1976), pp. 1067-1083; J. Huston McCulloch, "Measuring the Term Structure of Interest Rates," *Journal of Business* (January 1971), pp. 19-31; and J. Huston McCulloch, "The Tax Adjusted Yield Curve," *Journal of Finance* (June 1975), pp. 811-830.

[5] See, Oldrich A. Vasicek and H. Gifford Fong, "Term Structure Modeling Using Exponential Splines," *Journal of Finance* (May 1982), pp. 339-358. For an example of a dealer model, see Arnold Shapiro *et al.*, *Merrill Lynch Exponential Spline Model,* Merrill Lynch & Co., Global Securities Research & Economics Group, Fixed Income Analytics, August 8, 1994.

Exhibit 5: Comparison of Theoretical Spot Rates Using the Bootstrapping Methodology, the Merrill Lynch Exponential Spline Methodology, and Based on Coupon Strips (August 13, 1996)

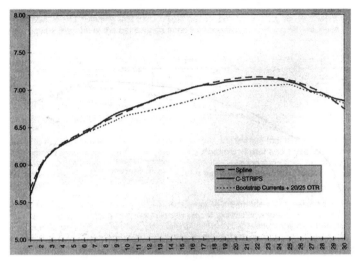

Source: Figure 8 in Philip H. Galdi and Shenglin Lu, *Analyzing Risk and Relative Value of Corporate and Government Securities*, Merrill Lynch & Co., Global Securities Research & Economics Group, Fixed Income Analytics, 1997, p. 12. Copyright ©1997 Merrill Lynch, Pierce, Fenner & Smith Incorporated.

The drawback of using all Treasury securities is that real-time information is not available for all issues.[6] To deal with this problem, Merrill Lynch, for example, has developed a real time spline model. This model uses only the on-the-run issues (and in some cases the previous on-the-run issue).

Exhibit 3 provides a comparison of the theoretical spot rate constructed on August 13, 1996 using coupon strips with those of the exponential spline methodology and the bootstrapping methodology. Exhibit 5 compares in graph form the spot rates constructed from bootstrapping the on-the-run issues plus the 20-year and 25-year off-the run issues, the Merrill Lynch spline methodology, and the coupon strips. Notice how close the spot rates based on the spline methodology are to the coupon strips, particularly after the 6-year maturity point.

THE DISCOUNT FUNCTION

The term structure is represented by the spot rate curve. We also know that the present value of $1 at any future date, *n*, when discounted at the spot rate for period *n* is:

---

[6] Galdi and Lu, *Analyzing Risk and Relative Value of Corporate and Government Securities*, p. 11.

$$\frac{\$1}{\left[1 + \left(\frac{\text{Spot rate for period } n}{2}\right)\right]^n}$$

For example, the present value of $1 five years from now using the spot rate for 10 periods in Exhibit 2, 5.2772%, is

$$\frac{\$1}{\left[1 + \left(\frac{0.052772}{2}\right)\right]^{10}} = 0.7707$$

This value can be viewed as the time value of $1 for a default-free cash flow to be received in five years. Equivalently, it is the value of a zero-coupon default-free security with a maturity of five years and a maturity value of $1.

The last column of Exhibit 2 shows the time value of $1 for each period. The set of time values for all periods is called the *discount function*.

APPLYING THE SPOT RATES TO PRICE A TREASURY COUPON SECURITY

To demonstrate how to use the spot rate curve, suppose that we want to price an 8% 10-year Treasury security. The price of this issue is the present value of the cash flows where each cash flow is discounted at the corresponding spot rate. This is illustrated in Exhibit 6.

The third column shows the cash flow for each period. The fourth column shows the spot rate curve taken from Exhibit 2. The corresponding discount function is shown in the next-to-the-last column taken from Exhibit 2. Multiplying the value in the discount function column by the cash flow gives the present value of the cash flow. The sum of the present value of the cash flows is equal to 115.2619. This is the theoretical value of this issue.

Exhibit 7 shows how to price a 6% 10-year Treasury issue. As indicated in Exhibit 2, the price of this issue is 100. This agrees with the theoretical value calculated in Exhibit 7.

WHY TREASURIES MUST BE PRICED BASED ON SPOT RATES

The price of a Treasury security is determined by the spot rates, not the yield to maturity of a Treasury coupon security of the same maturity. We will use an illustration to demonstrate the economic forces that will assure that the actual market price of a Treasury coupon security will not depart significantly from its theoretical value.

Exhibit 6: Determination of the Theoretical Price of an 8% 10-Year Treasury

Period	Years	Cash flow	Spot rate (%)	Discount function	Present Value
1	0.5	4.00	3.0000	0.9852	3.9409
2	1.0	4.00	3.3000	0.9678	3.8712
3	1.5	4.00	3.5053	0.9492	3.7968
4	2.0	4.00	3.9164	0.9254	3.7014
5	2.5	4.00	4.4376	0.8961	3.5843
6	3.0	4.00	4.7520	0.8686	3.4743
7	3.5	4.00	4.9622	0.8424	3.3694
8	4.0	4.00	5.0650	0.8187	3.2747
9	4.5	4.00	5.1701	0.7948	3.1791
10	5.0	4.00	5.2772	0.7707	3.0828
11	5.5	4.00	5.3864	0.7465	2.9861
12	6.0	4.00	5.4976	0.7222	2.8889
13	6.5	4.00	5.6108	0.6979	2.7916
14	7.0	4.00	5.6643	0.6764	2.7055
15	7.5	4.00	5.7193	0.6551	2.6205
16	8.0	4.00	5.7755	0.6341	2.5365
17	8.5	4.00	5.8331	0.6134	2.4536
18	9.0	4.00	5.9584	0.5895	2.3581
19	9.5	4.00	6.0863	0.5658	2.2631
20	10.0	104.00	6.2169	0.5421	56.3828
				Total	115.2619

Exhibit 7: Determination of the Theoretical Price of a 6% 10-Year Treasury

Period	Years	Cash flow	Spot rate (%)	Discount function	Present value
1	0.5	3.00	3.0000	0.9852	2.9557
2	1.0	3.00	3.3000	0.9678	2.9034
3	1.5	3.00	3.5053	0.9492	2.8476
4	2.0	3.00	3.9164	0.9254	2.7761
5	2.5	3.00	4.4376	0.8961	2.6882
6	3.0	3.00	4.7520	0.8686	2.6057
7	3.5	3.00	4.9622	0.8424	2.5271
8	4.0	3.00	5.0650	0.8187	2.4560
9	4.5	3.00	5.1701	0.7948	2.3843
10	5.0	3.00	5.2772	0.7707	2.3121
11	5.5	3.00	5.3864	0.7465	2.2396
12	6.0	3.00	5.4976	0.7222	2.1667
13	6.5	3.00	5.6108	0.6979	2.0937
14	7.0	3.00	5.6643	0.6764	2.0292
15	7.5	3.00	5.7193	0.6551	1.9654
16	8.0	3.00	5.7755	0.6341	1.9024
17	8.5	3.00	5.8331	0.6134	1.8402
18	9.0	3.00	5.9584	0.5895	1.7686
19	9.5	3.00	6.0863	0.5658	1.6973
20	10.0	103.00	6.2169	0.5421	55.8407
				Total	100.0000

To demonstrate this, consider the 8% 10-year Treasury security. Suppose that this Treasury security is priced based on the 6% yield to maturity of the 10-year maturity Treasury coupon security in Exhibit 2. Discounting all of the cash flows of the 8% 10-year Treasury security at 6% gives a present value of 114.88.

The question is, could this security trade at 114.88 in the market? Let's see what would happen if the 8% 10-year Treasury traded at 114.88. Suppose that a dealer firm buys this issue at 114.88 and strips it. By stripping it, we mean creating zero-coupon instruments as depicted in Exhibit 1. By stripping this issue, the dealer firm creates 20 zero-coupon instruments guaranteed by the U.S. Treasury.[7]

How much can the 20 zero-coupon instruments be sold for by the dealer firm? Expressed equivalently, at what yield can each of the zero-coupon instruments be sold? The answer is in Exhibit 2. The yield at which each zero-coupon instrument can be sold is the spot rate shown in the next-to-the-last column.

We can use Exhibit 6 to determine the proceeds that would be received per $100 of par value of the 8% 10-year issue stripped. The last column shows how much would be received for each coupon sold as a zero-coupon instrument. The total proceeds received from selling the zero-coupon Treasury securities created would be $115.2619 per $100 of par value of the Treasury issue purchased by the dealer. Since the dealer purchased the issue for $114.88, this would result in an arbitrage profit of $0.3819 per $100 of the 8% 10-year Treasury issue purchased.

To understand why the dealer has the opportunity to realize this arbitrage profit, look at the last column of Exhibit 3 which shows how much the dealer paid for each cash flow by buying the entire package of cash flows (i.e., by buying the issue). For example, consider the $4 coupon payment in four years. By buying the 10-year Treasury bond priced to yield 6%, the dealer effectively pays a price based on 6% (3% semiannual) for that coupon payment, or, equivalently, $3.1577. Under the assumptions of this illustration, however, investors were willing to accept a lower yield to maturity (the 4-year spot rate), 5.065% (2.5325% semiannual), to purchase a zero-coupon Treasury security with four years to maturity. Thus investors were willing to pay $3.2747. On this one coupon payment, the dealer realizes a profit equal to the difference between $3.2747 and $3.1577 (or $0.117). From all the cash flows, the total profit is $0.3819. In this instance, coupon stripping results in the sum of the parts being greater than the whole.

Suppose that, instead of the observed yield to maturity from Exhibit 2, the yields that investors want are the same as the theoretical spot rates that are shown in the exhibit. As can be seen in Exhibit 6, if we use these spot rates to discount the cash flows, the total proceeds from the sale of the zero-coupon Treasury securities would be equal to $115.2619, making coupon stripping uneconomic since the proceeds from stripping would be the same as the cost of purchasing the issue.

---

[7] As shown in Exhibit 1, 21 zero-coupon instruments are created since the last coupon and the maturity value are sold separately. In our illustrations, we do not make any distinction between the last coupon and maturity value.

In our illustration of coupon stripping, the price of the Treasury security is less than its theoretical price. Suppose instead that the price of the Treasury coupon security is greater than its theoretical price. In this case, investors can create a portfolio of zero-coupon Treasury securities such that the cash flows of the portfolio replicate the cash flows of the mispriced Treasury coupon security. By doing so, the investor will realize a yield higher than the yield on the Treasury coupon security. For example, suppose that the market price of the 10-year Treasury coupon security we used in our illustration is $116. An investor could buy 20 outstanding zero-coupon stripped Treasury securities with maturity values identical to the cash flows shown in the third column of Exhibit 6. The cost of purchasing this portfolio of stripped Treasury securities would be $115.2619. Thus, an investor is effectively purchasing a portfolio of stripped Treasury securities that has the same cash flows as an 8% 10-year Treasury coupon security at a cost of $115.2619 instead of $116.

It is the process of coupon stripping and reconstituting that will prevent the market price of Treasury securities from departing significantly from their theoretical value.

ZERO-VOLATILITY SPREAD

Traditional analysis of the yield premium for a non-Treasury bond involves calculating the difference between the yield to maturity (or yield to call) of the bond in question and the yield to maturity of a comparable maturity Treasury coupon security. The latter is obtained from the Treasury yield curve. For example, consider the following 10-year bonds:

Issue	Coupon	Price	Yield to maturity
Treasury	6%	100.00	6.00%
Non-Treasury	8%	104.19	7.40%

The yield spread for these two bonds as traditionally computed is 140 basis points (7.4% minus 6%). We refer to this traditional yield spread as the *nominal spread*.

The drawbacks of the nominal spread are (1) for both bonds, the yield fails to take into consideration the term structure of interest rates and (2) in the case of callable and/or putable bonds, expected interest rate volatility may alter the future cash flows of the non-Treasury bond. Here, we focus only on the first problem: failure to consider the spot rate curve. We will deal with the second problem in Chapters 6 and 8.

Determination of the Zero-Volatility Spread

The *zero-volatility spread* is a measure of the spread that the investor would realize over the entire Treasury spot rate curve if (1) the bond is held to maturity and (2) the spot rates do not change. It is not a spread off one point on the Treasury yield curve, as is the nominal spread.

Exhibit 8: Determination of the Zero-Volatility Spread for the 8% 10-Year Non-Treasury Issue Selling at 104.19 to Yield 7.4%

Period	Years	Cash flow	Spot rate (%)	Present value: Spread 100 bp	Present value: Spread 125 bp	Present value: Spread 146 bp
1	0.5	4.00	3.0000	3.9216	3.9168	3.9127
2	1.0	4.00	3.3000	3.8334	3.8240	3.8162
3	1.5	4.00	3.5053	3.7414	3.7277	3.7163
4	2.0	4.00	3.9164	3.6297	3.6121	3.5973
5	2.5	4.00	4.4376	3.4979	3.4767	3.4590
6	3.0	4.00	4.7520	3.3742	3.3497	3.3293
7	3.5	4.00	4.9622	3.2565	3.2290	3.2061
8	4.0	4.00	5.0650	3.1497	3.1193	3.0940
9	4.5	4.00	5.1701	3.0430	3.0100	2.9826
10	5.0	4.00	5.2772	2.9366	2.9013	2.8719
11	5.5	4.00	5.3864	2.8307	2.7933	2.7622
12	6.0	4.00	5.4976	2.7255	2.6862	2.6537
13	6.5	4.00	5.6108	2.6210	2.5801	2.5463
14	7.0	4.00	5.6643	2.5279	2.4855	2.4504
15	7.5	4.00	5.7193	2.4367	2.3929	2.3568
16	8.0	4.00	5.7755	2.3472	2.3023	2.2652
17	8.5	4.00	5.8331	2.2596	2.2137	2.1758
18	9.0	4.00	5.9584	2.1612	2.1148	2.0766
19	9.5	4.00	6.0863	2.0642	2.0174	1.9790
20	10.0	104.00	6.2169	51.1833	49.9638	48.9630
			Total	107.5414	105.7165	104.2145*

* Closest spread to four decimals.

The zero-volatility spread is the spread that will make the present value of the cash flows from the non-Treasury bond, when discounted at the Treasury spot rate plus the spread, equal to the non-Treasury bond's market price. A trial-and-error procedure is required to determine the zero-volatility spread.

To illustrate how this is done, let's use the non-Treasury bond in our previous illustration and the Treasury yield curve in Exhibit 2. The Treasury spot rates are reproduced in the fourth column of Exhibit 8. The third column in the exhibit lists the cash flows for the 8%, 10-year non-Treasury issue. The goal is to determine the spread that when added to all the Treasury spot rates will produce a present value for the cash flows of the non-Treasury bond equal to its market price, 104.19.

Suppose we select a spread of 100 basis points. To each Treasury spot rate shown in the fourth column 100 basis points is added. So, for example, the 5-year (period 10) spot rate is 6.2772% (5.2772% plus 1%). The spot rate plus 100 basis points is then used to calculate the present value of 107.5414. Because the present value is not equal to the non-Treasury issue's price (104.19), the zero-volatility spread is not 100 basis points. If a spread of 125 basis points is tried, it can be seen from the next-to-the-last column of Exhibit 6 that the present value is 105.7165; again, because this is not equal to the non-Treasury issue's price, 125 basis points is not the zero-volatility spread. The last column of Exhibit 8 shows the present value when a 146 basis point spread is tried. The present value is close to the non-Treasury issue's price. Therefore 146 basis points is the zero-volatility spread, compared to the nominal spread of 140 basis points.

Divergence Between Zero-Volatility Spread and Nominal Spread

Typically, for standard coupon paying bonds with a bullet maturity (i.e., a single payment of principal) the zero-volatility spread and the nominal spread will not differ significantly. In our example it is only 6 basis points.

For short-term issues, there is little divergence. The main factor causing any difference is the shape of the yield curve. The steeper the yield curve, the greater the difference. To illustrate this, consider the two yield curves shown in Exhibit 9. The yield for the longest maturity of both yield curves is 6%. The first yield curve is steeper than the one used in Exhibit 2; the second yield curve is flat, with the yield for all maturities equal to 6%.

Exhibit 9: Two Hypothetical Yield Curves

Period	Years	Steep curve (%)	Flat curve (%)
1	0.5	2.00	6.00
2	1.0	2.40	6.00
3	1.5	2.80	6.00
4	2.0	2.90	6.00
5	2.5	3.00	6.00
6	3.0	3.10	6.00
7	3.5	3.30	6.00
8	4.0	3.80	6.00
9	4.5	3.90	6.00
10	5.0	4.20	6.00
11	5.5	4.40	6.00
12	6.0	4.50	6.00
13	6.5	4.60	6.00
14	7.0	4.70	6.00
15	7.5	4.90	6.00
16	8.0	5.00	6.00
17	8.5	5.30	6.00
18	9.0	5.70	6.00
19	9.5	5.80	6.00
20	10.0	6.00	6.00

Exhibit 10: Determination of the Zero-Volatility Spread for the 8% 10-Year Non-Treasury Issue Selling at 104.19 to Yield 7.4% Assuming a Steep Yield Curve

Period	Years	Cash flow	Spot rate (%)	Spread 154 bp
1	0.5	4.00	2.0000	3.9304
2	1.0	4.00	2.4000	3.8469
3	1.5	4.00	2.8075	3.7501
4	2.0	4.00	2.9081	3.6631
5	2.5	4.00	3.0097	3.5745
6	3.0	4.00	3.1124	3.4845
7	3.5	4.00	3.3216	3.3810
8	4.0	4.00	3.8570	3.2326
9	4.5	4.00	3.9605	3.1334
10	5.0	4.00	4.2898	3.0011
11	5.5	4.00	4.5102	2.8820
12	6.0	4.00	4.6174	2.7799
13	6.5	4.00	4.7267	2.6784
14	7.0	4.00	4.8380	2.5775
15	7.5	4.00	5.0752	2.4551
16	8.0	4.00	5.1904	2.3554
17	8.5	4.00	5.5699	2.2088
18	9.0	4.00	6.1027	2.0366
19	9.5	4.00	6.2242	1.9399
20	10.0	104.00	6.4980	47.2910
			Total	104.2022

Exhibit 10 shows the spot rate curve for the first yield curve and that the zero-volatility spread is 154. Thus, with this steeper yield curve, the difference between the zero-volatility spread and the nominal spread is 14 basis points. Exhibit 11 shows that for the flat yield curve the zero-volatility spread is 140 basis points, the same as the nominal spread. This will always be the case for a flat yield curve.

The difference between the zero-volatility spread and the nominal spread is greater for issues in which the principal is repaid over time rather than only at maturity — that is, for amortizing securities compared to bullet-maturity securities. Thus the difference between the nominal spread and the zero-volatility spread will be considerably greater for sinking fund bonds, mortgage-backed securities, and asset backed securities in a steep yield curve environment.

THE TERM STRUCTURE OF CREDIT SPREADS

Thus far our focus in this chapter has been on the term structure of U.S. Treasury securities — default-free securities. The Treasury spot rates can then be used to value any default-free security. As we illustrated earlier, failure of Treasury securities to be priced according to the Treasury spot rates creates the opportunity for arbitrage profits or enhanced returns.

For a corporate bond, the theoretical price is not as easy to determine. The price of a corporate bond must reflect not only the spot rates for default-free bonds but also a risk premium to reflect default risk and any options embedded in the issue. For now, we will skip options embedded in bonds, a complexity addressed in later chapters.

In practice, the spot rates that have been used to discount the cash flows of corporate bonds are the Treasury spot rates plus a constant credit spread. For example, if the 6-month Treasury spot rate is 3%, and the 10-year Treasury spot rate is 6%, and a suitable credit spread is deemed to be 100 basis points, then a 4% spot rate is used to discount a 6-month cash flow of a corporate bond and a 7% discount rate to discount a 10-year cash flow.

Exhibit 11: Determination of the Zero-Volatility Spread for the 8% 10-Year Non-Treasury Issue Selling at 104.19 to Yield 7.4% Assuming a Flat Yield Curve

Period	Years	Cash flow	Spot rate (%)	Spread 140 bp
1	0.5	4.00	6.0000	3.8573
2	1.0	4.00	6.0000	3.7197
3	1.5	4.00	6.0000	3.5869
4	2.0	4.00	6.0000	3.4590
5	2.5	4.00	6.0000	3.3355
6	3.0	4.00	6.0000	3.2165
7	3.5	4.00	6.0000	3.1018
8	4.0	4.00	6.0000	2.9911
9	4.5	4.00	6.0000	2.8844
10	5.0	4.00	6.0000	2.7815
11	5.5	4.00	6.0000	2.6822
12	6.0	4.00	6.0000	2.5865
13	6.5	4.00	6.0000	2.4942
14	7.0	4.00	6.0000	2.4052
15	7.5	4.00	6.0000	2.3194
16	8.0	4.00	6.0000	2.2367
17	8.5	4.00	6.0000	2.1569
18	9.0	4.00	6.0000	2.0799
19	9.5	4.00	6.0000	2.0057
20	10.0	104.00	6.0000	50.2873
			Total	104.1876

The drawback of this approach is that there is no reason to expect the credit spread to be the same regardless of when the cash flow is expected to be received. Instead, it might be expected that the credit spread increases with the maturity of the corporate bond. That is, there is a term structure for credit spreads.

In practice, the difficulty in estimating a term structure for credit spreads is that unlike Treasury securities in which there is a wide-range of maturities from which to construct a Treasury spot rate curve, there are no issuers that offer a sufficiently wide range of corporate zero-coupon securities to construct a zero-coupon spread curve. Robert Litterman and Thomas Iben of Goldman Sachs describe a procedure to construct a generic zero-coupon spread curve by credit rating and industry using data provided from a trading desk.[8]

The basic principle is as follows.[9] Consider four hypothetical zero-coupon securities, two Treasury issues and two securities issued by the same corporation:

Type	Maturity	Price per $1 par	Yield (%)
Treasury	1 year	0.930	7.39
Corporate	1 year	0.926	7.84
Treasury	2 years	0.848	8.42
Corporate	2 years	0.840	8.91

Focus first on the two issues with one year to maturity. Investors are willing to pay 93.0 cents to receive $1 by purchasing the 1-year Treasury and 92.6 cents to receive $1 by purchasing the 1-year corporate security. The 4-cent difference produces a credit spread of 45 basis points (7.84% minus 7.39%). The lower price for the corporate security reflects default risk; that is, it reflects the probability that the issuer will default. In this simple illustration it is assumed that if default occurs, the investor does not realize anything. In practice, this is not true and the formulation can be modified to reflect this.

For the same expected return to result by holding either bond, the price of the corporate bond must be equal to the price of the Treasury times the probability of solvency (i.e., not defaulting). Thus,

Price of corporate zero
= Price of Treasury zero × (Probability of solvency)

or equivalently, since the probability of solvency is equal to one minus the probability of default,

Price of corporate zero
= Price of Treasury zero × (1 − Probability of default)

---

[8] Robert Litterman and Thomas Iben, "Corporate Bond Valuation and the Term Structure of Credit Spreads," *Journal of Portfolio Management* (Spring 1991), pp. 52-64. The original paper was published by Goldman Sachs in 1988.

[9] The numerical example is the one used by Litterman and Iben, pp. 53-54.

Solving for the probability of default,

$$\text{Probability of default} = 1 - \frac{\text{Price of corporate zero}}{\text{Price of Treasury zero}}$$

In our example,

$$\text{Probability of default} = 1 - \frac{0.926}{0.930} = 0.0043$$

Now let's focus on the two zero-coupon securities that mature two years from now. The 2-year corporate zero will pay off $1 in the second year only if the corporation that has issued both 1-year and 2-year securities does not default in either the first or the second year. The probability of default in the first year has already been determined (0.0043). The next step is to determine the conditional probability of default in the second year, given that the corporation does not default in the first year. Litterman and Iben refer to this probability as the "forward probability of default."

Given the assumption that the expected return from holding a Treasury zero for two years must equal the return from holding a corporate zero for two years times the probability of solvency, the forward probability of default can be calculated. In this example it is 0.0052. This procedure can be used to determine a term structure of credit spreads for zero-coupon corporates for a given issuer.

Exhibit 12 shows in tabular form a generic zero spread term structure for industrial corporations for each investment-grade credit rating as of September 8, 1993. Notice that the credit spread increases with maturity. This is a typical shape for the term structure of credit spreads. In addition, the shape of the term structure is not the same for all credit ratings. The lower the credit rating, the steeper the term structure.

One implication of an upward-sloping term structure for credit spreads is that it is inappropriate to discount the cash flows from a corporate bond at a constant spread to the Treasury spot rate curve. The short-term cash flows will be undervalued, and the long-term cash flows will be overvalued.

Exhibit 12: Generic Zero Spread Curves for Industrial Corporations by Credit Quality
(September 8, 1993)

Credit rating	Maturity (in years)								
	2	3	5	7	10	15	20	25	30
Aaa	22	25	28	31	33	37	41	45	48
Aa	28	32	36	38	41	49	57	65	71
A	38	47	52	58	63	71	79	88	94
Baa	55	71	77	83	89	98	107	116	123

Source: Goldman Sachs & Co.

Exhibit 13: Calculation of Value of a Hypothetical AAA Industrial 8% 10-Year Bond Using Benchmark Credit Structure

Period	Years	Cash flow	Spot rate (%)	Credit spread (%)	Credit structure (%)	Present value
1	0.5	4.00	3.0000	0.20	3.2000	3.9370
2	1.0	4.00	3.3000	0.20	3.5000	3.8636
3	1.5	4.00	3.5053	0.25	3.7553	3.7829
4	2.0	4.00	3.9164	0.30	4.2164	3.6797
5	2.5	4.00	4.4376	0.35	4.7876	3.5538
6	3.0	4.00	4.7520	0.35	5.1020	3.4389
7	3.5	4.00	4.9622	0.40	5.3622	3.3237
8	4.0	4.00	5.0650	0.45	5.5150	3.2177
9	4.5	4.00	5.1701	0.45	5.6201	3.1170
10	5.0	4.00	5.2772	0.50	5.7772	3.0088
11	5.5	4.00	5.3864	0.55	5.9364	2.8995
12	6.0	4.00	5.4976	0.60	6.0976	2.7896
13	6.5	4.00	5.6108	0.65	6.2608	2.6794
14	7.0	4.00	5.6643	0.70	6.3643	2.5799
15	7.5	4.00	5.7193	0.75	6.4693	2.4813
16	8.0	4.00	5.7755	0.80	6.5755	2.3838
17	8.5	4.00	5.8331	0.85	6.6831	2.2876
18	9.0	4.00	5.9584	0.90	6.8584	2.1801
19	9.5	4.00	6.0863	0.95	7.0363	2.0737
20	10.0	104.00	6.2169	1.00	7.2169	51.1833
					Total	108.4615

Benchmark Spot Rate Curve

When the generic zero spreads for a given credit quality and in a given industry are added to the default-free spot rates, the resulting credit term structure is used to value bonds of issuers of the same credit quality in the industry sector. This term structure is referred to as the *benchmark spot rate curve* or *benchmark zero-coupon rate curve*.

For example, Exhibit 13 reproduces the default-free spot rate curve in Exhibit 2. Also shown in the exhibit is a hypothetical generic zero spread for AAA industrial bonds. The resulting benchmark spot rate curve is in the next-to-the-last column. It is this spot rate curve that is used to value a AAA industrial bond. This is done in Exhibit 13 for a hypothetical 8% 10-year AAA industrial bond. The theoretical price is 108.4615.

Exhibit 14: Demonstration that the Zero-Volatility Spread is 40 Basis Points

Period	Years	Cash flow	Spot rate	Credit spread	40 bp spread	Present value
1	0.5	4.00	3.0000	0.20	3.6000	3.9293
2	1.0	4.00	3.3000	0.20	3.9000	3.8484
3	1.5	4.00	3.5053	0.25	4.1553	3.7607
4	2.0	4.00	3.9164	0.30	4.6164	3.6511
5	2.5	4.00	4.4376	0.35	5.1876	3.5193
6	3.0	4.00	4.7520	0.35	5.5020	3.3989
7	3.5	4.00	4.9622	0.40	5.7622	3.2788
8	4.0	4.00	5.0650	0.45	5.9150	3.1681
9	4.5	4.00	5.1701	0.45	6.0201	3.0630
10	5.0	4.00	5.2772	0.50	6.1772	2.9509
11	5.5	4.00	5.3864	0.55	6.3364	2.8383
12	6.0	4.00	5.4976	0.60	6.4976	2.7255
13	6.5	4.00	5.6108	0.65	6.6608	2.6127
14	7.0	4.00	5.6643	0.70	6.7643	2.5109
15	7.5	4.00	5.7193	0.75	6.8693	2.4103
16	8.0	4.00	5.7755	0.80	6.9755	2.3112
17	8.5	4.00	5.8331	0.85	7.0831	2.2137
18	9.0	4.00	5.9584	0.90	7.2584	2.1056
19	9.5	4.00	6.0863	0.95	7.4363	1.9990
20	10.0	104.00	6.2169	1.00	7.6169	49.2468
					Total	105.5423

Zero-Volatility Spread

In the same way that a zero-volatility spread relative to a default-free spot rate curve can be calculated, a zero-volatility spread to any benchmark spot rate curve can be calculated. To illustrate, suppose that a hypothetical AAA industrial bond with a coupon rate of 8% and a 10-year maturity is trading at 105.5423. The zero-volatility spread relative to the AAA industrial term structure is the spread that must be added to that term structure that will make the present value of the cash flows equal to the market price. In our illustration, the zero-volatility spread relative to this benchmark is 40 basis points, as shown in Exhibit 14.

Thus, when a zero-volatility spread is cited, it must be cited relative to some benchmark spot rate curve. This is necessary because it indicates the credit and sector risks that are being considered when the zero-volatility spread was calculated.

The Term Structure for Municipal Bonds

Unlike the taxable fixed-income market, there is no risk-free interest rate benchmark for the tax-exempt municipal market. Several benchmark curves are used in this market sector. In general, a benchmark yield curve is constructed for AAA quality rated general obligation and revenue bonds. The Delphis Hanover yield curve is a popular yield curve that is often quoted in the municipal market.

As in the taxable market, current coupon bonds are used for constructing the yield curve. However, unlike the Treasury market in which current coupon bonds are issued on regular cycles, no such practice is followed in the municipal market. In order to derive an appropriate yield curve, the AAA curve is generally derived from market observations on yields of newly issued bonds in the associated market sector.

Given the AAA yield curve, a AAA spot rate curve can be constructed using the bootstrapping methodology described earlier. As in the case of corporates, a term structure for municipal credit spreads can be developed and added to the AAA yield curve.

KEY POINTS

1. *The base interest rate in valuing fixed income securities is the rate on default-free securities and U.S. Treasury securities are viewed as default-free securities.*

2. *Because each cash flow of a fixed income security should be viewed as a zero-coupon instrument, to properly value fixed income securities, what is needed is the rate on zero-coupon default-free securities or, equivalently, the rate on zero-coupon Treasury securities.*

3. *The rate on a zero-coupon instrument is called the spot rate.*

4. *The Treasury yield curve graphically depicts the relationship between the yield on Treasury securities and maturity; however, the securities included are a combination of zero-coupon instruments (that is, Treasury bills) and Treasury coupon securities.*

5. *Since the U.S. Treasury does not issue zero-coupon securities with a maturity greater than one year, a theoretical spot rate curve must be constructed from the yield curve.*

6. *The collection of spot rates showing the relationship between theoretical spot rates and maturity is called the spot rate curve or the term structure of interest rates.*

7. *In estimating the theoretical spot rate curve, the following securities can be included: (1) on-the-run Treasury issues; (2) on-the-run Treasury issues and selected off-the-run Treasury issues; (3) all Treasury coupon securities and bills; and (4) Treasury coupon strips.*

8. *The bootstrapping methodology is utilized to construct the theoretical spot rate curve when either the on-the-run Treasury issues or on-the-run issues with selected off-the-run issues are the securities used.*

9. *The basic principle in bootstrapping a par coupon curve is that the value of the cash flows from an on-the-run Treasury issue is equal to par value.*

10. *When all Treasury coupon securities and bills are used, a statistical technique called the exponential spline methodology is used to construct the theoretical spot rate curve.*

11. *When Treasury strips are used as the theoretical spot rates, typically only the coupon strips are used.*

12. *The discount function is calculated from the theoretical spot rates and represents the present value of a $1 default-free cash flow or equivalently, the value of a default-free zero-coupon instrument with a $1 maturity value.*

13. *From a Treasury spot rate curve or discount function, the value of any default-free security can be determined.*

14. The economic force that assures that securities will be priced based on spot rates is the opportunity for government dealers to strip Treasury securities or for investors to risklessly enhance portfolio returns.

15. The traditional approach to measuring the yield premium for a non-Treasury bond is to calculate the nominal spread which is the difference between the yield of the bond in question and the yield of a comparable maturity Treasury coupon security.

16. The drawbacks of the traditional approach are that the yield used fails to take into consideration the term structure of interest rates and, in the case of callable and/or putable bonds, the effect of expected interest rate volatility on the cash flows of the non-Treasury bond is ignored.

17. To take into consideration the term structure of interest rates, a zero-volatility spread (or static spread) should be calculated.

18. The zero-volatility spread is a measure of the spread that the investor would realize over the entire Treasury spot rate curve if the bond is held to maturity.

19. Unlike the traditional or nominal spread measure, the zero-volatility spread is not a spread off one point on the Treasury yield curve but is a spread over the entire spot rate curve.

20. For bullet bonds, unless the yield curve is very steep, the nominal spread will not differ significantly from the zero-volatility spread; for securities where principal is repaid over time rather than just at maturity there can be a significant difference, particularly in a steep yield curve environment.

21. To value a security with credit risk, it is necessary to determine a term structure of credit risk or equivalently a zero-coupon credit spread.

22. Evidence suggests that the credit spread increases with maturity and the lower the credit rating, the steeper the curve.

23. An implication of an upward-sloping term structure for credit spreads is that it is inappropriate to discount the cash flows from a corporate bond at a constant spread to the Treasury spot rate curve.

24. Adding the zero-coupon credit for a particular credit quality within a sector to the Treasury spot rate curve gives the benchmark spot rate curve that should be used to value a security and from which a zero-volatility spread can be calculated.

Chapter 3

Forward Rates and
Term Structure Theories

The objectives of this chapter are to:

1. explain what is meant by forward rates;

2. demonstrate how forward rates can be calculated;

3. show the relationship between spot rates and forward rates;

4. explain the various theories of the term structure of interest rates and what they suggest about forward rates; and,

5. review the models used to explain the behavior of interest rates.

In the previous chapter, we saw how a default-free theoretical spot rate curve can be extrapolated from the Treasury yield curve. Additional information useful to market participants can be extrapolated from the Treasury yield curve: *forward rates*. These rates can be viewed as the market's consensus of future interest rates. This view, however, is predicated on a particular theory about the term structure of interest rates.

FORWARD RATES

Market participants typically have different views about what they expect future interest rates to be. Under a certain theory of the term structure of interest rates described later in this chapter and based on arbitrage arguments, the market's consensus of future interest rates can be extrapolated from the Treasury yield curve. These rates are called *forward rates*.

Examples of forward rates that can be calculated from the Treasury yield curve are the:

- 6-month forward rate six months from now
- 6-month forward rate three years from now
- 1-year forward rate one year from now
- 3-year forward rate two years from now
- 5-year forward rate three years from now

Since the forward rates are extrapolated from the Treasury yield curve, these rates are sometimes referred to as *implicit forward rates*.

To illustrate how forward rates are derived, we begin with the derivation of 6-month forward rates. The 6-month forward rates are sometimes referred to as *short forward rates*. The structure of short forward rates is called the *forward rate curve*.

Deriving 6-Month Forward Rates

To illustrate the process of extrapolating 6-month forward rates, we will use the yield curve and corresponding spot rate curve from Exhibit 1 of the previous chapter. These are reproduced in Exhibit 1.

Consider an investor who has a 1-year investment horizon and is faced with the following two alternatives:

Alternative 1: Buy a 1-year Treasury bill, or
Alternative 2: Buy a 6-month Treasury bill, and when it matures in six months buy another 6-month Treasury bill.

The investor will be indifferent toward the two alternatives if they produce the same return over the 1-year investment horizon. The investor knows the spot rate on the 6-month Treasury bill and the 1-year Treasury bill. However, he does not know what yield will be available on a 6-month Treasury bill that will be purchased six months from now. That is, he does not know the 6-month forward rate six months from now. Given the spot rates for the 6-month Treasury bill and the 1-year Treasury bill, the forward rate on a 6-month Treasury bill is the rate that equalizes the dollar return between the two alternatives.

To see how that rate can be determined, suppose that an investor purchased a 6-month Treasury bill for $X. At the end of six months, the value of this investment would be:

$$X(1 + z_1)$$

where z_1 is one-half the bond-equivalent yield (BEY) of the theoretical 6-month spot rate.

Let f represent one-half the forward rate (expressed as a BEY) on a 6-month Treasury bill available six months from now. If the investor were to renew his investment by purchasing that bill at that time, then the future dollars available at the end of one year from the $X investment would be:

$$X(1 + z_1)(1 + f)$$

Exhibit 1: Hypothetical Treasury Yield Curve and Resulting Spot Rate Curve

Period	Years	Yield to maturity (%)	Spot rate (%)
1	0.5	3.00	3.0000
2	1.0	3.30	3.3000
3	1.5	3.50	3.5053
4	2.0	3.90	3.9164
5	2.5	4.40	4.4376
6	3.0	4.70	4.7520
7	3.5	4.90	4.9622
8	4.0	5.00	5.0650
9	4.5	5.10	5.1701
10	5.0	5.20	5.2772
11	5.5	5.30	5.3864
12	6.0	5.40	5.4976
13	6.5	5.50	5.6108
14	7.0	5.55	5.6643
15	7.5	5.60	5.7193
16	8.0	5.65	5.7755
17	8.5	5.70	5.8331
18	9.0	5.80	5.9584
19	9.5	5.90	6.0863
20	10.0	6.00	6.2169

Exhibit 2: Graphical Depiction of the 6-Month Forward Rate Six Months from Now

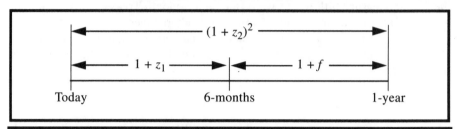

Now consider the alternative of investing in a 1-year Treasury bill. If we let z_2 represent one-half the BEY of the theoretical 1-year spot rate, then the future dollars available at the end of one year from the $X investment would be:

$$X (1 + z_2)^2$$

This is depicted in Exhibit 2.

Now, we are prepared to analyze the investor's choices and what this says about forward rates. The investor will be indifferent toward the two alternatives confronting him if he makes the same dollar investment ($X) and receives the same future dollars from both alternatives at the end of one year. That is, the investor will be indifferent if:

$$X (1 + z_1) (1 + f) = X (1 + z_2)^2$$

Solving for f, we get:

$$f = \frac{(1 + z_2)^2}{(1 + z_1)} - 1$$

Doubling f gives the BEY for the 6-month forward rate six months from now.

We can illustrate the use of this formula with the theoretical spot rates shown in Exhibit 1. From that exhibit, we know that:

6-month bill spot rate = 0.030, therefore z_1 = 0.0150
1-year bill spot rate   = 0.033, therefore z_2 = 0.0165

Substituting into the formula, we have:

$$f = \frac{(1.0165)^2}{(1.0150)} - 1 = 0.0180 = 1.8\%$$

Therefore, the forward rate on a 6-month Treasury security is 3.6% (1.8% × 2) BEY.

Let's confirm our results. If $X is invested in the 6-month Treasury bill at 1.5% and the proceeds then reinvested at the 6-month forward rate of 1.8%, the total proceeds from this alternative would be:

$X\,(1.015)\,(1.018) = 1.03327\,X$

Investment of \$X in the 1-year Treasury bill at one-half the 1-year rate, 1.0165%, would produce the following proceeds at the end of one year:

$X\,(1.0165)^2 = 1.03327\,X$

Both alternatives have the same payoff if the 6-month Treasury bill yield six months from now is 1.8% (3.6% on a BEY). This means that if an investor is guaranteed a 1.8% yield (3.6% BEY) on a 6-month Treasury bill six months from now, he will be indifferent toward the two alternatives.

The same line of reasoning can be used to obtain the 6-month forward rate beginning at any time period in the future. For example, the following can be determined:

- the 6-month forward rate three years from now
- the 6-month forward rate five years from now

The notation that we use to indicate 6-month forward rates is $_1f_m$ where the subscript 1 indicates a 1-period (6-month) rate and the subscript m indicates the period beginning m periods from now. When m is equal to zero, this means the current rate. Thus, the first 6-month forward rate is simply the current 6-month spot rate. That is,

$_1f_0 = z_1$

The general formula for determining a 6-month forward rate is:

$$_1f_m = \frac{(1 + z_{m+1})^{m+1}}{(1 + z_m)^m} - 1$$

For example, suppose that the 6-month forward rate four years (8 6-month periods) from now is sought. In terms of our notation, m is 8 and we seek $_1f_8$. The formula is then:

$$_1f_8 = \frac{(1 + z_9)^9}{(1 + z_8)^8} - 1$$

From Exhibit 1, since the 4-year spot rate is 5.065% and the 4.5-year spot rate is 5.1701%, z_8 is 2.5325% and z_9 is 2.58505%. Then,

$$_1f_8 = \frac{(1.0258505)^9}{(1.025325)^8} - 1 = 3.005\%$$

Doubling this rate gives a 6-month forward rate four years from now of 6.01%.

Exhibit 3: Six-Month Forward Rates:
The Short-Term Forward Rate Curve

Notation	Forward Rate
$_1f_0$	3.00
$_1f_1$	3.60
$_1f_2$	3.92
$_1f_3$	5.15
$_1f_4$	6.54
$_1f_5$	6.33
$_1f_6$	6.23
$_1f_7$	5.79
$_1f_8$	6.01
$_1f_9$	6.24
$_1f_{10}$	6.48
$_1f_{11}$	6.72
$_1f_{12}$	6.97
$_1f_{13}$	6.36
$_1f_{14}$	6.49
$_1f_{15}$	6.62
$_1f_{16}$	6.76
$_1f_{17}$	8.10
$_1f_{18}$	8.40
$_1f_{19}$	8.72

Exhibit 3 shows all of the 6-month forward rates for the Treasury yield curve and corresponding spot rate curve shown in Exhibit 1. The set of these forward rates is the *short-term forward-rate curve*.

Relationship between Spot Rates and Short-Term Forward Rates

Suppose an investor invests X in a 3-year zero-coupon Treasury security. The total proceeds three years (six periods) from now would be:

$$X (1 + z_6)^6$$

The investor could instead buy a 6-month Treasury bill and reinvest the proceeds every six months for three years. The future dollars or dollar return will depend on the 6-month forward rates. Suppose that the investor can actually reinvest the proceeds maturing every six months at the calculated 6-month forward rates shown in Exhibit 3. At the end of three years, an investment of X would generate the following proceeds:

$$X (1 + z_1) (1 + {_1f_1}) (1 + {_1f_2}) (1 + {_1f_3}) (1 + {_1f_4}) (1 + {_1f_5})$$

Since the two investments must give the same proceeds at the end of four years, the two previous equations can be equated:

$$X (1 + z_6)^6 = X (1 + z_1) (1 + {}_1f_1) (1 + {}_1f_2) (1 + {}_1f_3) (1 + {}_1f_4) (1 + {}_1f_5)$$

Solving for the 3-year (6-period) spot rate, we have:

$$z_6 = [(1 + z_1) (1 + {}_1f_1) (1 + {}_1f_2) (1 + {}_1f_3) (1 + {}_1f_4) (1 + {}_1f_5)]^{\frac{1}{6}} - 1$$

This equation tells us that the 3-year spot rate depends on the current 6-month spot rate and the five 6-month forward rates. In fact, the right-hand side of this equation is a geometric average of the current 6-month spot rate and the five 6-month forward rates.

Let's use the values in Exhibits 1 and 3 to confirm this result. Since the 6-month spot rate in Exhibit 1 is 3%, z_1 is 1.5% and therefore

$$z_6 = [(1.015) (1.018) (1.0196) (1.02575) (1.0327) (1.03165)]^{\frac{1}{6}} - 1$$
$$= 0.023761 = 2.3761\%$$

Doubling this rate gives 4.7522%. This agrees with the spot rate shown in Exhibit 1.

In general, the relationship between a T-period spot rate, the current 6-month spot rate, and the 6-month forward rates is as follows:

$$z_T = [(1 + z_1) (1 + {}_1f_1) (1 + {}_1f_2) ... (1 + {}_1f_{T-1})]^{1/T} - 1$$

Therefore, discounting at the forward rates will give the same present value as discounting at spot rates. This means that calculating the zero-volatility spread over the Treasury spot rate curve is the same as calculating the zero-volatility spread over the Treasury forward rate curve.

Forward Rates for Any Period

We can take the analysis of forward rates further. It is not necessary to limit ourselves to 6-month forward rates. The Treasury yield curve can be used to calculate the forward rate for any time in the future for any investment horizon.

To demonstrate how this is done, we must redefine our earlier notation. Before we defined ${}_1f_m$ as the 1-period (or 6-month) forward rate m periods from now. We will now let ${}_nf_m$ be the forward rate for an investment of n periods beginning m periods from now. This is depicted in Exhibit 4. For example, ${}_4f_6$ is the 4-period forward rate beginning six periods from now.

Now let's see how the spot rates can be used to calculate forward rates for a period greater than six months. We assume in the illustration that there are zero-coupon Treasury securities available. The existence of these securities is not necessary for determination of the forward rates. The assumption just simplifies the presentation.

Exhibit 4: : Graphical Depiction of Forward Rates

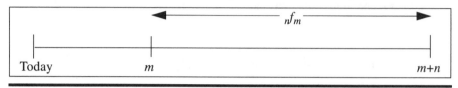

Suppose that an investor with a 5-year investment horizon is considering the following two alternatives:

Alternative 1:   Buy a 5-year (10-period) zero-coupon Treasury security, or

Alternative 2:   Buy a 3-year (6-period) zero-coupon Treasury security, and when it matures in three years buy a 2-year zero-coupon Treasury security.

By investing $\$X$ in a 5-year zero-coupon Treasury security today, the investor will have the following at the end of five years:

$$X (1 + z_{10})^{10}$$

where z_{10} is one-half the BEY of the theoretical 10-period spot rate.

With the second alternative, the amount available at the end of three years from investing $\$X$ in a 3-year zero-coupon Treasury security would be:

$$X (1 + z_6)^6$$

The amount at the end of five years depends on the forward rate for a 2-year investment beginning three years from now. In terms of our formula, it depends on $_4f_6$. The amount at the end of five years would then be:

$$X (1 + z_6)^6 (1 + {}_4f_6)^4$$

The investor will be indifferent toward the two alternatives confronting him if he makes the same dollar investment ($\$X$) and receives the same future dollars from both alternatives at the end of five years. That is, the investor will be indifferent if:

$$X (1 + z_{10})^{10} = X (1 + z_6)^6 (1 + {}_4f_6)^4$$

Solving for $_4f_6$, we get:

$${}_4f_6 = \left[\frac{(1 + z_{10})^{10}}{(1 + z_6)^6} \right]^{1/4} - 1$$

Doubling $_4f_6$ gives the BEY for the 2-year forward rate three years from now.

We can illustrate the use of this formula with the theoretical spot rates shown in Exhibit 1. From that exhibit, we know that the:

5-year spot rate = 5.2772%, therefore z_{10} = 0.026386
3-year spot rate = 4.7520%, therefore z_6 = 0.023760

Substituting these into the formula, we have:

$$_4f_6 = \left[\frac{(1.026386)^{10}}{(1.023760)^6}\right]^{1/4} - 1 = 0.03034 = 3.034\%$$

Therefore, the 2-year forward rate three years from now is 6.068% (3.034% × 2) on a BEY.

In general, the formula for any forward rate is:

$$_nf_m = \left[\frac{(1 + z_{m+n})^{m+n}}{(1 + z_m)^m}\right]^{1/n} - 1$$

Forward Rate as a Hedgeable Rate

A natural question about forward rates is how well they do at predicting future interest rates. Studies have demonstrated that forward rates do not do a good job at predicting future interest rates.[1] Then, why the big deal about understanding forward rates? The reason is that forward rates indicate how an investor's expectations must differ from the market consensus in order to make the correct decision.

A forward rate may not be realized. That is irrelevant. The fact is that a forward rate indicates to the investor if his expectation about a rate in the future is less than the corresponding forward rate, then he would be better off investing now to lock in the forward rate. For this reason, as well as others explained later, some market participants prefer not to talk about forward rates as being market consensus rates. Instead they refer to forward rates as being *hedgeable rates*.

THEORIES OF THE TERM STRUCTURE OF INTEREST RATES

If we plot the term structure — the yield to maturity, or the spot rate, at successive maturities against maturity — what is it likely to look like?

Exhibit 5 shows three shapes that have appeared with some frequency over time. Panel A shows an upward-sloping yield curve; that is, yield rises steadily as maturity increases. This shape is commonly referred to as a "normal" or "positive" yield curve. Panel B shows a downward-sloping or "inverted" yield curve, where yields decline as maturity increases. Panel C shows a "flat" yield curve. Two major theories have evolved to account for these observed shapes of the yield curve: the *expectations theory* and the *market segmentation theory*.

---

[1] Eugene F. Fama, "Forward Rates as Predictors of Future Spot Rates," *Journal of Financial Economics* Vol. 3, No. 4, 1976, pp. 361-377.

Exhibit 5: Three Observed Yield Curve Shapes

Yields on 10/24/94 — Normal

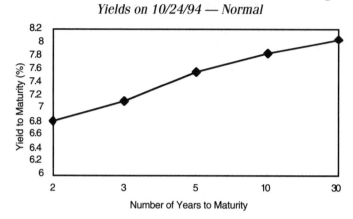

Yields on 12/28/89 — Flat

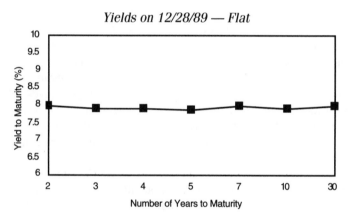

Yields on 3/3/89 — Inverted

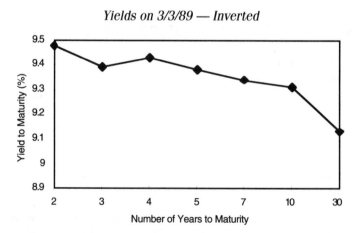

Exhibit 6: Term Structure Theories

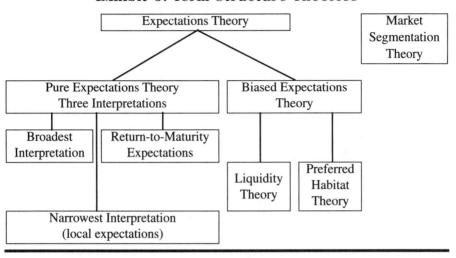

There are several forms of the expectations theory — the *pure expectations theory*, the *liquidity theory*, and the *preferred habitat theory*. All share a hypothesis about the behavior of short-term forward rates and also assume that the forward rates in current long-term bonds are closely related to the market's expectations about future short-term rates. These three theories differ, however, on whether other factors also affect forward rates, and how. The pure expectations theory postulates that no systematic factors other than expected future short-term rates affect forward rates; the liquidity theory and the preferred habitat theory assert that there are other factors. Accordingly, the last two forms of the expectations theory are sometimes referred to as *biased expectations theories*. The relationship among the various theories is described below and summarized in Exhibit 6.

The Pure Expectations Theory

According to the pure expectations theory, forward rates exclusively represent expected future rates. Thus, the entire term structure at a given time reflects the market's current expectations of the family of future short-term rates. Under this view, a rising term structure must indicate that the market expects short-term rates to rise throughout the relevant future. Similarly, a flat term structure reflects an expectation that future short-term rates will be mostly constant, while a falling term structure must reflect an expectation that future short-term rates will decline.

Drawbacks of the Theory

The pure expectations theory suffers from one shortcoming, which, qualitatively, is quite serious. It neglects the risks inherent in investing in bonds. If forward rates were perfect predictors of future interest rates, then the future prices of bonds would be known with certainty. The return over any investment period would be certain and independent of the maturity of the instrument acquired. However, with the uncertainty about future interest rates and, therefore, about future prices of bonds, these instruments become risky investments in the sense that the return over some investment horizon is unknown.

There are two risks that cause uncertainty about the return over some investment horizon. The first is the uncertainty about the price of the bond at the end of the investment horizon. For example, an investor who plans to invest for five years might consider the following three investment alternatives: (1) invest in a 5-year bond and hold it for five years; (2) invest in a 12-year bond and sell it at the end of five years; and, (3) invest in a 30-year bond and sell it at the end of five years. The return that will be realized for the second and third alternatives is not known because the price of each of these bonds at the end of five years is unknown. In the case of the 12-year bond, the price will depend on the yield on 7-year bonds five years from now; and the price of the 30-year bond will depend on the yield on 25-year bonds five years from now. Since forward rates implied in the current term structure for a 7-year bond five years from now and a 25-year bond five years from now are not perfect predictors of the actual future rates, there is uncertainty about the price for both bonds five years from now. Thus, there is price risk; that is, the price of the bond may be lower than currently expected at the end of the investment horizon. As explained in the next chapter, an important feature of the interest rate risk is that it increases with the length of the bond's maturity.

The second risk involves the uncertainty about the rate at which the proceeds from a bond that matures prior to the end of the investment horizon can be reinvested until the maturity date, that is, reinvestment risk. For example, an investor who plans to invest for five years might consider the following three alternative investments: (1) invest in a 5-year bond and hold it for five years; (2) invest in a 6-month instrument and, when it matures, reinvest the proceeds in 6-month instruments over the entire 5-year investment horizon; and, (3) invest in a 2-year bond and, when it matures, reinvest the proceeds in a 3-year bond. The risk in the second and third alternatives is that the return over the 5-year investment horizon is unknown because rates at which the proceeds can be reinvested until the end of the investment horizon are unknown.

Interpretations of the Theory

There are several interpretations of the pure expectations theory that have been put forth by economists. These interpretations are not exact equivalents nor are they consistent with each other, in large part because they offer different treatments of the two risks associated with realizing a return that we have just explained.[2]

The broadest interpretation of the pure expectations theory suggests that investors expect the return for any investment horizon to be the same, regardless

---

[2] These formulations are summarized by John Cox, Jonathan Ingersoll, Jr., and Stephen Ross, "A Re-examination of Traditional Hypotheses About the Term Structure of Interest Rates," *Journal of Finance* (September 1981), pp. 769-799.

of the maturity strategy selected.[3] For example, consider an investor who has a 6-month investment horizon. According to this theory, it makes no difference if a 5-year, 12-year, or 30-year bond is purchased and held for five years since the investor expects the return from all three bonds to be the same over the 5-year investment horizon. A major criticism of this very broad interpretation of the theory is that, because of price risk associated with investing in bonds with a maturity greater than the investment horizon, the expected returns from these three very different investments should differ in significant ways.[4]

A second interpretation, referred to as the *local expectations* form of the pure expectations theory, suggests that the return will be the same over a short-term investment horizon starting today. For example, if an investor has a 6-month investment horizon, buying a 5-year, 10-year or 20-year bond will produce the same 6-month return.

This is illustrated in Exhibit 7 for a 6-month investment horizon for three of the bonds in Exhibit 1 — the 1-year, 5-year, and 10-year issues. For the 6-month issue in Exhibit 1, the total return is the 6-month spot rate of 3%. Panel A of Exhibit 7 shows the cash flows for the 1-year issue six months from now. If the short-term forward rate is realized, the 6-month forward rate is 3.6% as indicated in Exhibit 3. The price of the 1-year issue six months from now when discounted at the 6-month forward rate is shown in Exhibit 7. Adding this price to the coupon rate and dividing by the initial price of 100 gives a 6-month total return of 1.5% and a 1-year total return of 3%. This is the same total return as the 6-month issue. Panels B and C of Exhibit 7 show the same calculations for the 5-year and 10-year issues assuming that the 6-month forward rates shown in Exhibit 3 are realized 6-months from now. As can be seen, the total return is 3%. Thus, in each case, the total return over a 6-month horizon is the same and it is equal to the current 6-month spot rate.

It has been demonstrated that the local expectations formulation, which is narrow in scope, is the only interpretation of the pure expectations theory that can be sustained in equilibrium.[5]

The third and final interpretation of the pure expectations theory suggests that the return that an investor will realize by rolling over short-term bonds to some investment horizon will be the same as holding a zero-coupon bond with a maturity that is the same as that investment horizon. (A zero-coupon bond has no reinvestment risk, so that future interest rates over the investment horizon do not affect the return.) This variant is called the *return-to-maturity expectations* interpretation. For example, let's once again assume that an investor has a 5-year investment horizon. By buying a 5-year zero-coupon bond and holding it to maturity, the investor's return is the difference between the maturity value and the price of the bond, divided by the price of the bond. According to the return-to-maturity expectations, the same return will be realized by buying a 6-month instrument and rolling it over for five years. At this time, the validity of this interpretation is subject to considerable doubt.

---

[3] F. Lutz, "The Structure of Interest Rates," *Quarterly Journal of Economics* (1940-41), pp. 36-63.
[4] Cox, Ingersoll and Ross, pp. 774-775.
[5] Cox, Ingersoll, and Ross.

Exhibit 7: Total Return Over 6-Month Investment Horizon if 6-Month Forward Rates are Realized

Panel A: Total return on 1-year issue if forward rates are realized			
Period	Cash flow ($)	Six-month forward rate (%)	Price at horizon ($)
1	101.650	3.60	99.85265

Price at horizon: 99.85265	Total proceeds: 101.5027
Coupon: 1.65	Total return: 3.00%

Panel B: Total return on 5-year issue if forward rates are realized			
Period	Cash flows ($)	Six-month forward rate (%)	Present value ($)
1	2.600	3.60	2.55403
2	2.600	3.92	2.50493
3	2.600	5.15	2.44205
4	2.600	6.54	2.36472
5	2.600	6.33	2.29217
6	2.600	6.23	2.22293
7	2.600	5.79	2.16039
8	2.600	6.01	2.09736
9	102.600	6.24	80.26096
		Total:	98.89954

Price at horizon: 98.89954	Total proceeds: 101.4995
Coupon: 2.60	Total return: 3.00%

Panel C: Total return on 10-year issue if forward rates are realized			
Period	Cash flows ($)	Six-month forward rate (%)	Present value ($)
1	3.000	3.60	2.94695
2	3.000	3.92	2.89030
3	3.000	5.15	2.81775
4	3.000	6.54	2.72853
5	3.000	6.33	2.64482
6	3.000	6.23	2.56492
7	3.000	5.79	2.49275
8	3.000	6.01	2.42003
9	3.000	6.24	2.34681
10	3.000	6.48	2.27316
11	3.000	6.72	2.19927
12	3.000	6.97	2.12520
13	3.000	6.36	2.05970
14	3.000	6.49	1.99497
15	3.000	6.62	1.93105
16	3.000	6.76	1.86791
17	3.000	8.10	1.79521
18	3.000	8.40	1.72285
19	103.000	8.72	56.67989
		Total:	98.50208

Price at horizon: 98.50208	Total proceeds: 101.5021
Coupon: 3.00	Total return: 3.00%

Biased Expectations Theories

There are two forms of the biased expectations theory: the liquidity theory and the preferred habitat theory.

The Liquidity Theory

We have explained that the drawback of the pure expectations theory is that it does not consider the risks associated with bond investments. We have just shown that there is indeed risk in holding a long-term bond for one period, and that risk increases with the bond's maturity because maturity and price volatility are directly related.

Given this uncertainty, and considering that investors typically do not like uncertainty, some economists and financial analysts have suggested a different theory. This theory states that investors will hold longer-term maturities if they are offered a long-term rate higher than the average of expected future rates by a risk premium that is positively related to the term to maturity.[6] Put differently, the forward rates should reflect both interest rate expectations and a "liquidity" premium (really a risk premium), and the premium should be higher for longer maturities.

According to this theory, which is called the *liquidity theory of the term structure*, forward rates will not be an unbiased estimate of the market's expectations of future interest rates because they embody a liquidity premium. Thus, an upward-sloping yield curve may reflect expectations that future interest rates either (1) will rise, or (2) will be unchanged or even fall, but with a liquidity premium increasing fast enough with maturity so as to produce an upward-sloping yield curve.

The Preferred Habitat Theory

Another theory, known as the *preferred habitat theory*, also adopts the view that the term structure reflects the expectation of the future path of interest rates as well as a risk premium. However, the preferred habitat theory rejects the assertion that the risk premium must rise uniformly with maturity.[7] Proponents of the preferred habitat theory say that the latter conclusion could be accepted if all investors intend to liquidate their investment at the shortest possible date while all borrowers are anxious to borrow long. This assumption can be rejected since institutions have holding periods dictated by the nature of their liabilities.

The preferred habitat theory asserts that if there is an imbalance between the supply and demand for funds within a given maturity range, investors and borrowers will not be reluctant to shift their investing and financing activities out of their preferred maturity sector to take advantage of any imbalance. However, to do so, investors must be induced by a yield premium in order to accept the risks associated with shifting funds out of their preferred sector. Similarly, borrowers can only be induced to raise funds in a maturity sector other than their preferred sector by a sufficient cost savings to compensate for the corresponding funding risk.

---

[6] John R. Hicks, *Value and Capital* (London: Oxford University Press, 1946), second ed., pp. 141-145.

[7] Franco Modigliani and Richard Sutch, "Innovations in Interest Rate Policy," *American Economic Review* (May 1966), pp. 178-197.

Thus, this theory proposes that the shape of the yield curve is determined by both expectations of future interest rates and a risk premium, positive or negative, to induce market participants to shift out of their preferred habitat. Clearly, according to this theory, yield curves sloping up, down, or flat are all possible.

Market Segmentation Theory

The *market segmentation theory* also recognizes that investors have preferred habitats dictated by the nature of their liabilities. This theory also proposes that the major reason for the shape of the yield curve lies in asset/liability management constraints (either regulatory or self-imposed) and/or creditors (borrowers) restricting their lending (financing) to specific maturity sectors.[8] However, the market segmentation theory differs from the preferred habitat theory in that it assumes that neither investors nor borrowers are willing to shift from one maturity sector to another to take advantage of opportunities arising from differences between expectations and forward rates. Thus, for the segmentation theory, the shape of the yield curve is determined by the supply of and demand for securities within each maturity sector.

MODELS DESCRIBING THE BEHAVIOR OF INTEREST RATES

Term structure theory is concerned with the behavior of interest rates; it identifies the factors that are expected to explain the movement of interest rates. Whatever the factors are, they are random in nature. That is, the future value of a factor that is expected to explain the movement of interest rates is not known with certainty. Thus, it is necessary to specify a statistical process that describes the behavior of these factors and is a reasonable characterization of their actual behavior.

The most common model used to describe the behavior of interest rates is one which assumes that short-term rates follow some statistical process and that other interest rates in the term structure are related to short-term rates. The short rate is the only one that is assumed to drive the rates of all other maturities. Hence, these models are referred to as *one-factor models*. The other rates are not randomly determined once the short rate is specified. Using arbitrage arguments, the equilibrium rate for all other maturities is determined. Three formulations of one-factor models are described in the appendix to this chapter.

There are also two-factor models that have been proposed. One factor in all these models is the short rate. The different models specify a second factor. In the model proposed by Brennan and Schwartz, the second factor is a long-term rate.[9] In the two-factor developed by Fong and Vasicek, the second factor is the volatility of short rates.[10]

---

[8] This theory was suggested in J.M. Culbertson, "The Term Structure of Interest Rates," *Quarterly Journal of Economics* (November 1957), pp. 489-504.

[9] Michael J. Brennan and Eduardo S. Schwartz, "A Continuous Time Approach to the Pricing of Bonds," *Journal of Banking and Finance* (July 1979), pp. 133-155.

[10] H. Gifford Fong and Oldrich A. Vasicek, "Fixed-Income Volatility Management," *Journal of Portfolio Management* (Summer 1991), pp. 41-46.

KEY POINTS

1. *Using arbitrage arguments, the market's consensus of future interest rates can be extrapolated from the Treasury yield curve or equivalently, the spot rate curve.*

2. *These rates are called forward rates or implied forward rates and the set of short-term (6-month) forward rates is the short forward rate curve.*

3. *The spot rate for a given period is related to the forward rates, specifically, the spot rate is a geometric average of the current 6-month spot rate and the subsequent 6-month forward rates.*

4. *Because of the relationship between spot and forward rates, discounting at the forward rates will give the same value for a security as discounting at the spot rates.*

5. *Calculating the zero-volatility spread over the Treasury spot rate curve is the same as calculating that spread over the Treasury forward rate curve.*

6. *Historically, different shapes have been observed for the Treasury yield curve: a normal or positive yield curve, a downward-sloping or inverted yield curve, and a flat yield curve.*

7. *The two major theories for explaining the observed shapes of the yield curve are the expectations theory and the market segmentation theory.*

8. *The three forms of the expectations theory (the pure expectations theory, the liquidity theory, and the preferred habitat theory) assume that the forward rates in current long-term bonds are closely related to the market's expectations about future short-term rates.*

9. *The three forms of the expectations theory differ on whether other factors also affect forward rates, and how.*

10. *The pure expectations theory postulates that no systematic factors other than expected future short-term rates affect forward rates.*

11. *Because forward rates are not perfect predictors of future interest rates, the pure expectations theory suffers from one shortcoming: it neglects the risks (interest rate risk and reinvestment risk) associated with investing in bonds.*

12. *The broadest interpretation of the pure expectations theory suggests that investors expect the return for any investment horizon to be the same, regardless of the maturity strategy selected.*

13. The local expectations form of the pure expectations theory suggests that the return of every maturity bond will be the same over a short-term investment horizon starting today and it is this narrow interpretation that economists have demonstrated is the only interpretation that can be sustained in equilibrium.

14. The return-to-maturity expectations interpretation of the pure expectations theory suggests that the return that an investor will realize by rolling over short-term bonds to some investment horizon will be the same as holding a zero-coupon bond with a maturity that is the same as that investment horizon.

15. The liquidity theory and the preferred habitat theory assert that there are other factors that affect forward rates and these two theories are therefore referred to as biased expectations theories.

16. The liquidity theory states that investors will hold longer-term maturities only if they are offered a risk premium and therefore forward rates should reflect both interest rate expectations and a liquidity risk premium.

17. The preferred habitat theory in addition to adopting the view that forward rates reflect the expectation of the future path of interest rates as well as a risk premium argues that the risk premium need not reflect a liquidity premium but the demand and supply of funds in a given maturity range.

18. The market segmentation theory also recognizes that investors have preferred maturity sectors dictated by the nature of their liabilities but it goes further than the preferred habitat theory by assuming that neither investors nor borrowers are willing to shift from one maturity sector to another to take advantage of opportunities arising from differences between expectations and forward rates.

19. To model the term structure, it is necessary to identify the factors that affect the behavior of interest rates and to specify a statistical process that describes the behavior of those factors and is a reasonable characterization of their actual behavior.

20. The one-factor model which assumes that changes in the short rate determines the term structure is the most commonly used model.

APPENDIX:
ONE-FACTOR MODELS OF THE TERM STRUCTURE

One-factor models of the term structure are formulated in terms of how they describe the dynamics of the short rate; that is, they specify how the short rate changes for small changes in the underlying variables that affect its value. In this appendix, we discuss the various formulations of the one-factor model.

SOME BASICS

To introduce the term structure dynamic models, some basic concepts from probability theory must be explained.

Random Variable

In one-factor models, the short rate is a *random* or *stochastic variable* because its value over time changes in an uncertain way. A random variable is defined as a variable which can have more than one possible future outcome.

A random variable can be classified as either a *continuous variable* or a *discrete variable*. A continuous variable is one that has no break. For example, consider the random variable of interest, the short rate. Suppose that the short rate can be between 0% and 25% and that it can take on any value within this range of probable outcomes. Thus, in moving from, say, 3% to 4%, the short rate can take on a value of 3.79217%. A discrete variable, by contrast, has breaks or jumps. For example, if in moving from 3% to 4% the short rate is restricted to taking on only values in 20 basis point increments (i.e., 3.2%, 3.4%, 3.6%, and 3.8%) it would be classified as a discrete variable. In the development of the models in this chapter, we assume that the random variables are continuous.

Stochastic Process

While the value of the short rate at some future time is uncertain, the pattern by which it changes over time can be assumed. In statistical terminology, this pattern or behavior is called a *stochastic process* or *probability distribution*. Thus, when we say that it is necessary to describe the dynamics of the short rate, we mean that it is necessary to specify the stochastic process that describes the movement of the short rate.

Discrete-Time Versus Continuous-Time Stochastic Processes

Stochastic processes can be classified according to when the value of the random variable can change. When the value of the random variable can change at only fixed points in time, the stochastic process that describes the random process is called a *discrete-time stochastic process*. If, however, the random variable can change at any point in time (no matter how small the time interval), the stochastic process is called a *continuous-time stochastic process*.

In the models that we describe in this appendix, we assume a continuous-time stochastic process; that is, we assume continuous trading. The assumption that the random variable is continuous and that the stochastic process is a continuous-time stochastic process allows the use of calculus to derive important results.

Standard Wiener Process

There are several types of continuous-time stochastic processes. A simple stochastic process for describing the dynamics of the short rate is a *standard Wiener process* and is expressed in equation form as follows:

$$dr = b \, dt + \sigma \, dx \tag{1}$$

where

$$
\begin{aligned}
dr &= \text{change in the short rate} \\
b &= \text{expected direction of rate change} \\
dt &= \text{length of time interval} \\
\sigma &= \text{standard deviation of changes in the short rate} \\
dx &= \text{random process}
\end{aligned}
$$

Equation (1) states that the change in the short rate (dr) over a very small interval of time (dt) depends on: (1) the expected direction of the change in the short rate (b) and (2) a random process (dx).

The expected direction of the change in the short rate (b) is called the *drift rate*. The random nature of the change in the short rate comes from the random variable x in equation (1).

In a standard Wiener process it is assumed that the random variable x over a very small time interval is normally distributed with a mean of zero and a standard deviations of one.[11] The change in the short rate will then be proportional to the value of the random variable, the proportionality depending on the standard deviation of the change in the short rate (σ). It is also assumed that the change in the short rate for any two different short intervals of time are independent.

Given the above assumptions, two properties of the standard Wiener process follow:

> *Property 1:* The expected value of the change in the short rate is equal to the drift rate (b). If the drift rate is assumed to be equal to zero, this means that the expected value of the change in the short rate is zero and therefore the expected value for the short rate is its current value.

> *Property 2:* The variance of the change in the short rate over some interval of T is equal to T and its standard deviation is the square root of T.

---

[11] Statistically, this means that x is drawn from a standardized normal distribution.

Ito Process

A special case of the standard Wiener process is to assume that both the drift rate and the standard deviation of the change in the short rate is a function of (i.e., depends on) the level of the short rate and time. This is expressed as follows:

$$dr = b(r,t)\, dt + \sigma(r,t)\, dx \tag{2}$$

All of the symbols are the same as in equation (1).

The notation $b(r,t)$ means that the drift rate depends on the short rate r and time t. Similarly, $\sigma(r,t)$ means that the standard deviation of the change in the short rate depends on the short rate and time. This special case of the standard Wiener process as formulated in equation (2) is called an *Ito process*.

ALTERNATIVE SPECIFICATIONS OF THE ONE-FACTOR MODELS

It is the Ito process that is used in modeling the short-term rate. To describe the dynamics of the short rate it is necessary to specify the dynamics of the two terms in the Ito process:

1. dynamics of the drift term, $b(r,t)$, and
2. dynamics of the variance or volatility term, $\sigma(r,t)$

It is the specification of the variance term that characterizes a model of the term structure as a *one-factor model*.

Dynamics of the Drift Term

In the Ito process to describe changes in the short rate over time, one formulation is to assume that the drift rate follows a *mean-reversion process* as described below:

$$b(r,t) = \alpha(\bar{r} - r)$$

where

α = the speed of adjustment
$\bar{r}$ = the long-run stable mean of the short rate

The mean-reverting process in the drift term drives the short rate to converge toward its long-run stable mean with the appropriate speed of adjustment (α).

Dynamics of the Variance Term

Three alternative specifications of the variance term have been suggested in the financial economics literature.[12] In each formulation, the variance term does not

---

[12] For a discussion of other formulations and empirical evidence on their relative performance, see K.C. Chan, G. Andrew Karolyi, Francis A. Longstaff, and Anthony B. Sanders, "An Empirical Comparison of Alternative Models of the Short-Term Interest Rate," *Journal of Finance* (July 1992), pp. 1209-1227.

depend on time. Because of this, the resulting term structure model is called a one-factor model. That is, each formulation has the following form:

$$\sigma(r,t) = \sigma(r)$$

which means that the variance is independent of t.

Vasicek Specification
The first specification, suggested by Oldrich Vasicek in 1977,[13] is

$$\sigma(r,t) = \sigma$$

This means that volatility is independent of both the level of the short rate and time.

Dothan Specification
In 1978, Uri Dothan[14] suggested the following specification for volatility:

$$\sigma(r,t) = \sigma r$$

This specification assumes that volatility is related to the level of the short rate, but independent of time. Thus, the higher the level of the short rate, the greater the volatility of rates.

Cox-Ingersoll-Ross Specification
In 1985, John Cox, Jonathan Ingersoll, and Stephen Ross (CIR)[15] suggested the following specification which has subsequently been used in most sophisticated models of the term structure of interest rates:

$$\sigma(r, t) = \sigma\sqrt{r}$$

The CIR model, also called the *square-root model*, indicates that (1) volatility increases with the short rate and (2) negative interest rates cannot occur.

Mean-Reverting Square Root Diffusion Model
A popular formula for describing a one-factor model is to assume that the drift rate is mean reverting as described earlier and the variance follows the CIR or square-root model. The resulting stochastic process for the short rate is then:

$$dr = \alpha(\bar{r} - r)dt + \sigma\sqrt{r}dx$$

This model is sometimes referred to as the *mean-reverting square-root diffusion process*. This assumed stochastic process of the short rate has shown to be a reasonable approximation of interest rate behavior.

---

[13] Oldrich A. Vasicek, "An Equilibrium Characterization of the Term Structure," *Journal of Financial Economics* (1977), pp. 177-188.

[14] L. Uri Dothan, "On the Term Structure of Interest Rates," *Journal of Financial Economics* (1978), pp. 59-69.

[15] John C. Cox, Jonathan E. Ingersoll, Jr, and Stephen A. Ross, "A Theory of the Term Structure of Interest Rates," *Econometrica* (1985), pp. 385-407.

Chapter 4

Measuring Price Sensitivity to Interest Rate Changes

The objectives of this chapter are to:

1. review the relationship between the price and the yield of a fixed income security;

2. illustrate the price volatility properties of an option-free bond;

3. explain why the calculation of the duration of a security requires a valuation model;

4. provide a general formula that can be used to calculate the duration of any security assuming a parallel shift in the yield curve;

5. explain why the traditional duration measure, modified duration, is of limited value in determining the duration of a security with an embedded option;

6. distinguish between modified duration and effective duration;

7. explain what the convexity measure of a bond is; and,

8. distinguish between standard convexity and effective convexity.

While the focus of this book is on the valuation of fixed income securities, investors are also concerned with how the value of a security will change when interest rates change. The responsiveness of a security's price to interest rate changes is popularly referred to as *duration*.

PRICE VOLATILITY CHARACTERISTICS OF OPTION-FREE BONDS

A fundamental principle of an option-free bond (that is, a bond that does not have any embedded options) is that the price of the bond changes in the opposite direction from a change in the bond's yield. Exhibit 1 illustrates this property for four hypothetical bonds, where the bond prices are shown assuming a par value of $100.

When the price/yield relationship for any option-free bond is graphed, it exhibits the shape shown in Exhibit 2. Notice that as the yield rises, the price of the option-free bond declines. However, this relationship is not linear (that is, it is not a straight line). The shape of the price/yield relationship for any option-free bond is referred to as *convex*. The price/yield relationship that we have discussed refers to an instantaneous change in yield.

Properties of Option-Free Bonds

Exhibit 3 uses the four hypothetical bonds in Exhibit 1 to show the percentage change in each bond's price for various changes in the yield, assuming that the initial yield for all four bonds is 6%. An examination of Exhibit 3 reveals several properties concerning the price volatility of an option-free bond.

Exhibit 1: Price/Yield Relationship for Four Hypothetical Option-Free Bonds

	Price			
Yield (%)	6%/5 year	6%/20year	9%/5 year	9%/20year
4.00	108.9826	127.3555	122.4565	168.3887
5.00	104.3760	112.5514	117.5041	150.2056
5.50	102.1600	106.0195	115.1201	142.1367
5.90	100.4276	101.1651	113.2556	136.1193
5.99	100.0427	100.1157	112.8412	134.8159
6.00	100.0000	100.0000	112.7953	134.6722
6.01	99.9574	99.8845	112.7494	134.5287
6.10	99.5746	98.8535	112.3373	133.2472
6.50	97.8944	94.4479	110.5280	127.7605
7.00	95.8417	89.3225	108.3166	121.3551
8.00	91.8891	80.2072	104.0554	109.8964

Exhibit 2: Price/Yield Relationship for an Option-Free Bond

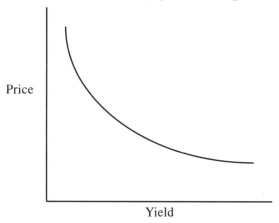

Exhibit 3: Instantaneous Percentage Price Change for Four Hypothetical Bonds
(Initial Yield for all Four Bonds is 6%)

New Yield (%)	Percent Price Change			
	6%/5 year	6%/20year	9%/5 year	9%/20year
4.00	8.98	27.36	8.57	25.04
5.00	4.38	12.55	4.17	11.53
5.50	2.16	6.02	2.06	5.54
5.90	0.43	1.17	0.41	1.07
5.99	0.04	0.12	0.04	0.11
6.01	−0.04	−0.12	−0.04	−0.11
6.10	−0.43	−1.15	−0.41	−1.06
6.50	−2.11	−5.55	−2.01	−5.13
7.00	−4.16	−10.68	−3.97	−9.89
8.00	−8.11	−19.79	−7.75	−18.40

Property 1: Although the prices of all option-free bonds move in the opposite direction from the change in yield, the percentage price change is not the same for all bonds.

Property 2: For small changes in yield, the percentage price change for a given bond is roughly the same, whether the yield increases or decreases.

Property 3: For large changes in yield, the percentage price change is not the same for an increase in yield as it is for a decrease in yield.

Property 4: For a large change in yield of an equal number of basis points, the percentage price increase is greater than the percentage price decrease.

The implication of Property 4 is that if an investor is long a bond, the price appreciation that will be realized if the yield decreases is greater than the capital loss that will be realized if the yield rises by the same number of basis points. For an investor who is short a bond, the reverse is true: the potential capital loss is greater than the potential capital gain if the yield changes by a given number of basis points.

An explanation for these four properties of bond price volatility lies in the convex shape of the price/yield relationship.

Characteristics of a Bond that Affect its Price Volatility

There are two characteristics of an option-free bond that determine its price volatility that can be verified by examining Exhibit 3: coupon and term to maturity.

Characteristic 1: For a given term to maturity and initial yield, the lower the coupon rate the greater the price volatility of a bond.

Characteristic 2: For a given coupon rate and initial yield, the longer the term to maturity, the greater the price volatility.

An implication of the second characteristic is that investors who want to increase a portfolio's price volatility because they expect interest rates to fall, all other factors being constant, should hold bonds with long maturities in the portfolio. To reduce a portfolio's price volatility in anticipation of a rise in interest rates, bonds with short-term maturities should be held in the portfolio.

The Effects of Yield to Maturity

We cannot ignore the fact that credit considerations cause different bonds to trade at different yields, even if they have the same coupon and maturity. How, then, holding other factors constant, does the yield to maturity affect a bond's price volatility? As it turns out, the higher the yield to maturity that a bond trades at, the lower the price volatility.

To see this, we can compare a 6% 20-year bond initially selling at a yield of 6%, and a 6% 20-year bond initially selling at a yield of 10%. The former is initially at a price of 100, and the latter carries a price of 65.68. Now, if the yields on both bonds increase by 100 basis points, the first bond trades down by 10.68 points (10.68%). After the assumed increase in yield, the second bond will trade at a price of 59.88, for a price decline of only 5.80 (or 8.83%). Thus, we see that the bond that trades at a lower yield is more volatile in both percentage price change and absolute price change, as long as the other bond characteristics are the same.

A possibly more relevant comparison of bond price volatility is that of comparing bonds that trade at different yields but starting them all on the same footing (e.g., by comparing only bonds trading at par). For par bonds trading at different yields but with the same maturity, the lower yielding bonds still exhibit both greater absolute price change and percentage price change for a given change in yield.

An implication of this is that, for a given change in yields, price volatility is lower when yield levels in the market are high, and price volatility is higher when yield levels are low.

MEASURING INTEREST RATE RISK

Now we know that coupon and maturity affect a security's price volatility when yield changes, and that the level of interest rates affects price volatility. What is needed is a measure that encompasses these three factors that affect a security's price volatility when yields change. The most obvious way to measure the price sensitivity of a security to changes in interest rates is to change rates by a small number of basis points and calculate how the value of a security will change.

To do this, we introduce the following notation. Let

Δy = change in rate used to calculate new values
V_+ = estimated value if yield is increased by Δy
V_- = estimated value if yield is decreased by Δy
V_0 = initial price (per \$100 of par value)

There are two key points to keep in mind in the foregoing discussion. First, the change in yield referred to above is the same change in yield for all maturities. This assumption is commonly referred to as a *parallel yield curve shift assumption*. Thus, the foregoing discussion about the price sensitivity of a security to interest rate changes is limited to parallel shifts in the yield curve. Later in this chapter we will address the case where the yield curve shifts in a nonparallel manner.

Second, the notation refers to the estimated value of the security. This value is obtained from a valuation model. Consequently, the resulting measure of the price sensitivity of a security to interest rates changes is only as good as the valuation model employed to obtain the estimated value of the security.

Now let's focus on the measure of interest. We are interested in the percentage change in the price of a security when interest rates change. The percentage change in price per basis point change is found by dividing the percentage price change by the number of basis points (Δy times 100). That is:

$$\frac{V_- - V_0}{V_0(\Delta y)100}$$

Similarly, the percentage change in price per basis point change for an increase in yield of Δy times 100 is:

$$\frac{V_0 - V_+}{V_0(\Delta y)100}$$

As explained earlier, the percentage price change for an increase and decrease in interest rates will not be the same. Consequently, the average percentage price change per basis point change in yield can be calculated. This is done as follows:

$$\frac{1}{2}\left[\frac{V_- - V_0}{V_0(\Delta y)100} + \frac{V_0 - V_+}{V_0(\Delta y)100}\right]$$

or equivalently,

$$\frac{V_- - V_+}{2V_0(\Delta y)100}$$

The approximate percentage price change for a 100 basis point change in yield is found by multiplying the previous formula by 100. The name popularly used to refer to this change is *duration*. Thus,

$$\text{Duration} = \frac{V_- - V_+}{2V_0(\Delta y)} \tag{1}$$

To illustrate this formula, consider the following option-free bond: a 9% coupon 20-year bond trading to yield 6%. The initial price or value (V_0) is 134.6722. Suppose the yield is changed by 20 basis points. If the yield is decreased to 5.8%, the value of this bond (V_-) would be 137.5888. If the yield is increased to 6.2%, the value of this bond (V_+) would be 131.8439.

Thus,

$$\Delta y = 0.0020$$
$$V_+ = 131.8439$$
$$V_- = 137.5888$$
$$V_0 = 134.6722$$

Substituting these values into the duration formula,

$$\text{Duration} = \frac{137.5888 - 131.8439}{2(134.6722)(0.002)} = 10.66$$

The duration of a security can be interpreted as the approximate percentage change in price for a 100 basis point parallel shift in the yield curve. Thus a bond with a duration of 4.8 will change by approximately 4.8% for a 100 basis point parallel shift in the yield curve. For a 50 basis point parallel shift in the yield curve, the bond's price will change by approximately 2.4%; for a 25 basis point parallel shift in the yield curve, 1.2%, etc.

Modified Duration Versus Effective Duration

A popular form of duration that is used by practitioners is *modified duration*. Modified duration is the approximate percentage change in a bond's price for a 100 basis point parallel shift in the yield curve assuming that the bond's cash flows do *not* change when the yield curve shifts. What this means is that in calculating the values of V_- and V_+ in equation (1), the cash flows used to calculate V_0 are used. Therefore, the change in the bond's price when the yield curve is shifted by a small number of basis points is due solely to discounting at the new yield level.

Exhibit 4: Modified Duration Versus Effective Duration

Duration
Interpretation: Generic description of the sensitivity of a bond's price (as a percentage of initial price) to a parallel shift in the yield curve

Modified Duration	*Effective Duration*
Duration measure in which it is assumed that yield changes do not change the expected cash flows	Duration in which recognition is given to the fact that yield changes may change the expected cash flows

The assumption that the cash flows will not change when the yield curve shifts in a parallel fashion makes sense for option-free bonds such as noncallable Treasury securities. This is because the payments made by the U.S. Department of the Treasury to a holder of its obligations do not change when the yield curve changes. However, the same cannot be said for callable and putable bonds and mortgage-backed securities. For these securities, a change in yield will alter the expected cash flows.

The valuation models that we will describe in Chapters 6, 7, and 8 take into account how shifts in the yield curve will affect cash flows. Thus, when V_- and V_+ are the values produced from these valuation models, the resulting duration takes into account both the discounting at different interest rates and how the cash flows change. When duration is calculated in this manner, it is referred to as *effective duration* or *option-adjusted duration*. Exhibit 4 summarizes the distinction between modified duration and effective duration.

The difference between modified duration and effective duration for fixed income securities with an embedded option can be quite dramatic. For example, a callable corporate bond could have a modified duration of 5 but an effective duration of 4. For certain collateralized mortgage obligations, the modified duration could be 8 and the effective duration 25! Thus, using modified duration as a measure of the price sensitivity of a security to a parallel shift in the yield curve would be misleading. The more appropriate measure for any security with an embedded option is effective duration.

Relationship to Macaulay Duration

Before leaving this topic, it is worth comparing the modified duration formula presented above to that commonly found in the literature. It is common in the literature to find the following formula for modified duration:[1]

$$\frac{1}{(1 + \text{yield}/k)}\left[\frac{1PVCF_1 + 2PVCF_2 + 3PVCF_3 + \dots + nPVCF_n}{k \times \text{Price}}\right] \quad (2)$$

---

[1] More specifically, this is the formula for modified duration for a bond on a coupon anniversary date.

where

k = number of periods, or payments, per year (e.g., $k = 2$ for semiannual pay bonds and $k = 12$ for monthly pay bonds)

n = number of periods until maturity (i.e., number of years to maturity times k)

yield = yield to maturity of the bond

$PVCF_t$ = present value of the cash flow in period t discounted at the yield to maturity

The expression in the bracket for the modified duration formula in equation (2) is a measure formulated in 1938 by Frederick Macaulay.[2] This measure is popularly referred to as *Macaulay duration*. Thus, modified duration is commonly expressed as:

$$\text{Modified duration} = \frac{\text{Macaulay duration}}{(1 + \text{yield}/k)}$$

The general formulation for duration as given by equation (1) provides a short-cut procedure for determining a bond's modified duration. Because it is easier to calculate the modified duration using the short-cut procedure, many vendors of analytical software will use equation (1) rather than equation (2) to reduce computation time. But, once again, it must be emphasized that modified duration is a flawed measure of a bond's price sensitivity to interest rate changes for a bond with an embedded option.

Price Sensitivity to Nonparallel Yield Curve Shifts

Both modified duration and effective duration assume that any change in interest rates is the result of a parallel shift in the yield curve. For some fixed income securities, the price sensitivity to most nonparallel shifts will be very close to the estimated price sensitivity for a parallel shift in the yield curve. This is generally true for option-free bonds with a bullet maturity. However, for sinking-fund bonds and bonds with embedded options, particularly mortgage-backed securities and asset-backed securities, the price sensitivity to a nonparallel shift in the yield curve can be quite different from that estimated for a parallel shift.

Several measures have been proposed in the literature to estimate the price sensitivity of a bond to nonparallel yield curve shifts.[3] A discussion of these measures is beyond the scope of this chapter.

---

[2] Frederick Macaulay, *Some Theoretical Problems Suggested by the Movement of Interest Rates, Bond Yields, and Stock Prices in the U.S. Since 1856* (New York: National Bureau of Economic Research, 1938).

[3] See, for example, Thomas E. Klaffky, Y.Y. Ma, and Ardavan Nozari, "Managing Yield Curve Exposure: Introducing Reshaping Durations," *Journal of Fixed Income* (December 1992), pp. 5-15; Robert R. Reitano, "Non-Parallel Yield Curve Shifts and Immunization," *Journal of Portfolio Management* (Spring 1992), pp. 36-43; Thomas Y. Ho, "Key Rate Durations: Measures of Interest Rate Risk," *Journal of Fixed Income* (September 1992), pp. 29-44; Brian D. Johnson and Kenneth R. Meyer, "Managing Yield Curve Risk in an Index Environment," *Financial Analysts Journal* (November/December 1989), pp. 51-59; Chapter 3 in Frank J. Fabozzi and H. Gifford Fong, *Advanced Fixed Income Portfolio Management* (Chicago: Probus Publishing, 1994); and, Ravi E. Dattatreya and Frank J. Fabozzi, "The Risk Point Method for Measuring and Controlling Yield Curve Risk," *Financial Analysts Journal* (July-August 1995), pp. 45-54.

CONVEXITY

Notice that the duration measure indicates that regardless of whether the yield curve is shifted up or down, the approximate percentage price change is the same. However, this does not agree with the properties of a bond's price volatility described earlier in this chapter. Specifically, Property 2 states that for small changes in yield the percentage price change will be the same for an increase or decrease in yield. Property 3 states that for large changes in yield this is not true. This suggests that duration is only a good approximation of the percentage price change for a small change in yield.

To see this, consider once again the 9% 20-year bond selling to yield 6% with a duration of 10.66. If yields increase instantaneously by 10 basis points (from 6% to 6.1%), then using duration the approximate percentage price change would be −1.066% (−10.66% divided by 10, remembering that duration is the percentage price change for a 100 basis point change in yield). Notice from Exhibit 3 that the actual percentage price change is −1.07%. Similarly, if the yield decreases instantaneously by 10 basis points (from 6.00% to 5.90%), then the percentage change in price would be +1.066%. From Exhibit 3, the actual percentage price change would be +1.07%. This example illustrates that for small changes in yield, duration does an excellent job of approximating the percentage price change.

Instead of a small change in yield, let's assume that yields increase by 200 basis points, from 6% to 8%. The approximate percentage price change is −21.32% (−10.66% times 2). As can be seen from Exhibit 3, the actual percentage change in price is only −18.40%. Moreover, if the yield decreased by 200 basis points from 6% to 4%, the approximate percentage price change based on duration would be +21.32%, compared to an actual percentage price change of +25.04%. Thus, the approximation is not as good for a 200 basis point change in yield.

Duration is in fact a first approximation for a small parallel shift in the yield curve. The approximation can be improved by using a second approximation. This approximation is referred to as a bond's *convexity*.[4] The use of this term in the industry is unfortunate since the term convexity is also used to describe the shape or curvature of the price/yield relationship, as explained earlier in this chapter. The convexity measure of a security is the approximate change in price that is not explained by duration.

Measuring Convexity

The convexity of any bond can be approximated using the following formula:

---

[4] Mathematically, any function can be estimated by a series of approximations referred to as a Taylor series. Each approximation or term of the Taylor series is based on the corresponding derivative. For a bond, duration is the first approximation to price and is related to the first derivative of the bond's price. The convexity measure is the second approximation and related to the second derivative of the bond's price. It turns out that in general the first two approximations do a good job of estimating the bond's price so no additional derivatives are needed. The derivation is provided in Chapter 4 of Frank J. Fabozzi, *Bond Markets, Analysis, and Strategies* (Englewood Cliffs, N.J.: Prentice Hall, 1993).

$$\text{Convexity} = \frac{V_+ + V_- - 2V_0}{2V_0(\Delta y)^2} \tag{3}$$

For our hypothetical 9% 20-year bond selling to yield 6%, we know that

Δy = 0.0020
V_+ = 131.8439
V_- = 137.5888
V_0 = 134.6722

Substituting these values into the convexity formula,

$$\text{Convexity} = \frac{137.5888 + 131.8439 - 2(134.6722)}{2(134.6722)(0.002)^2} = 81.96$$

Percentage Price Change Due to Convexity

Given the convexity measure, the approximate percentage change in price due to the bond's convexity that is not explained by duration is:

$\text{Convexity} \times (\Delta y)^2$

For example, for the 9% coupon bond maturing in 20 years, the approximate percentage price change due to convexity if the yield increases from 6% to 8% is

$$81.96 \times (0.02)^2 = 0.0328 = 3.28\%$$

If the yield decreases from 6% to 4%, the approximate percentage price change due to convexity would also be 3.28%.

The approximate percentage price change based on both duration and convexity is found by simply adding the two estimates. So, for example, if yields change from 6% to 8%, the estimated percentage price change would be:

Duration   = -21.32%
Convexity = $+3.28\%$
Total   = -18.04%

The actual percentage price change is −18.40%. For a decrease of 200 basis points, from 6% to 4%, the approximate percentage price change would be as follows:

Duration   = $+21.32\%$
Convexity = $+3.28\%$
Total   = $+24.60\%$

The actual percentage price change is +25.04%. Thus, both duration and convexity together do a good job of estimating the sensitivity of a bond's price change to large changes in yield.

While it is easy to interpret what duration means, it is more difficult to interpret the convexity measure because it is multiplied by the square of the change in yield. Basically, convexity is the rate of change of duration when yields change.[5]

Standard Convexity and Effective Convexity

The prices used in equation (3) to calculate convexity can be obtained by either assuming that when the yield curve shifts in a parallel way the expected cash flows do not change or they do change. In the former case, the resulting convexity is referred to as *standard convexity*.[6] Actually, in the industry, convexity is not qualified by the adjective standard. Thus, in practice the term convexity typically means the cash flows are assumed not to change when yields change. *Effective convexity* or *option-adjusted convexity,* in contrast, assumes that the cash flows do change when yields change. This is the same distinction made for duration.

As with duration, for bonds with embedded options there could be quite a difference between the calculated standard convexity and effective convexity. In fact, for all option-free bonds, either convexity measure will have a positive value. For callable bonds and mortgage-backed securities, the calculated effective convexity can be negative when the calculated standard convexity gives a positive value.

---

[5] More specifically, convexity is the rate of change of a bond's dollar price change (or dollar duration).

[6] The formula for standard convexity is

$$\frac{1(2)PVCF_1 + 2(3)PVCF_2 + 3(4)PVCF_3 + ... + n(n+1)PVCF_n}{2(1+\text{yield}/k)^2\ k^2\ \text{Price}}$$

Using this formula, the standard convexity for the 9% 20-year bond selling to yield 6% is 82.04. While this number is slightly different from that obtained using equation (3), when we use this measure to obtain the approximate percentage price change due to convexity, the result will be the same.

KEY POINTS

1. *The price of an option-free bond moves inversely with a change in yield.*

2. *The price/yield relationship for an option-free bond is convex.*

3. *A property of an option-free bond is that for a small change in yield, the percentage price change is roughly the same, whether the yield increases or decreases.*

4. *A property of an option-free bond is that for a large change in yield, the percentage price change is not the same for an increase in yield as it is for a decrease in yield.*

5. *A property of an option-free bond is that for a large change in basis points of a given amount, the percentage price increase is greater than the percentage price decrease.*

6. *The coupon and maturity of an option-free bond affect its price volatility.*

7. *For a given term to maturity and initial yield, the lower the coupon rate the greater the price volatility of a bond.*

8. *For a given coupon rate and initial yield, the longer the term to maturity, the greater the price volatility.*

9. *For a given change in yield, price volatility is less when yield levels in the market are high than when yield levels are low.*

10. *The percentage price change of a bond can be estimated by changing the yield by a small number of basis points and estimating how the price changes.*

11. *The duration of a bond measures the approximate percentage price change for a 100 basis point change in yield, assuming a parallel shift in the yield curve.*

12. *Modified duration is the approximate percentage change in a bond's price for a 100 basis point parallel shift in the yield curve assuming that the bond's cash flows do not change when the yield curve shifts.*

13. *Modified duration is not a useful measure of the price sensitivity for securities with embedded options.*

14. *Effective duration or option-adjusted duration is the approximate percentage price change of a bond for a 100 basis point parallel shift in the yield curve allowing for the cash flows to change as a result of the change in yield.*

15. *The difference between modified duration and effective duration for fixed income securities with an embedded option can be quite dramatic.*

16. *Both modified duration and effective duration assume that any change in interest rates is the result of a parallel shift in the yield curve.*

17. *There are duration measures that allow for a nonparallel shift in the yield curve.*

18. *The estimate of the price sensitivity of a bond based on duration can be improved by using a bond's convexity.*

19. *The convexity of a bond measures how quickly its duration changes as yield changes.*

20. *As with duration, the convexity of a bond can be measured assuming that the cash flows do not change when yield changes (standard convexity) or assuming that it does change when yield changes (effective convexity).*

Chapter 5

Overview of the Valuation of Bonds with Embedded Options

The objectives of this chapter are to:

1. *explain the disadvantages of the call feature from a bondholder's perspective and therefore why potential investors want to receive compensation for the risk that the issue might be called;*

2. *review the traditional methodology used to evaluate callable bonds;*

3. *provide a conceptual framework for thinking about how to value bonds with embedded options;*

4. *review the factors that affect the value of an option;*

5. *explain what is meant by the option-adjusted spread; and,*

6. *describe what modeling risk is.*

Thus far, our discussion of bond valuation has been limited to bonds in which neither the issuer nor the bondholder has the option to alter a bond's cash flows. In Chapters 5, 6, 7, and 8 we look at how to value bonds with embedded options. We begin our discussion with the most common type of embedded option — a call option.

DISADVANTAGES OF CALLABLE BONDS

The holder of a callable bond has given the issuer the right to call the issue prior to the maturity date. A mortgage-backed security is also a callable security since homeowners have the right to pay off all or part of the mortgage loan balance at any time. Asset-backed securities share this feature.

The presence of a call option results in two disadvantages to the bondholder. First, callable bonds expose bondholders to reinvestment risk since an issuer may call a bond when the yield on bonds in the market is lower than the issue's coupon rate. For example, if the coupon rate on a callable corporate bond is 13% and prevailing market yield is 7%, the issuer will benefit by calling the 13% issue and refunding it with a 7% issue. From the investor's perspective, the proceeds received will have to be reinvested at a lower interest rate.

Second, the price appreciation potential for a callable bond in a declining interest rate environment is limited. The price of the callable bond will not rise as much as an otherwise comparable noncallable bond. This can be seen in Exhibit 1. The price/yield relationship for an option-free (i.e., noncallable/nonputable) bond is convex. The convex curve a–a' shows the price/yield relationship. The exhibit also shows the price/yield relationship for an otherwise equivalent callable bond as depicted by the shape of the curve denoted by a–b.

Exhibit 1: Price/Yield Relationship for an Option-Free Bond and a Callable Bond

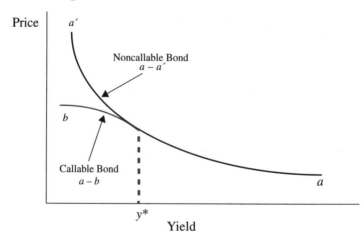

The reason for the shape of the price/yield relationship for the callable bond is as follows. When the prevailing market yield for comparable bonds is higher than the coupon rate on the bond, it is unlikely that the issuer will call the bond. For example, if a bond's coupon rate is 7% and the prevailing yield on comparable bonds is 13%, it is highly improbable that the issuer will call the outstanding issue. Since the bond is unlikely to be called, the callable bond will have the same price/yield relationship as a noncallable bond. However, even when the coupon rate is just below the market yield, investors may not pay the same price for the callable bond had it been noncallable because there is still the chance that the market yield may drop further making it beneficial for the issuer to call the bond.

The exact yield level at which investors begin to view the issue likely to be called may not be known, but we do know that there is some level. In Exhibit 1, at yield levels below y^*, the price/yield relationship for the callable bond departs from the price/yield relationship for the noncallable bond. If, for example, the market yield is such that a noncallable bond would be selling for 109, but as the callable bond would be called at 104, investors would not pay 109. If they did and the bond is called, investors would receive 104 (the call price) for a bond they purchased for 109. Notice that for a range of yields below y^*, there is price compression — that is, there is limited price appreciation as yields decline. The portion of the callable bond price/yield relationship below y^* is said to be *negatively convex*.

Negative convexity means that the price appreciation will be less than the price depreciation for a large change in yield of a given number of basis points. For a bond that is option-free and exhibits positive convexity, the price appreciation will be greater than the price depreciation for a large change in yield of a given number of basis points. The price changes resulting from bonds exhibiting positive convexity and negative convexity can be expressed as follows:

Change in interest rates	Absolute value of percentage price change for:	
	Positive Convexity	Negative Convexity
−100 basis points	X%	less than Y%
+100 basis points	less than X%	Y%

Since investors are exposed to reinvestment risk and truncated price appreciation potential due to negative convexity, they must be compensated for these risks. The key in valuing callable bonds is to adjust the price to reflect these risks. Or equivalently, the key is to adjust the price for the value of the call option that creates these risks.

STATIC VALUATION METHODOLOGY

The traditional approach to valuing callable bonds has been in terms of the yield to worst. This yield measure is found by calculating the yield to maturity and the yield to call for every call date, and then selecting the lowest of all of the calculated yields.

There are several drawbacks of this approach. First, it assumes that the issue will be called on the date used in the yield to worst calculation. Second, it gives no recognition to the volatility of interest rates which would affect future interest rates and therefore whether the issue will be called in the future. Thus, the traditional valuation analysis can best be described as static valuation analysis since only a single interest rate scenario is used.

Another pitfall of the traditional valuation approach is that in the valuation of bonds only one yield, the yield to worst, is used to discount all cash flows to the assumed call or maturity date. As we noted in previous chapters, the appropriate discount rates are based on the theoretical spot rates.

To resolve this pitfall, a zero-volatility spread can be calculated. As explained in Chapter 2, the zero-volatility spread is defined as the constant spread that is added to the issuer's spot rate curve that will make the present value of the cash flows to either the assumed call date or maturity date equal to the market price. It is called a zero-volatility spread since it assumes a zero-volatility interest rate scenario; that is, it assumes no volatility of interest rates in the future.

The zero-volatility spread therefore is a spread over the entire theoretical spot rate curve of the issuer, not a single point on the issuer's on-the-run yield curve. As shown in Chapter 2, the magnitude of the difference between the traditional or nominal spread and the zero-volatility yield spread depends on the steepness of the yield curve: the steeper the curve, the greater the difference between the two values. In a relatively flat interest rate environment, the difference between the traditional yield spread and the zero-volatility spread will be small.

THE COMPONENTS OF A BOND
WITH AN EMBEDDED OPTION

To develop an analytical framework for valuing a bond with an embedded option, it is necessary to decompose a bond into its component parts. A callable bond is a bond in which the bondholder has sold the issuer an option (more specifically, a call option) that allows the issuer to repurchase the contractual cash flows of the bond from the bond's call date until the maturity date.

Consider the following two bonds: (1) an 8% coupon bond with 20 years to maturity that is callable in five years at 104 and (2) a 10-year 9% coupon bond callable immediately at par. For the first bond, the bondholder owns a 5-year noncallable bond and has sold a call option granting the issuer the right to call away from the bondholder 15 years of cash flows 5 years from now for a price of 104. The investor who owns the second bond has a 10-year noncallable bond and has sold a call option granting the issuer the right to immediately call the entire 10-year contractual cash flows, or any cash flows remaining at the time the issue is called, for 100.

Effectively, the owner of a callable bond is entering into two separate transactions. First, the investor buys a noncallable bond from the issuer for which he pays some price. Then, the investor sells the issuer a call option for which he receives the option price. Therefore, we can summarize the position of a callable bondholder as follows:

long a callable bond = long a noncallable bond + short a call option

In terms of price, the price of a callable bond is equal to the price of the two components parts. That is,

price of a callable bond = price of a noncallable bond – price of a call option

The reason the call option price is subtracted from the price of the non-callable bond is that when the bondholder sells a call option, he receives the option price. Graphically, this can be seen in Exhibit 1. The difference between the price of the noncallable bond and the callable bond at a given yield is the value of the embedded call option.

Actually, the position is more complicated than we just described. The issuer may be entitled to call the bond at the first call date and any time thereafter, or at the first call date and any subsequent coupon anniversary date. Thus the investor has effectively sold an American-type call option to the issuer but the call price varies with the date the call option is exercised. This is because the call schedule for a bond may have a different call price depending on the call date. Moreover, the underlying bond for the call option is the remaining coupon payments that would have been made by the issuer had the bond not been called. For exposition purposes, it is easier to understand the principles associated with the investment characteristics of callable bonds by describing the investor's position as long a noncallable bond and short a call option.

The same logic applies to putable bonds. In the case of a putable bond, the bondholder has the right to sell the bond to the issuer at a designated price and time. A putable bond can be broken into two separate transactions. First, the investor buys a nonputable bond. Second, the investor buys a put option from the issuer that allows the investor to sell the bond to the issuer. Therefore, the position of a putable bondholder can be described as:

long a putable bond = long a nonputable bond + long a put option

The price of a putable bond is then

price of a putable bond = price of a nonputable bond + price of a put option

Factors Affecting the Value of an Option

Now that we know that the value of a bond is affected by the value of an embedded option, it would be helpful to know what factors affect the value of an option.

Intrinsic Value

The option value is a reflection of the option's *intrinsic value* and any additional amount over its intrinsic value. The premium over intrinsic value is often referred to as the *time value*. The intrinsic value of an option is its economic value if it is exercised immediately. If no positive economic value would result from exercising the option immediately, then the intrinsic value is zero.

For a call option, the intrinsic value is positive if the current price of the underlying security is greater than the strike price. The intrinsic value is then the difference between the two prices. If the strike price of a call option is greater than or equal to the current price of the security, the intrinsic value is zero. For example, if the strike price for a call option is 100 and the current price for the security is 105, the intrinsic value is 5. That is, an option buyer exercising the option and simultaneously selling the underlying security would realize 105 from the sale of the security, which would be covered by acquiring the security from the option writer for 100, thereby netting a 5 gain.

When an option has intrinsic value, it is said to be *in the money*. When the strike price of a call option exceeds the current price of the security, the call option is said to be *out of the money*; it has no intrinsic value. An option for which the strike price is equal to the current price of the security is said to be *at the money*. Both at-the-money and out-of-the-money options have an intrinsic value of zero because they not profitable to exercise.

For a put option, the intrinsic value is equal to the amount by which the current price of the security is below the strike price. For example, if the strike price of a put option is 100 and the current price of the security is 92, the intrinsic value is 8. The buyer of the put option who exercises the put option and simultaneously sells the underlying security will net 8 by exercising this option since the security will be sold to the writer for 100 and purchased in the market for 92. The intrinsic value is zero if the strike price is less than or equal to the current market price. For our put option with a strike price of 100, the option would be: (1) in the money when the security's price is less than 100, (2) out of the money when the security's price exceeds 100, and (3) at the money when the security's price is equal to 100.

The relationships are summarized in Exhibit 2.

Exhibit 2: Relationship Between Security Price, Strike Price, and Intrinsic Value

If Security price > Strike price	Call option	Put Option
Intrinsic value	Security price – Strike price	Zero
Jargon	In-the-money	Out-of-the money
If Security price < Strike price	Call option	Put Option
Intrinsic value	Zero	Strike price – Security price
Jargon	Out-of-the money	In-the-money
If Security price = Strike price	Call option	Put Option
Intrinsic value	Zero	Zero
Jargon	At-the money	At-the money

Exhibit 3: Summary of Factors that Affect the Price of an American Option

Factor	Effect of an increase of factor on:	
	Call price	Put price
Current price of underlying security	increase	decrease
Strike price	decrease	increase
Time to expiration of option	increase	increase
Expected interest rate volatility	increase	increase
Short-term interest rate	increase	decrease
Coupon payments	decrease	increase

Time Value

The time value of an option is the amount by which the option price exceeds its intrinsic value. The option buyer hopes that, at some time prior to expiration, changes in the market price of the underlying security will increase the value of the rights conveyed by the option. For this prospect, the option buyer is willing to pay a premium above the intrinsic value.

For example, if the price of a call option with a strike price of 100 is 9 when the current price of the security is 105, the time value of this option is 4 (9 minus its intrinsic value of 5). Had the current price of the security been 90 instead of 105, then the time value of this option would be the entire 9 because the option has no intrinsic value.

Factors that Influence an Option's Value

There are six factors that influence the value of an option in which the underlying security is a fixed income instrument:

1. current price of the underlying security;
2. strike price;
3. time to expiration of the option;
4. expected interest rate volatility over the life of the option;
5. short-term risk-free interest rate over the life of the option; and
6. coupon payments over the life of the option.

The impact of each of these factors may depend on whether (1) the option is a call or a put, and (2) the option is an American option or a European option. A summary of the effect of each factor on American put and call option prices is presented in Exhibit 3.

Current Price of the Underlying Security

The option price will change as the price of the underlying security changes. For a call option, as the price of the underlying security increases (holding all other factors constant), the option price increases. The opposite holds for a put option: as the price of the underlying security increases, the price of a put option decreases.

Strike Price

All other factors equal, the lower the strike price, the higher the price of a call option. For put options, the higher the strike price, the higher the option price.

Time to Expiration of the Option

An option is a "wasting asset." That is, after the expiration date passes the option has no value. Holding all other factors equal, the longer the time to expiration of the option, the greater the option price. This is because, as the time to expiration decreases, less time remains for the underlying security's price to rise (for a call buyer) or to fall (for a put buyer) — that is, to compensate the option buyer for any time value paid — and, therefore, the probability of a favorable price movement decreases. Consequently, for American options, as the time remaining until expiration decreases, the option price approaches its intrinsic value.

Expected Interest Rate Volatility Over the Life of the Option

All other factors equal, the greater the expected interest rate volatility (as measured by the standard deviation or variance) of the interest rate, the more an investor would be willing to pay for the option, and the more an option writer would demand for it. This is because the greater the expected volatility, the greater the probability that the price of the underlying security will move in favor of the option buyer at some time before expiration.

Short-Term Risk-Free Interest Rate Over the Life of the Option

Buying the underlying security ties up one's money. Buying an option on the same quantity of the underlying security makes the difference between the security price and the option price available for investment at the risk-free rate. All other factors constant, the higher the short-term risk-free interest rate, the greater the cost of buying the underlying security and carrying it to the expiration date of the call option. Hence, the higher the short-term risk-free interest rate, the more attractive the call option will be relative to the direct purchase of the underlying security. As a result, the higher the short-term risk-free interest rate, the greater the price of a call option. An increase in short-term rates decreases the value of a put option. This is because it makes a short sale of the security more attractive in comparison to a put.

Coupon Payments Over the Life of the Option

Coupon payments on the underlying security tend to decrease the price of a call option because they make it more attractive to hold the underlying security than to hold the option. For put options, coupon payments on the underlying security tend to increase their price.

Valuation Methodologies

There are two main approaches to the valuation of bonds with embedded options. These are:

1. the binomial lattice method, or simply, binomial method, and
2. the Monte Carlo simulation method, or simply, Monte Carlo method.

There are two things that are common to both methods. First, each begins with an assumption as to the statistical process that is assumed to generate the term structure of interest rates. Second, each method is based on the principle that arbitrage profits cannot be generated.

In the chapters to follow, we discuss each method. For now, here is a quick overview. In the binomial method, an interest rate tree is "grown." The tree is then used to determine whether the embedded option will be exercised at a given point on the tree and what the value will be at that point. In the Monte Carlo simulation method, interest rate paths are generated. On each interest rate path, a cash flow is determined taking into consideration the possible exercise of the embedded option. The present value of the cash flows on each interest rate path is then calculated. The average of the present value over all the interest rate paths is the value of the bond.

Option-Adjusted Spread

What an investor seeks to do is to buy securities whose value is greater than their market price. A valuation model such as the two described above allows an investor to estimate the value of a security, which at this point would be sufficient to determine the fairness of the price of the security. That is, the investor can say that this bond is 1 point cheap or 2 points cheap, and so on.

A valuation model need not stop here, however. Instead, it can convert the divergence between the price observed in the market for the security and the value derived from the model into a yield spread measure. This step is necessary since most market participants find it more convenient to think about yield spread than about price differences.

The *option-adjusted spread* (OAS) was developed as a measure of the yield spread that can be used to convert dollar differences between value and price. Thus, basically, the OAS is used to reconcile value with market price. But what is it a "spread" over? As we shall see when we describe the two valuation methodologies, the OAS is a spread over the issuer's spot rate curve or benchmark. The spot rate curve itself is not a single curve, but a series of spot rate curves that allow for changes in forward rates.

The reason that the resulting spread is referred to as "option-adjusted" is because the cash flows of the security whose value we seek are adjusted to reflect any embedded options. In contrast, the zero-volatility spread does not consider how the cash flows will change when interest rates change in the future. That is, the zero-volatility spread assumes that interest rate volatility is zero. Consequently, the zero-volatility spread is also referred to as the *zero-volatility OAS*.

While the product of a valuation model is the OAS, the process can be worked in reverse. For a specified OAS, the valuation model can determine the theoretical value of the security that is consistent with that OAS.

Option Cost

The implied cost of the option embedded in any security can be obtained by calculating the difference between the OAS at the assumed volatility of interest rates and the zero-volatility spread. That is,

Option cost = Zero-volatility spread – Option-adjusted spread

The reason that the option cost is measured in this way is as follows. In an environment of no interest rate volatility, the investor would earn the zero-volatility spread. When future interest rates are uncertain, the spread is different because of any embedded option; the OAS reflects the spread after adjusting for this option. Therefore, the option cost is the difference between the spread that would be earned in a zero-volatility interest rate environment (the zero-volatility spread, or equivalently, the zero-volatility OAS) and the spread after adjusting for any embedded option (the OAS).

For callable bonds and mortgage passthrough securities, the option cost is positive. This is because the borrower's ability to alter the cash flows will result in an OAS that is less than the zero-volatility spread. In the case of a putable bond, the OAS is greater than the zero-volatility spread so that the option cost is negative. This occurs because of the investor's ability to alter the cash flows.

In general, when the option cost is positive, this means that the investor has sold or is short an option. This is true for callable bonds and mortgage passthrough securities. A negative value for the option cost means that the investor has purchased or is long an option. A putable bond is an example of this negative option cost. There are certain securities in the mortgage-backed securities market that also have an option cost that is negative.

The relationships are summarized below:

Sign of option cost	Interpretation
Positive	Investor has sold or is short an option
Negative	Investor has purchased or is long an option

While the option cost as described above is measured in basis points, it can be translated into a dollar price.

Modeling Risk

The user of any valuation model is exposed to *modeling risk*. This is the risk that the output of the model is incorrect because the assumptions upon which it is based are incorrect. Consequently, it is imperative that the results of a valuation model be stress-tested for modeling risk by altering the assumptions.

KEY POINTS

1. *It is necessary to have a framework for the analysis of bonds with embedded options.*

2. *The potential investor in a callable bond must be compensated for the risk that the issuer will call the bond prior to the stated maturity date.*

3. *The two disadvantages faced by an investor in callable bonds are reinvestment risk and truncated price appreciation when yields decline (that is, negative convexity).*

4. *The traditional methodology for valuing bonds with embedded options relies on the yield to worst.*

5. *One drawback of the traditional methodology is that it assumes a zero-volatility environment for interest rates in the future and is therefore referred to as a static valuation methodology.*

6. *Another drawback of the traditional methodology is that it fails to recognize the term structure of interest rates.*

7. *To value a bond with an embedded option it is necessary to understand that the bond can be decomposed into an option-free component and an option component.*

8. *Because of the embedded option component, it is necessary to understand what factors affect the value of an option.*

9. *The value of an option can be decomposed into intrinsic value and time value.*

10. *The six factors that affect the value of an option are the current price of the underlying security, strike price, time to expiration of the option, expected interest rate volatility over the life of the option, short-term risk-free interest rate over the life of the option, and coupon payments over the life of the option.*

11. *There are two valuation methodologies that are being used to value bonds with embedded options: the binomial lattice model and the Monte Carlo simulation model.*

12. *The two methodologies seek to determine the fair or theoretical value of the bond.*

13. *The option-adjusted spread (OAS) converts the cheapness or richness of a bond into a spread over the future possible spot rate curves.*

14. *The spread is option adjusted because it allows for future interest rate volatility to affect the cash flows.*

15. *The cost of the embedded option is measured as the difference between the zero-volatility spread and the option-adjusted spread.*

16. *The zero-volatility spread is also referred to as the static spread and the zero volatility OAS.*

17. *The user of a valuation model is exposed to modeling risk and should test the sensitivity of the model to alternative assumptions.*

Chapter 6

Binomial Model I: Valuing Callable Bonds

The objectives of this chapter are to:

1. explain what is meant by a binomial interest rate tree;

2. explain how a binomial interest rate tree is constructed to be consistent with the prices for the on-the-run issues of an issuer and a given volatility assumption;

3. demonstrate how a binomial interest rate tree can be used to value an option-free bond and a callable bond;

4. explain how the value of the embedded call option is determined;

5. explain how the option-adjusted spread is calculated using the binomial model; and,

6. show how effective duration and effective convexity are calculated using the binomial model.

The binomial model is a popular methodology for valuing not only callable and putable bonds but also a wide range of interest rate structured notes, and options on bonds. Our focus in this chapter is the application of the binomial model to value callable bonds. In the next chapter we will see how to apply this model to value other bond structures.

VALUING OPTION-FREE BONDS: A REVIEW

Let's review the valuation of option-free bonds. We must determine the on-the-run yield curve for the particular issuer whose bonds we want to value. The starting point is the Treasury's on-the-run yield curve. To obtain a particular issuer's on-the-run yield curve, an appropriate credit spread is added to each on-the-run Treasury issue. The credit spread need not be constant for all maturities. For example, as explained in Chapter 2, the credit spread may increase with maturity.

In our illustration, we use the following hypothetical on-the-run issue for an issuer:

Maturity	Yield to maturity	Market Price
1 year	3.5%	100
2 years	4.2%	100
3 years	4.7%	100
4 years	5.2%	100

Each bond is trading at par value (100) so the coupon rate is equal to the yield to maturity. We will simplify the illustration by assuming annual-pay bonds.

Using the bootstrapping methodology explained in Chapter 2, the spot rates are given below:

Year	Spot Rate
1	3.5000%
2	4.2147%
3	4.7345%
4	5.2707%

The corresponding one-year forward rates are:

Current 1-year forward rate	3.500%
1-year forward rate one year from now	4.935%
1-year forward rate two years from now	5.784%
1-year forward rate three years from now	6.893%

Now consider an option-free bond with four years remaining to maturity and a coupon rate of 6.5%. The value of this bond can be calculated in one of two ways, both producing the same value. First, the cash flows can be discounted at the spot rates as shown below:

$$\frac{\$6.5}{(1.035)^1} + \frac{\$6.5}{(1.042147)^2} + \frac{\$6.5}{(1.047345)^3} + \frac{\$100 + \$6.5}{(1.052707)^4} = \$104.643$$

The second way is to discount by the 1-year forward rates as shown below:

$$\frac{\$6.5}{(1.035)} + \frac{\$6.5}{(1.035)(1.04935)} + \frac{\$6.5}{(1.035)(1.04935)(1.05784)}$$

$$+ \frac{\$100 + \$6.5}{(1.035)(1.04935)(1.05784)(1.06893)} = \$104.643$$

BINOMIAL INTEREST RATE TREE[1]

Once we allow for embedded options, consideration must be given to interest rate volatility. This can be done by introducing a *binomial interest rate tree*. This tree is nothing more than a graphical depiction of the one-period or short rates over time based on some assumption about interest rate volatility. How this tree is constructed is illustrated below.

Exhibit 1 shows an example of a binomial interest rate tree. In this tree, each node (bold circle) represents a time period that is equal to one year from the node to its left. Each node is labeled with an N, representing node, and a subscript that indicates the path that the 1-year rate took to get to that node. L represents the lower of the two 1-year rates and H represents the higher of the two 1-year rates. For example, node N_{HH} means to get to that node the following path for 1-year rates occurred: the 1-year rate realized is the higher of the two rates in the first year and then the higher of the 1-year rates in the second year.[2]

Look first at the point denoted by just N in Exhibit 1. This is the root of the tree and is nothing more than the current 1-year spot rate, or equivalently the current 1-year rate, which we denote by r_0. What we have assumed in creating this tree is that the 1-year rate can take on two possible values the next year and the two rates have the same probability of occurring. One rate will be higher than the other. It is assumed that the 1-year rate can evolve over time based on a random process called a lognormal random walk with a certain volatility.

We use the following notation to describe the tree in the first year. Let

σ = assumed volatility of the 1-year rate

$r_{1,L}$ = the lower 1-year rate one year from now

$r_{1,H}$ = the higher 1-year rate one year from now

---

[1] The model described in this chapter was presented in Andrew J. Kalotay, George O. Williams, and Frank J. Fabozzi, "A Model for the Valuation of Bonds and Embedded Options," *Financial Analysts Journal* (May-June 1993), pp. 35-46.

[2] Note that N_{HL} is equivalent to N_{LH} in the second year and that in the third year N_{HHL} is equivalent to N_{HLH} and N_{LHH} and that N_{HLL} is equivalent to N_{LHL}. We have simply selected one label for a node.

Exhibit 1: Four-Year Binomial Interest Rate Tree

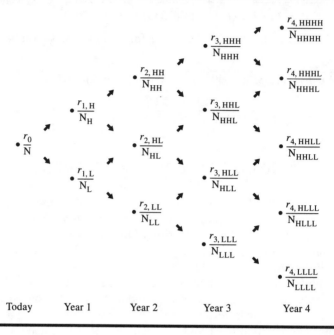

| Today | Year 1 | Year 2 | Year 3 | Year 4 |

The relationship between $r_{1,L}$ and $r_{1,H}$ is as follows:

$$r_{1,H} = r_{1,L}(e^{2\sigma})$$

where e is the base of the natural logarithm 2.71828.

For example, suppose that $r_{1,L}$ is 4.4448% and σ is 10% per year, then:

$$r_{1,H} = 4.4448\%(e^{2 \times 0.10}) = 5.4289\%$$

In the second year, there are three possible values for the 1-year rate, which we will denote as follows:

$r_{2,LL}$ = 1-year rate in second year assuming the lower rate in the first year and the lower rate in the second year

$r_{2,HH}$ = 1-year rate in second year assuming the higher rate in the first year and the higher rate in the second year

$r_{2,HL}$ = 1-year rate in second year assuming the higher rate in the first year and the lower rate in the second year or equivalently the lower rate in the first year and the higher rate in the second year

The relationship between $r_{2,LL}$ and the other two 1-year rates is as follows:

$$r_{2,HH} = r_{2,LL}(e^{4\sigma}) \quad \text{and} \quad r_{2,HL} = r_{2,LL}(e^{2\sigma})$$

So, for example, if $r_{2,LL}$ is 4.6958%, then assuming once again that σ is 10%, then

$$r_{2, HH} = 4.6958\%(e^{4 \times 0.10}) = 7.0053\%$$

and

$$r_{2, HL} = 4.6958\%(e^{2 \times 0.10}) = 5.7354\%$$

In the third year there are four possible values for the 1-year rate, which are denoted as follows: $r_{3,HHH}$, $r_{3,HHL}$, $r_{3,HLL}$, and $r_{3,LLL}$, and whose first three values are related to the last as follows:

$$r_{3,HHH} = r_{3,LLL}(e^{6\sigma})$$
$$r_{3,HHL} = r_{3,LLL}(e^{4\sigma})$$
$$r_{3,HLL} = r_{3,LLL}(e^{2\sigma})$$

Exhibit 1 shows the notation for a 4-year binomial interest rate tree. We can simplify the notation by letting r_t be the 1-year rate t years from now for the lower rate since all the other short rates t years from now depend on that rate. Exhibit 2 shows the interest rate tree using this simplified notation.

Exhibit 2: Four-Year Binomial Interest Rate Tree with One-Year Rates*

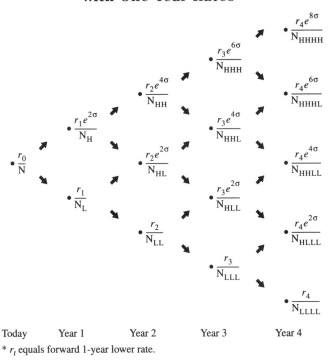

Today   Year 1   Year 2   Year 3   Year 4

* r_t equals forward 1-year lower rate.

Before we go on to show how to use this binomial interest rate tree to value bonds, let's focus on two issues here. First, what does the volatility parameter σ represent? Second, how do we find the value of the bond at each node?

Volatility and the Standard Deviation

It can be shown that the standard deviation of the 1-year rate is equal to $r_0\sigma$.[3] The standard deviation is a statistical measure of volatility. We discuss this measure and its estimation in Chapter 15.

It is important to see that the process that we assumed generates the binomial interest rate tree (or equivalently the short rates), implies that volatility is measured relative to the current level of rates. For example, if σ is 10% and the 1-year rate (r_0) is 4%, then the standard deviation of the 1-year rate is 4% $\times$ 10% = 0.4% or 40 basis points. However, if the current 1-year rate is 8%, the standard deviation of the 1-year rate would be 8% $\times$ 10% or 80 basis points.

Determining the Value at a Node

To find the value of the bond at a node, we first calculate the bond's value at the two nodes to the right of the node we are interested in. For example, in Exhibit 2, suppose we want to determine the bond's value at node N_H. The bond's value at node N_{HH} and N_{HL} must be determined. Hold aside for now how we get these two values because as we will see the process involves starting from the last year in the tree and working backwards to get the final solution we want, so these two values will be known.

Effectively what we are saying is that if we are at some node, then the value at that node will depend on the future cash flows. In turn, the future cash flows depend on (1) the bond's value one year from now and (2) the coupon payment one year from now. The latter is known. The former depends on whether the 1-year rate is the higher or lower rate. The bond's value depending on whether the rate is the higher or lower rate is reported at the two nodes to the right of the node that is the focus of our attention. So, the cash flow at a node will be either (1) the bond's value if the 1-year rate is the higher rate plus the coupon payment, or (2) the bond's value if the 1-year rate is the lower rate plus the coupon payment. For example, suppose that we are interested in the bond's value at N_H. The cash flow will be either the bond's value at N_{HH} plus the coupon payment, or the bond's value at N_{HL} plus the coupon payment.

To get the bond's value at a node we follow the fundamental rule for valuation: the value is the present value of the expected cash flows. The appropriate discount rate to use is the 1-year rate at the node. Now there are two present val-

---

[3] This can be seen by noting that

$$e^{2\sigma} \approx 1 + 2\sigma$$

Then the standard deviation of the 1-year rate is

$$\frac{re^{2\sigma} - r}{2} \approx \frac{r + 2\sigma r - r}{2} = \sigma r$$

ues in this case: the present value if the 1-year rate is the higher rate and one if it is the lower rate. Since it is assumed that the probability of both outcomes is equal, an average of the two present values is computed. This is illustrated in Exhibit 3 for any node assuming that the 1-year rate is r_* at the node where the valuation is sought and letting:

$$V_H = \text{the bond's value for the higher 1-year rate}$$
$$V_L = \text{the bond's value for the lower 1-year rate}$$
$$C = \text{coupon payment}$$

Using our notation, the cash flow at a node is either:

$$V_H + C \text{ for the higher 1-year rate}$$
$$V_L + C \text{ for the lower 1-year rate}$$

The present value of these two cash flows using the 1-year rate at the node, r_*, is:

$$\frac{V_H + C}{(1 + r_*)} = \text{present value for the higher 1-year rate}$$

$$\frac{V_L + C}{(1 + r_*)} = \text{present value for the lower 1-year rate}$$

Then, the value of the bond at the node is found as follows:

$$\text{Value at a node} = \frac{1}{2}\left[\frac{V_H + C}{(1 + r_*)} + \frac{V_L + C}{(1 + r_*)}\right]$$

Exhibit 3: Calculating a Value at a Node

Bond's value in
higher-rate state
1-year forward
↓
• $V_H + C$ ← Cash flow in
higher-rate state

1-year rate
at node where → $\dfrac{V}{r_*}$ •
bond's value
is sought

• $V_L + C$ ← Cash flow in
lower-rate state
Bond's value in
lower-rate state
1-year forward

Exhibit 4: The 1-Year Rates for Year 1
Using the 2-Year 4.2% On-the-Run Issue: First Trial

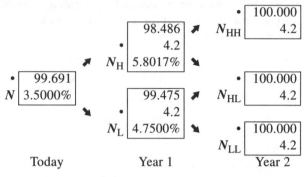

Today	Year 1	Year 2

CONSTRUCTING THE BINOMIAL INTEREST RATE TREE

To see how to construct the binomial interest rate tree, let's use the assumed on-the-run yields we used earlier. We will assume that volatility, σ, is 10% and construct a 2-year tree using the 2-year bond with a coupon rate of 4.2%.

Exhibit 4 shows a more detailed binomial interest rate tree with the cash flow shown at each node. We'll see how all the values reported in the exhibit are obtained. The root rate for the tree, r_0, is simply the current 1-year rate, 3.5%.

In the first year there are two possible 1-year rates, the higher rate and the lower rate. What we want to find is the two 1-year rates that will be consistent with the volatility assumption, the process that is assumed to generate the short rates, and the observed market value of the bond. There is no simple formula for this. It must be found by an iterative process (i.e., trial-and-error). The steps are described and illustrated below.

Step 1: Select a value for r_1. Recall that r_1 is the lower 1-year rate. In this first trial, we *arbitrarily* selected a value of 4.75%.

Step 2: Determine the corresponding value for the higher 1-year rate. As explained earlier, this rate is related to the lower 1-year rate as follows: $r_1 \, e^{2\sigma}$. Since r_1 is 4.75%, the higher 1-year rate is 5.8017% (= 4.75% $e^{2 \times 0.10}$). This value is reported in Exhibit 4 at node N_H.

Step 3: Compute the bond value's one year from now. This value is determined as follows:

> *3a.* Determine the bond's value two years from now. In our example, this is simple. Since we are using a 2-year bond, the bond's value is its maturity value ($100) plus its final coupon payment ($4.2). Thus, it is $104.2.

3b. Calculate the present value of the bond's value found in *3a* for the higher rate in the second year. The appropriate discount rate is the higher 1-year rate, 5.8017% in our example. The present value is $98.486 (= $104.2/ 1.058017). This is the value of V_H that we referred to earlier.

3c. Calculate the present value of the bond's value assumed in *3a* for the lower rate. The discount rate assumed for the lower 1-year rate is 4.75%. The present value is $99.475 (= $104.2/1.0475) and is the value of V_L.

3d. Add the coupon to both V_H and V_L to get the cash flow at N_H and N_L, respectively. In our example we have $102.686 for the higher rate and $103.675 for the lower rate.

3e. Calculate the present value of the two values using the 1-year rate r_*. At this point in the valuation, r_* is the root rate, 3.50%. Therefore,

$$\frac{V_H + C}{1 + r_*} = \frac{\$102.686}{1.035} = \$99.213$$

and

$$\frac{V_L + C}{1 + r_*} = \frac{\$103.675}{1.035} = \$100.169$$

Step 4: Calculate the average present value of the two cash flows in Step 3. This is the value we referred to earlier as

$$\text{Value at a node} = \frac{1}{2}\left[\frac{V_H + C}{(1 + r_*)} + \frac{V_L + C}{(1 + r_*)}\right]$$

In our example, we have

$$\text{Value at a node} = \frac{1}{2}[\$99.213 + \$100.169] = \$99.691$$

Step 5: Compare the value in Step 4 to the bond's market value. If the two values are the same, then the r_1 used in this trial is the one we seek. This is the 1-year rate that would then be used in the binomial interest rate tree for the lower rate and used to calculate the corresponding higher rate. If, instead, the value found in Step 4 is not equal to the market value of the bond, this means that the value r_1 in this trial is not the 1-year rate that is consistent with (1) the volatility assumption, (2) the process assumed to generate the 1-year rate, and (3) the observed market value of the bond. In this case, the five steps are repeated with a different value for r_1.

When r_1 is 4.75%, a value of $99.691 results in Step 4 which is less than the observed market price of $100. Therefore, 4.75% is too large and the five steps must be repeated trying a lower rate for r_1.

Let's jump right to the correct rate for r_1 in this example and rework steps 1 through 5. This occurs when r_1 is 4.4448%. The corresponding binomial interest rate tree is shown in Exhibit 5.

Exhibit 5: The 1-Year Rates for Year 1
Using the 2-Year 4.2% On-the-Run Issue

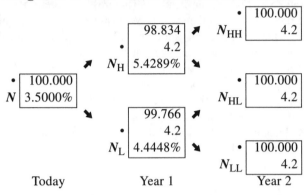

Today   Year 1   Year 2

Step 1: In this trial we select a value of 4.4448% for r_1, the lower 1-year rate.

Step 2: The corresponding value for the higher 1-year rate is 5.4289% (= 4.4448% $e^{2\times0.10}$).

Step 3: The bond's value one year from now is determined as follows:

    3a. The bond's value two years from now is $104.2, just as in the first trial.

    3b. The present value of the bond's value found in *3a* for the higher 1-year rate, V_H, is $98.834 (= $104.2/1.054289).

    3c. The present value of the bond's value found in *3a* for the lower 1-year rate, V_L, is $99.766 (= $104.2/1.044448).

    3d. Adding the coupon to V_H and V_L, we get $103.034 as the cash flow for the higher rate and $103.966 as the cash flow for the lower rate.

    3e. The present value of the two cash flows using the 1-year rate at the node to the left, 3.5%, gives

$$\frac{V_H + C}{1 + r_*} = \frac{\$103.034}{1.035} = \$99.550$$

and,

$$\frac{V_L + C}{1 + r_*} = \frac{\$103.966}{1.035} = \$100.450$$

Step 4: The average present value is $100, which is the value at the node.

Step 5: Since the average present value is equal to the observed market price of $100, r_1 or $r_{1,L}$ is 4.4448%, and $r_{1,H}$ is 5.4289%.

We can "grow" this tree for one more year by determining r_2. Now we will use the 3-year on-the-run issue, the 4.7% coupon bond, to get r_2. The same five steps are used in an iterative process to find the 1-year rates in the tree two years from now.

Our objective is now to find the value of r_2 that will produce a bond value of $100 (since the 3-year on-the-run issue has a market price of $100) and is consistent with (1) a volatility assumption of 10%, (2) a current 1-year rate of 3.5%, and (3) the two rates one year from now of 4.4448% (the lower rate) and 5.4289% (the higher rate).

We will explain how this is done using Exhibit 6. Let's look at how we get the information in the exhibit. The maturity value and coupon payment are shown in the boxes at the four nodes in year 3. Since the 3-year on-the-run issue has a maturity value of $100 and a coupon payment of $4.7, these values are the same in the box shown at each node. For the three nodes in year 2 the coupon payment of $4.7 is shown. Unknown at these three nodes are (1) the three rates two years from now and (2) the value of the bond in year 2. For the two nodes in year 1, the coupon payment is known, as are the 1-year rates in year 1. These are the rates found earlier. The value of the bond, which depends on the bond values at the nodes to the right, are unknown at these two nodes. All of the unknown values are indicated by a question mark.

Exhibit 7 is the same as Exhibit 6 complete with the values previously unknown. As can be seen from Exhibit 7, the value of r_2, or equivalently $r_{2,LL}$, which will produce the desired result is 4.6958%. We showed earlier that the corresponding rates $r_{2,HL}$ and $r_{2,HH}$ would be 5.7354% and 7.0053%, respectively. To verify that these are the 1-year rates two years from now, work backwards from the four nodes at the right of the tree in Exhibit 7. For example, the value in the box at N_{HH} is found by taking the value of $104.7 at the two nodes to its right and discounting at 7.0053%. The value is $97.846. (Since it is the same value for both nodes to the right, it is also the average value.) Similarly, the value in the box at N_{HL} is found by discounting $104.70 by 5.7354% and at N_{LL} by discounting at 4.6958%. The same procedure used in Exhibits 4 and 5 is used to get the values at the other nodes.

Exhibit 6: Information for Deriving the 1-Year Rates for Year 2 Using the 3-Year 4.7% On-the-Run Issue

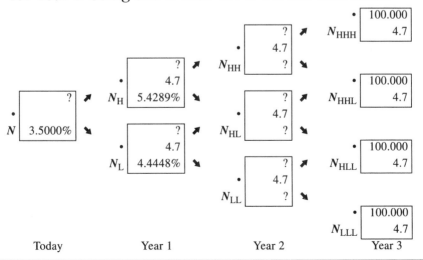

Exhibit 7: The 1-Year Rates for Year 2 Using the 3-Year 4.7% On-the-Run Issue

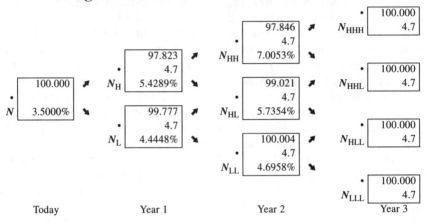

| Today | Year 1 | Year 2 | Year 3 |

Exhibit 8: Binomial Interest Rate Tree for Valuing Up to a 4-Year Bond for Issuer (10% Volatility Assumed)

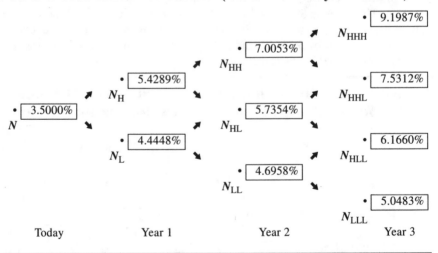

| Today | Year 1 | Year 2 | Year 3 |

VALUING AN OPTION-FREE BOND WITH THE TREE

Exhibit 8 shows the 1-year rates or binomial interest rate tree that can then be used to value any bond for this issuer with a maturity up to four years. To illustrate how to use the binomial interest rate tree, consider a 6.5% option-free bond with four years remaining to maturity. Also assume that the issuer's on-the-run yield curve is the one given earlier and hence the appropriate binomial interest rate tree is the one in Exhibit 8. Exhibit 9 shows the various values in the discounting process, and produces a bond value of $104.643.

It is important to note that this value is identical to the bond value found earlier when we discounted at either the spot rates or the 1-year forward rates. We should expect to find this result since our bond is option free. This clearly demonstrates that the valuation model is consistent with the standard valuation model for an option-free bond.

VALUING A CALLABLE BOND

Now we will demonstrate how the binomial interest rate tree can be applied to value a callable bond. The valuation process proceeds in the same fashion as in the case of an option-free bond, but with one exception: when the call option may be exercised by the issuer, the bond value at a node must be changed to reflect the lesser of its values if it is not called (i.e., the value obtained by applying the recursive valuation formula described above) and the call price.

Exhibit 9: Valuing an Option-Free Bond with Four Years to Maturity and a Coupon Rate of 6.5% (10% Volatility Assumed)

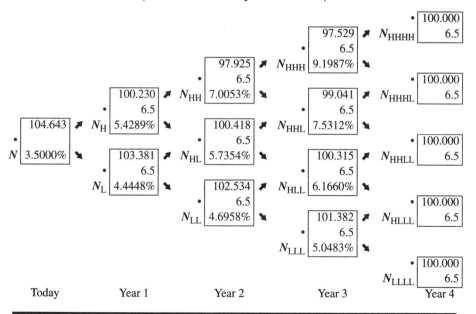

Exhibit 10: Valuing a Callable Bond with Four Years to Maturity, a Coupon Rate of 6.5%, and Callable in One Year at 100 (10% Volatility Assumed)

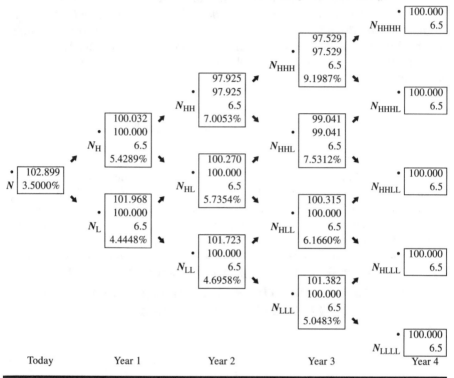

For example, consider a 6.5% bond with four years remaining to maturity that is callable in one year at $100. Exhibit 10 shows two values at each node of the binomial interest rate tree. The discounting process explained above is used to calculate the first of the two values at each node. The second value is the value based on whether the issue will be called. For simplicity, let's assume that this issuer calls the issue if it exceeds the call price. Then, in Exhibit 10 at nodes N_L, N_H, N_{LL}, N_{HL}, N_{LLL}, and N_{HLL}, the values from the recursive valuation formula are $101.968, $100.032, $101.723, $100.270, $101.382, and $100.315. These values exceed the assumed call price ($100) and therefore the second value is $100 rather than the calculated value. It is the second value that is used in subsequent calculations. The root of the tree indicates that the value for this callable bond is $102.899.

The question that we have not addressed in our illustration, which is nonetheless important, is the circumstances under which the issuer will call the bond. A detailed explanation of the call rule is beyond the scope of this chapter. Basically, it involves determining when it would be economical for the issuer on an after-tax basis to call the issue.

Exhibit 11: Valuing a Callable Bond with Four Years to Maturity, a Coupon Rate of 6.5%, and with a Call Price Schedule (10% Volatility Assumed)

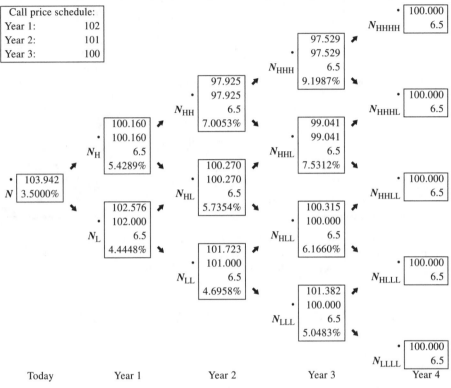

Suppose instead that the call price schedule is 102 in year 1, 101 in year 2, and 100 in year 3. Also assume that the bond will not be called unless it exceeds the call price for that year. Exhibit 11 shows the value at each node and the value of the callable bond. The call price schedule results in a greater value for the callable bond, $103.942 compared to $102.899 when the call price is 100 in each year.

Determining the Call Option Value

As explained in Chapter 5, the value of a callable bond is equal to the value of an option-free bond minus the value of the call option. This means that:

Value of a call option = Value of an option-free bond – Value of a callable bond

We have just seen how the value of an option-free bond and the value of a callable bond can be determined. The difference between the two values is therefore the value of the call option.

Exhibit 12: Binomial Interest Rate Tree for Valuing up to a 4-Year Bond for Issuer (20% Volatility Assumed)

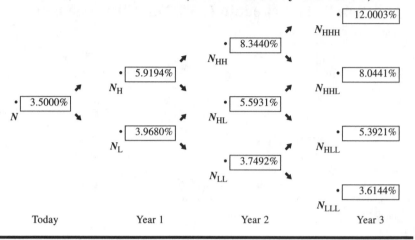

In our illustration, the value of the option-free bond is $104.643. If the call price is $100 in each year and the value of the callable bond is $102.899, the value of the call option is $1.744 (= $104.634 − $102.899).

VOLATILITY AND THE THEORETICAL VALUE

In our illustration, interest rate volatility was assumed to be 10%. The volatility assumption has an important impact on the theoretical value. More specifically, the higher the expected volatility, the higher the value of an option. The same is true for an option embedded in a bond. Correspondingly, this affects the value of a bond with an embedded option.

For example, for a callable bond, a higher interest rate volatility assumption means that the value of the call option increases and, since the value of the option-free bond is not affected, the value of the callable bond must be lower.

We will demonstrate this using the on-the-run yield curve in our previous illustrations. In the previous illustrations, we assumed interest rate volatility of 10%. To show the effect of higher volatility, we will assume volatility of 20%. Exhibit 12 gives the corresponding binomial interest rate tree. Exhibit 13 verifies that the binomial interest rate tree provides the same value for the option-free bond, $104.643.

Exhibit 14 shows the calculation for the callable bond assuming interest rate volatility of 20%. For the callable bond it is assumed that the issue is callable at par beginning in year 1. The value of the callable bond is $102.108 if volatility is assumed to be 20% compared to $102.899 if volatility is assumed to be 10%.

Exhibit 13: Valuing an Option-Free Bond with Four Years to Maturity and a Coupon Rate of 6.5% (20% Volatility Assumed)

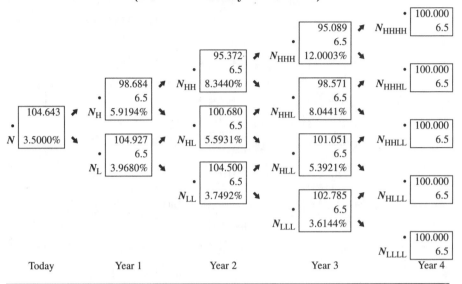

| Today | Year 1 | Year 2 | Year 3 | Year 4 |

In the construction of the binomial interest rate, it was assumed that volatility is the same for each year. The methodology can be extended to incorporate a term structure of volatility.

OPTION-ADJUSTED SPREAD

Suppose the market price of the 4-year 6.5% callable bond is $102.218 and the theoretical value assuming 10% volatility is $102.899. This means that this bond is cheap by $0.681 according to the valuation model. As explained in the previous chapter, bond market participants prefer to think not in terms of a bond's price being cheap or expensive in dollar terms but rather in terms of a yield spread — a cheap bond trades at a higher yield spread and an expensive bond at a lower yield spread.

The option-adjusted spread is the constant spread that when added to all the 1-year rates on the binomial interest rate tree that will make the theoretical value equal to the market price. In our illustration, if the market price is $102.218, the OAS would be the constant spread added to every rate in Exhibit 8 that will make the theoretical value equal to $102.218. The solution in this case would be 35 basis points. This can be verified in Exhibit 15 which shows the value of this issue by adding 35 basis points to each rate.

Exhibit 14: Valuing a Callable Bond with Four Years to Maturity, a Coupon Rate of 6.5%, and Callable in One Year at 100 (20% Volatility Assumed)

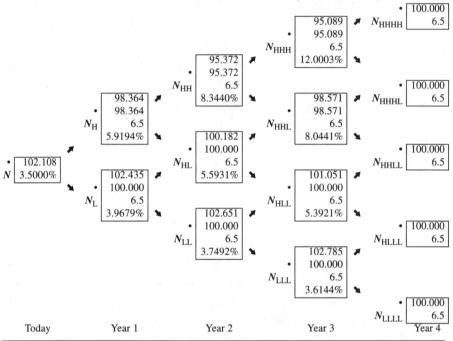

| Today | Year 1 | Year 2 | Year 3 | Year 4 |

As with the value of a bond with an embedded option, the OAS will depend on the volatility assumption. For a given bond price, the higher the interest rate volatility assumed, the lower the OAS for a callable bond. For example, if volatility is 20% rather than 10%, the OAS would be –6 basis points as can be seen from Exhibit 16.

This illustration clearly demonstrates the importance of the volatility assumption. Assuming volatility of 10%, the OAS is 35 basis points. At 20% volatility, the OAS declines and, in this case is negative and therefore the bond is overvalued.

EFFECTIVE DURATION AND EFFECTIVE CONVEXITY

In Chapter 4, we explained that effective duration and effective convexity are the appropriate interest rate risk measures (assuming a parallel shift in the yield curve) for a bond with an embedded option. The formulas are as follows:

$$\text{Effective duration} = \frac{V_- - V_+}{2V_0(\Delta y)}$$

Exhibit 15: Demonstration that the Option-Adjusted Spread is 35 Basis Points For a 6.5% Callable Bond Selling at 102.218 (Assuming 10% Volatility)

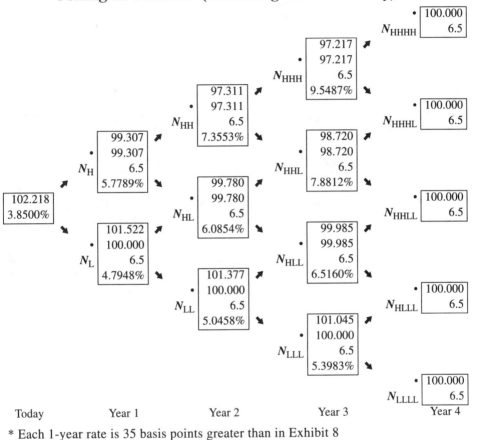

Today   Year 1   Year 2   Year 3   Year 4

* Each 1-year rate is 35 basis points greater than in Exhibit 8

$$\text{Effective convexity} = \frac{V_+ + V_- - 2V_0}{2V_0(\Delta y)^2}$$

where

Δy = change in rate used to calculate new values

V_+ = estimated value if yield is increased by Δy

V_- = estimated value if yield is decreased by Δy

V_0 = initial price (per \$100 of par value)

Exhibit 16: Demonstration that the Option-Adjusted Spread is –6 Basis Points for a 6.5% Callable Bond (Assuming 20% Volatility)*

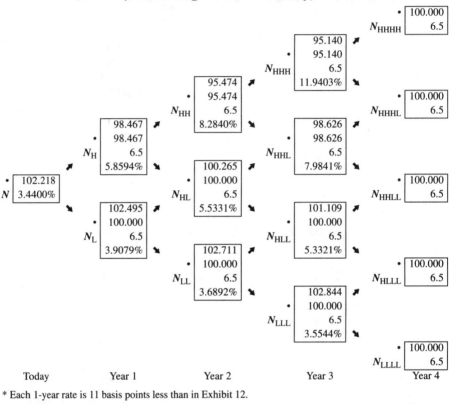

* Each 1-year rate is 11 basis points less than in Exhibit 12.

The procedure for calculating the value of V_+ to use in the formula is as follows:

Step 1: Calculate the OAS for the issue.

Step 2: Shift the on-the-run yield curve up by a small number of basis points (Δy).

Step 3: Construct a binomial interest rate tree based on the new yield curve in Step 2.

Step 4: To each of the 1-year rates in the binomial interest rate tree, add the OAS to obtain an "adjusted tree."

Step 5: Use the adjusted tree found in Step 4 to determine the value of the bond, which is V_+.

Exhibit 17: Determination of V₊ for Calculating Effective Duration and Convexity*

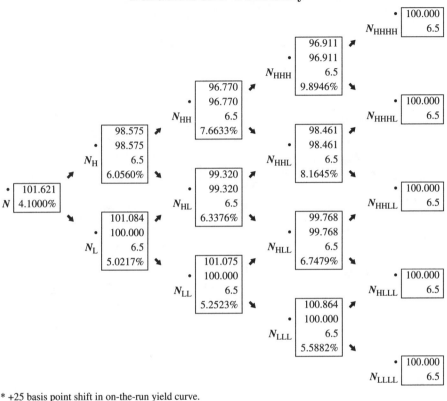

* +25 basis point shift in on-the-run yield curve.

To determine the value of V₋, the same five steps are followed except that in Step 2, the on-the-run yield curve is shifted down by a small number of basis points (Δy).

To illustrate how V₊ and V₋ are determined in order to calculate effective duration and effective convexity, we will use the same on-the-run yield curve that we have used in our previous illustrations assuming a volatility of 10%. The 4-year callable bond with a coupon rate of 6.5% and callable at par selling at 102.218 will be used in this illustration. The OAS for this issue is 35 basis points.

Exhibit 17 shows the adjusted tree by shifting the yield curve up by an arbitrarily small number of basis points, 25 basis points, and then adding 35 basis points (the OAS) to each 1-year rate. The adjusted tree is then used to value the bond. The resulting value, V₊, is 101.621. Exhibit 18 shows the adjusted tree by shifting the yield curve down by 25 basis points and then adding 35 basis points to each 1-year rate. The resulting value, V₋, is 102.765.

Exhibit 18: Determination of V– for Calculating Effective Duration and Convexity*

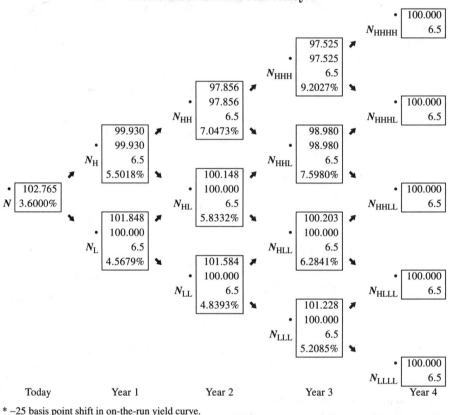

| | Today | Year 1 | Year 2 | Year 3 | Year 4 |

* –25 basis point shift in on-the-run yield curve.

The results are summarized below:

$$\Delta y = 0.0025$$
$$V_+ = 101.621$$
$$V_- = 102.765$$
$$V_0 = 102.218$$

Therefore,

$$\text{Effective duration} = \frac{102.765 - 101.621}{2(102.218)(0.0025)} = 2.24$$

$$\text{Effective convexity} = \frac{101.621 + 102.765 - 2(102.218)}{2(102.218)(0.0025)^2} = -39.1321$$

Notice that this callable bond exhibits negative convexity.

THE CHALLENGE OF IMPLEMENTATION

To transform the basic interest rate tree into a practical tool requires several refinements. For one thing, the spacing of the node lines in the tree must be much finer. However, the fine spacing required to value short-dated securities becomes computationally inefficient if one seeks to value, say, 30-year bonds. While one can introduce time-dependent node spacing, caution is required; it is easy to distort the term structure of volatility. Other practical difficulties include the management of cash flows that fall between two nodes.

KEY POINTS

1. *The binomial model involves generating an interest rate tree based on (1) an issuer's on-the-run yield curve, (2) an assumed interest rate generation process, and (3) an assumed interest rate volatility.*

2. *The binomial interest rate tree is constructed by trial and error.*

3. *The binomial interest rate tree provides the appropriate volatility-dependent 1-period rates that should be used to discount the expected cash flows of a bond.*

4. *The uncertainty of interest rates is introduced into the model by introducing the volatility of interest rates.*

5. *The standard deviation is a statistical measure of volatility.*

6. *The process assumes that the volatility of interest rates is measured relative to the current level of rates.*

7. *Using the binomial interest rate tree the value of any bond can be determined.*

8. *In valuing a callable bond using the binomial interest rate tree, the cash flows at a node are modified to take into account the call option.*

9. *The value of the embedded call option is the difference between the value of an option-free bond and the value of the callable bond.*

10. *The volatility assumption has an important impact on the theoretical value.*

11. *The option-adjusted spread is the constant spread that when added to the short rates in the binomial interest rate tree will produce a valuation for the bond equal to the market price of the bond.*

12. *The required values for calculating effective duration and effective convexity are found by shifting the on-the-run yield curve, calculating a new binomial interest rate tree, and then determining the required values after adjusting the tree by adding the OAS to each short rate.*

13. *To transform the basic binomial interest rate tree into a practical tool requires several refinements.*

Chapter 7

Binomial Model II: Valuing Other Bond Structures

The objectives of this chapter are to:

1. demonstrate how the binomial model can be used to value a putable bond;

2. explain how the binomial model can accommodate multiple embedded options;

3. explain how the binomial model can be used to value a step-up callable note;

4. explain how the binomial model can be used to value a range note;

5. show how the binomial model can be used to value a capped floater; and,

6. explain how a bond with an accelerated sinking fund option is valued.

In Chapter 6, we described the binomial model, how a binomial interest rate tree is constructed, and how the tree can be used to value a callable bond. In this chapter, we look at how the binomial model can be used to value other bond structures — putable bonds, callable step-up notes, range notes, and capped floating-rate notes. The binomial model can also handle bonds with multiple or interrelated embedded options such as a bond that is both callable and putable. Finally, we look at how the accelerated sinking fund option affects the value of a bond.

VALUING A PUTABLE BOND

A putable bond is one in which the bondholder has the right to force the issuer to pay off the bond prior to the maturity date. To illustrate how the binomial model can be used to value a putable bond, suppose that a 6.5% bond with four years remaining to maturity is putable in one year at par ($100). Also assume that the appropriate binomial interest rate tree for this issuer is the one in Exhibit 8 of Chapter 6 and the bondholder exercises the put if the bond's price is less than par.

Exhibit 1 shows the binomial interest rate tree with the bond value altered at three nodes (N_{HH}, N_{HHH}, and N_{HHL}) because the bond value at these nodes is less than $100, the assumed value at which the bond can be put. The value of this putable bond is $105.327.

Since the value of an option-free bond can be expressed as the value of a putable bond minus the value of a put option on that bond, this means that:

Value of a put option = Value of an option-free bond − Value of a putable bond

In our example, since the value of the putable bond is $105.327 and the value of the corresponding option-free bond is $104.643, the value of the put option is −$0.684. The negative sign indicates the issuer has sold the option, or equivalently, the investor has purchased the option.

Exhibit 12 of Chapter 6 shows the binomial tree assuming 20% volatility. Exhibit 2 shows the value of the putable bond assuming 20% volatility. The value of this putable bond is $106.010 at 20%, which is greater than its value at 10% volatility ($105.327).

Suppose that a bond is both putable and callable. The procedure for valuing such a structure is to adjust the value at each node to reflect whether the issue would be put or call. To illustrate this, consider the 4-year callable bond analyzed in the previous chapter that had a call schedule. The valuation of this issue is shown in Exhibit 11 of the previous chapter. Suppose the issue is putable in year 3 at par value. Exhibit 3 shows how to value this callable/putable issue. In year 3, the put value is shown as the second value in the two boxes where the value at the top of the box is less than par. The value of this callable/putable issue is $104.413, which is greater than the callable issue whose value is $103.942.

Exhibit 1: Valuing a Putable Bond with Four Years to Maturity, a Coupon Rate of 6.5%, and Putable in One Year at 100 (10% Volatility Assumed)

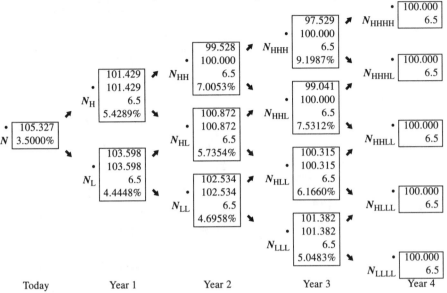

Today   Year 1   Year 2   Year 3   Year 4

Exhibit 2: Valuing a Putable Bond with Four Years to Maturity, a Coupon Rate of 6.5%, and Putable in One Year at 100 (20% Volatility Assumed)

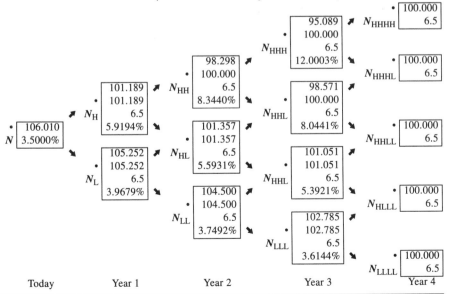

Today   Year 1   Year 2   Year 3   Year 4

Exhibit 3: Valuing a Putable/Callable Issue (10% Volatility Assumed)

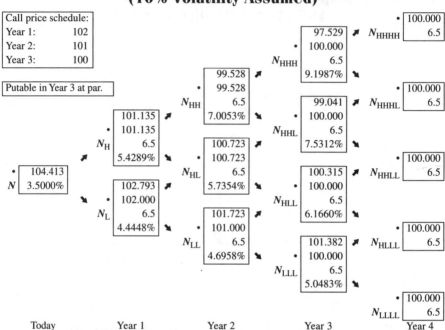

| Today | Year 1 | Year 2 | Year 3 | Year 4 |

VALUING A STEP-UP CALLABLE NOTE

Step-up callable notes are callable fixed income instruments whose coupon rate is increased (i.e., "stepped up") at designated times. When the coupon rate is increased only once over the security's life, it is said to be a *single step-up callable note*. A *multiple step-up callable note* is a step-up callable note whose coupon is increased more than one time over the life of the security.

To illustrate how the binomial model can be used to value step-up callable notes, let's begin with a single step-up callable note. Suppose that a 4-year step-up callable note pays 4.25% for two years and then 7.5% for two more years. Assume that this note is callable at par at the end of Year 2 and Year 3. We will use the binomial interest rate tree given in Exhibit 8 of Chapter 6 to value this note.

Exhibit 4 shows the value of a corresponding single step-up *noncallable* note. The valuation procedure is identical to that performed in Exhibit 9 of Chapter 6 except that the coupon in the box at each node reflects the step-up terms. The value is $102.082. Exhibit 5 shows that the value of the single step-up callable note is $100.031. The value of the embedded call option is equal to the difference in the step-up noncallable note value and the step-up callable note value, $2.051.

Exhibit 4: Valuing a Single Step-Up Noncallable Note with Four Years to Maturity (10% Volatility Assumed)

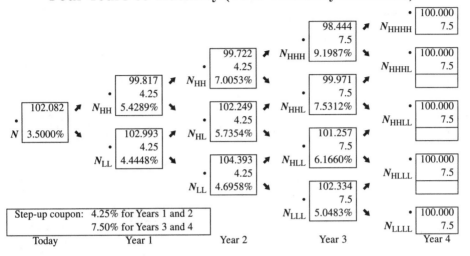

Exhibit 5: Valuing a Single Step-Up Callable Note with Four Years to Maturity, Callable in Two Years at 100 (10% Volatility Assumed)

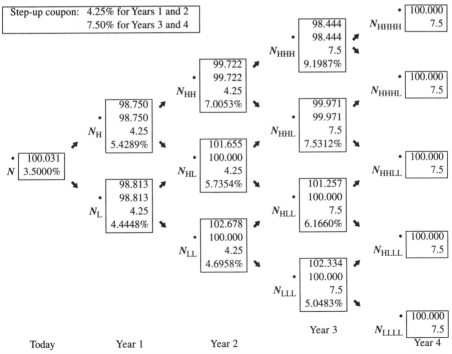

Exhibit 6: Valuing a Multiple Step-Up Noncallable Note with Four Years to Maturity (10% Volatility Assumed)

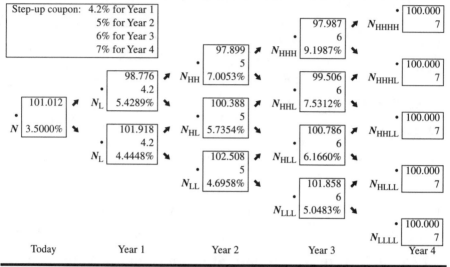

The procedure is the same for a multiple step-up callable note. Suppose that a multiple step-up callable note has the following coupon rates: 4.2% in Year 1, 5% in Year 2, 6% in Year 3, and 7% in Year 4. Also assume that the note is callable at the end of Year 1 at par. Exhibit 6 shows that the value of this note if it noncallable is $101.012. The value of the multiple step-up callable note is $99.996 as shown in Exhibit 7. The value of the embedded call option is $1.016.

VALUING A RANGE NOTE

A *range note* is a security that pays the reference rate with no spread if the reference rate is within a band. If the reference rate falls outside of the band (lower or upper), the coupon rate is zero. The band increases over time.

To illustrate, suppose that the reference rate is the 1-year rate we have been using in our illustrations. Suppose further that the bands are as shown below:

	Year 1	Year 2	Year 3
Lower limit of range	4.50%	5.25%	6.00%
Upper limit of range	5.50%	6.75%	8.00%

Using the binomial interest rate tree in Exhibit 8 of Chapter 6, Exhibit 8 shows how to value a 3-year range note. The coupon rate at each node is the forward rate if the rate is within the band and zero otherwise. The value of this range note is $96.773. Exhibit 9 shows the value of the range note if the coupon rate is the 1-year rate plus a spread of 200 basis points. This means that at each node, the coupon rate is increased by 200 basis points. In this case, the value of the range note is $99.965.

Exhibit 7: Valuing a Multiple Step-Up Noncallable Note with Four Years to Maturity, and Callable in One Year at 100 (10% Volatility Assumed)

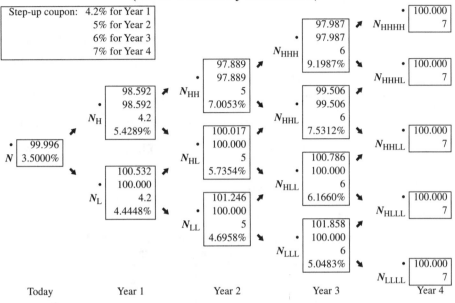

| Today | Year 1 | Year 2 | Year 3 | Year 4 |

Exhibit 8: Valuing a Range Note with Three Years to Maturity (10% Volatility Assumed)

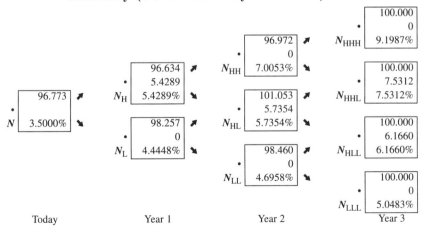

| Today | Year 1 | Year 2 | Year 3 |

Coupon Schedule: 1-year rate unless rate is outside bands below.

	Year 1	Year 2	Year 3
Lower limit of range	4.50%	5.25%	6.00%
Upper limit of range	5.50%	6.75%	8.00%

Exhibit 9: Valuing a Range Note with Three Years to Maturity with the Coupon Rate Equal to the 1-Year Rate Plus 200 Basis Points (10% Volatility Assumed)

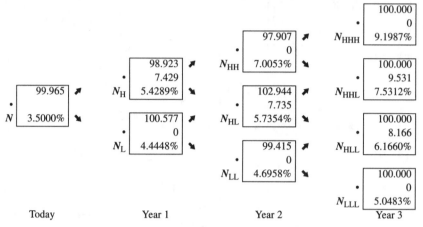

Today   Year 1   Year 2   Year 3

Coupon Schedule: 1-year rate plus 200 basis points, unless rate is outside bands below.

	Year 1	Year 2	Year 3
Lower limit of range	4.50%	5.25%	6.00%
Upper limit of range	5.50%	6.75%	8.00%

Range notes can also be putable. The procedure for valuing a putable range note is the same as illustrated in Exhibit 1.

VALUING A CAPPED FLOATING-RATE NOTE

The valuation of a capped floating-rate note using the binomial model requires that the coupon rate be adjusted based on the 1-year rate (which is assumed to be the reference rate). Exhibit 10 shows the binomial tree and the relevant values at each node for a floater whose coupon rate is the 1-year rate flat and in which there are no restrictions on the coupon rate.

The valuation procedure is identical to that for the other structures described with one exception. While the coupon rate is set at the beginning of the period, it is paid in arrears. In the valuation procedure, the coupon rate set for the next period is shown in the box at which the rate is determined. For example, in Exhibit 10, the coupon rate shown in the top box in Year 2 is 7.0053 as determined by the 1-year rate at that node. Since the payment will not be made until the next year, the value of 100 shown in the same box is determined by using the standard procedure but discounting the coupon rate in the same box. For example, let's see how we get the value of 100 in the top box in Year 2. The procedure is to calculate the average of the two present values of the bond value and coupon. Since the bond values and coupons are the same, the present value is simply:

$$\frac{100 + 7.0053}{1.070053} = 100$$

Suppose that the floater has a cap of 7.25%. Exhibit 11 shows how this floater would be valued. At each node where the short rate exceeds 7.25%, a coupon of $7.25 is substituted. The value of this capped floater is 99.724. Thus, the cost of the cap is the difference between par and 99.724. If the cap for this floater was 7.75% rather than 7.25%, it can be shown that the value of this floater would be 99.858. That is, the higher the cap, the closer the capped floater will trade to par.

ASSESSING HOW THE ACCELERATED SINKING FUND OPTION AFFECTS THE VALUE OF A BOND

In Chapter 1, we described the accelerated sinking fund provision. This provision is an option granted to the issuer to accelerate the retirement of the principal above that required by the sinking fund requirement. It will be beneficial for the issuer to do so if rates decline below the issue's coupon rate. The value of a bond with an accelerated sinking fund provision is equal to the value of an otherwise option-free bond minus the value of the accelerated sinking fund option. We show how the value of the accelerated sinking fund option is estimated using the binomial model.

Exhibit 10: Valuing a Floating-Rate Note with No Cap (10% Volatility Assumed)

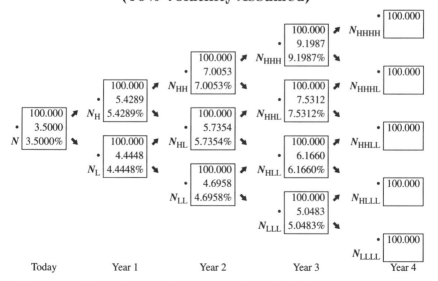

Note: The coupon rate shown at a node is the coupon rate to be received in the next year.

Exhibit 11: Valuing a Floating Rate Note with a 7.25% Cap (10% Volatility Assumed)

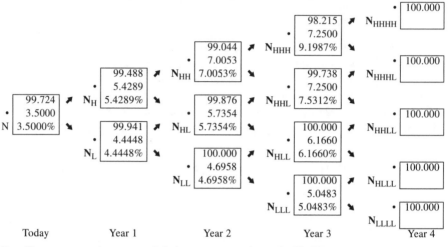

Note: The coupon rate shown at a node is the coupon rate to be received in the next year.

We will use an illustration to show how this is done. Consider a 4-year 6.5% coupon bond. Suppose that $100 million of this issue is outstanding and that the sinking fund provision requires that the issuer retire $20 million each year for the next three years. Suppose that the issuer may retire at par value an *additional* $10 million in each of the next three years. Effectively, this is a European call option for each of the next three years on $10 million of the issue.

Assume that the appropriate binomial interest rate tree is the one that we have been using in our previous illustrations assuming 10% volatility. We will assume that the issuer will exercise the right to retire the additional $10 million in any year in which the value at a node exceeds the par value. Exhibit 12 shows the tree for three years along with the value of the bond at each node.

Let's look at how to value the first accelerated call option to retire $10 million at par in Year 1. This is a 1-year European call option on $10 million par value of a 6.5% bond. Look at Exhibit 13a. There are two nodes. The value at both nodes must be determined. Look first at the upper box of the two nodes. The bond's value is 100.23. The issuer will exercise the option to accelerate payment since it exceeds par value. The value of this accelerated sinking fund option in Year 1 at that node per $100 par value is $0.23. Since the option is to retire $10 million par value, the value of this option in Year 1 at that node is $23,000. Similarly, the value of the option to retire $10 million in Year 1 at the lower node is $338,100. The value at the root can now be determined. This is found by taking the average present value of the two nodes at Year 1, discounting at the root rate of 3.5%. That is:

$$\frac{1}{2}\left(\frac{\$23,000}{1.035} + \frac{\$338,100}{1.035}\right) = \$174,444$$

Exhibit 12: Binomial Tree with Rates and Bond Values for Years 1, 2, and 3 for a 4-Year 6.5% Option-Free Bond

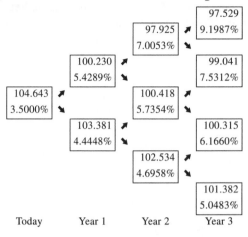

			97.529
		97.925 ↗	9.1987%
		7.0053% ↘	
	100.230 ↗		99.041
	5.4289% ↘		7.5312%
104.643 ↗		100.418 ↗	
3.5000% ↘		5.7354% ↘	
	103.381 ↗		100.315
	4.4448% ↘		6.1660%
		102.534 ↗	
		4.6958% ↘	
			101.382
			5.0483%
Today	Year 1	Year 2	Year 3

Let's do one more year, Year 2. Exhibit 13b shows at each node in Year 2 the bond's value. The top node has a value that is less than $100. This means that the issuer will not exercise the right to retire the additional $10 million. The value of the accelerated sinking fund provision at that node is zero. The value of the accelerated sinking fund provision at the other two nodes is positive since the bond's value at each node exceeds par. For the middle node it is $41,800 and for the lower node it is $253,400. The values are then present valued to Year 1 by using the interest rates to the node at the left. For example, to get the value of the accelerated sinking fund option in the top box at Year 1, the values of $0 and $41,800 are discounted at 5.4289% and averaged. The value is $19,824. The value at the lower node is $141,319 found by discounting $41,800 and $253,400 at 4.4448%. To get the value at the root, the average present value of $19,824 and $141,319 when discounted at 3.5% is computed. As shown in Exhibit 13b, the average present value is $77,847 and is therefore the value of the option to retire $10 million additional in Year 2.

Exhibit 13c shows the value of the accelerated sinking fund option to retire an additional $10 million in Year 3. The value is $25,600. Adding up the values found in Exhibits 13a, 13b, and 13c gives the value of the accelerated sinking fund option to retire $10 million in each of the next three years. The value is $277,891 ($174,444 + $77,847 + 25,600).

Now we must determine the value of a bond adjusting for the value of the accelerated sinking fund option. We know that the value of a 6.5% 4-year bond option-free bond is $104.643 per $100 of par value. Therefore, the value of the $100 million issue is $104.643 million. The value of the accelerated sinking fund option is $277,891. Thus, the value of $100 million par value adjusted for the accelerated sinking fund option is $104,643,000 minus $277,891, or $104,365,109. The value per $100 par is $104.365.

Exhibit 13: Valuing the Accelerated Sinking Fund Option

Bond: 4-year 6.5% coupon
Accelerated sinking fund option: $10 million additional in Years 1, 2, and 3

(a) Valuation of the option to retire $10 million in Year 1 at par

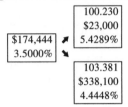

(b) Valuation of the option to retire $10 million in Year 2 at par

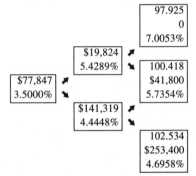

(c) Valuation of the option to retire $10 million in Year 3 at par

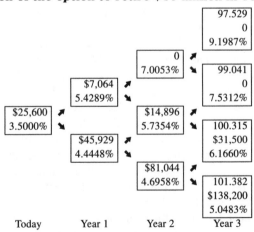

The same computational procedure described here for calculating the value of the accelerated sinking fund option will be used in valuing an option in Chapter 13 and a cap and floor in Chapter 15.

KEY POINTS

1. *For a bond with any embedded option or options, application of the binomial model requires that the value at each node of the tree be adjusted based on whether or not the option will be exercised.*

2. *The binomial model can be used to value bonds with multiple or interrelated embedded options by determining at each node of the tree whether or not one of the options will be exercised.*

3. *With a putable bond, the option will be exercised if the value at a node is less than the price at which the bondholder can put the bond to the issuer.*

4. *The value of a putable bond is greater than the value of an otherwise option-free bond.*

5. *The binomial model can be used to value a single step-up callable note or a multiple step-up callable note.*

6. *A range note is valued by adjusting the coupon at each node of the tree based on whether or not the interest rate falls within the range — in which case the coupon rate is the rate at the node — or is outside the range — in which case the coupon rate at the node is zero.*

7. *To value a floating-rate note that has a cap, the coupon at each node of the tree is adjusted by determining whether or not the cap is reached at a node; if the rate at a node does exceed the cap, the rate at the node is the capped rate rather than the rate determined by the floater's coupon formula.*

8. *The accelerated sinking fund provision is an option granted to the issuer to increase the amount retired when interest rates decline below the issue's coupon rate.*

9. *To value the accelerated sinking fund option, the value of each period's option is determined at each node on the tree and the present value of these option values is calculated using the rates on the tree.*

10. *The value of a bond with an accelerated sinking fund provision is equal to the value of an otherwise option-free bond minus the value of the accelerated sinking fund option.*

Chapter 8

Monte Carlo Model for Valuing Mortgage-Backed Securities

The objectives of this chapter are to:

1. provide an overview of mortgage-backed securities — passthroughs, stripped mortgage-backed securities, and collateralized mortgage obligations — and their cash flows characteristics;

2. explain the prepayment conventions for generating the cash flows of a mortgage-backed security;

3. describe the factors that affect prepayments;

4. explain why the Monte Carlo model is used to value mortgage-backed securities;

5. show how interest rate paths are simulated in a Monte Carlo model;

6. demonstrate how the Monte Carlo model can be used to determine the theoretical value of a mortgage-backed security;

7. explain how the option-adjusted spread, effective duration, and effective convexity are computed using the Monte Carlo model;

8. explain how the option cost is calculated in the Monte Carlo model;

9. discuss the complexities of modeling collateralized mortgage obligations;

10. *discuss some technical issues in the Monte Carlo model;*

11. *illustrate with actual deals how the OAS derived from the Monte Carlo model can be used to identify cheap and rich CMO tranches; and,*

12. *demonstrate modeling risk.*

The second model for valuing bonds with embedded options is the Monte Carlo simulation, or simply Monte Carlo, model. The model involves simulating a sufficiently large number of potential interest rate paths in order to assess the value of a security along these different paths. This model is the most flexible of the two valuation methodologies for valuing interest rate sensitive instruments where the history of interest rates is important. Mortgage-backed securities are commonly valued using this model. We begin with a description of mortgage-backed securities.

OVERVIEW OF MORTGAGE-BACKED SECURITIES

Mortgage-backed securities are securities backed by a pool (collection) of mortgage loans. While any type of mortgage loans, residential or commercial, can be used as collateral for a mortgage-backed security, most are backed by residential mortgages. Mortgage-backed securities include the following securities: (1) mortgage passthrough securities, (2) collateralized mortgage obligations, and (3) stripped mortgage-backed securities. The latter two mortgage-backed securities are referred to as *derivative mortgage-backed securities* because they are created from mortgage passthrough securities.

Mortgages

We begin our discussion with the raw material for a mortgage-backed security (MBS) — the mortgage loan. A *mortgage loan*, or simply mortgage, is a loan secured by the collateral of some specified real estate property which obliges the borrower to make a predetermined series of payments. There are many types of mortgage designs available in the United States. A *mortgage design* is a specification of the interest rate, term of the mortgage, and manner in which the borrowed funds are repaid. Below we describe the three most popular mortgage designs: (1) the fixed-rate, level-payment, fully amortized mortgage, (2) the adjustable-rate mortgage, and (3) the balloon mortgage. The interest rate on the mortgage loan is called the *mortgage rate* or *contract rate*. Our focus is on residential mortgage loans.

Fixed-Rate, Level-Payment, Fully Amortized Mortgage

The basic idea behind the design of the fixed-rate, level payment, fully amortized mortgage is that the borrower pays interest and repays principal in equal installments over an agreed-upon period of time, called the maturity or term of the mortgage. The frequency of payment is typically monthly. Each monthly mortgage payment for this mortgage design is due on the first of each month and consists of:

1. interest of $\frac{1}{12}$th of the annual interest rate times the amount of the outstanding mortgage balance at the beginning of the previous month, and
2. a repayment of a portion of the outstanding mortgage balance (principal).

The difference between the monthly mortgage payment and the portion of the payment that represents interest equals the amount that is applied to reduce the outstanding mortgage balance. The monthly mortgage payment is designed so that after the last scheduled monthly payment of the loan is made, the amount of the outstanding mortgage balance is zero (i.e. the mortgage is fully repaid or amortized). *The portion of the monthly mortgage payment applied to interest declines each month and the portion applied to reducing the mortgage balance increases.* The reason for this is that as the mortgage balance is reduced with each monthly mortgage payment, the interest on the mortgage balance declines. Since the monthly mortgage payment is fixed, an increasingly larger portion of the monthly payment is applied to reduce the principal in each subsequent month.

Every mortgage loan must be serviced. Servicing of a mortgage loan involves collecting monthly payments and forwarding proceeds to owners of the loan; sending payment notices to mortgagors; reminding mortgagors when payments are overdue; maintaining records of principal balances; administering an escrow balance for real estate taxes and insurance purposes; initiating foreclosure proceedings if necessary; and, furnishing tax information to mortgagors when applicable.

The servicing fee is a portion of the mortgage rate. If the mortgage rate is 8.125% and the servicing fee is 50 basis points, then the investor receives interest of 7.625%. The interest rate that the investor receives is said to be the *net interest* or *net coupon*.

The cash flows described above assume that the homeowner does not pay off any portion of the mortgage balance prior to the scheduled due date. But homeowners do pay off all or part of their mortgage balance prior to the maturity date. Payments made in excess of the scheduled principal repayments are called *prepayments*. We'll look more closely at the factors that affect prepayment behavior later in this chapter. The effect of prepayments is that the amount and timing of the cash flows from a mortgage are not known with certainty. This is true for all mortgage loans, not just fixed-rate, level-payment, fully amortized mortgages.

Adjustable-Rate Mortgages

An *adjustable-rate mortgage* (ARM) is a loan in which the mortgage rate is reset periodically in accordance with some appropriately chosen reference rate. Outstanding ARMs call for resetting the mortgage rate every month, six months, year, two years, three years, or five years. Two categories of reference rates have been used in ARMS: (1) market-determined rates and (2) calculated cost of funds for thrifts. The reference rate will have an important impact on the performance of an ARM and how it is priced. The most popular reference is a market-determined rate — the weekly average yield of constant maturity 1-year Treasuries. The cost of funds index for thrifts is calculated based on the monthly weighted average interest cost for liabilities of thrifts. The most popular is the Eleventh Federal Home Loan Bank Board District Cost of Funds Index (COFI).

The monthly mortgage payments of an ARM are affected by other features. These features are periodic caps and lifetime rate caps and floors. Periodic caps limit the amount that the mortgage rate may increase or decrease at the reset date. The periodic rate cap is expressed in percentage points. The most common rate cap on annual reset loans is 2%. Most ARMs have an upper limit on the mortgage rate that can be charged over the life of the loan.

Balloon Mortgages

In a *balloon mortgage* the borrower is given long-term financing by the lender but at specified future dates the mortgage rate is renegotiated. Thus, the lender is providing long-term funds for what is effectively a short-term borrowing, how short depending on the frequency of the renegotiation period. Effectively it is a short-term balloon loan in which the lender agrees to provide financing for the remainder of the term of the mortgage. The balloon payment is the original amount borrowed less the amount amortized.

Mortgage Passthrough Securities

A *mortgage passthrough security* is a security created when one or more holders of mortgages form a pool (collection) of mortgages and sell shares or participation certificates in the pool. A pool may consist of several thousand or only a few mortgages. The cash flows of a mortgage passthrough security depend on the cash flows of the underlying mortgages. The cash flows consist of monthly mortgage payments representing interest, the scheduled repayment of principal, and any prepayments.

Payments are made to security holders each month. Neither the amount nor the timing, however, of the cash flows from the pool of mortgages are identical to that of the cash flows passed through to investors. The monthly cash flows for a passthrough are less than the monthly cash flows of the underlying mortgages by an amount equal to servicing and other fees. The other fees are those charged by the issuer or guarantor of the passthrough for guaranteeing the issue. The coupon rate on a passthrough, called the *passthrough coupon rate*, is less than the mortgage rate on the underlying pool of mortgage loans by an amount equal to the servicing fee and guarantee fee. The latter is a fee charged by a guarantor.

Not all of the mortgages that are included in a pool of mortgages that are securitized have the same mortgage rate and the same maturity. Consequently, when describing a passthrough security, a weighted average coupon rate and a weighted average maturity are determined. A *weighted average coupon rate*, or WAC, is found by weighting the mortgage rate of each mortgage loan in the pool by the amount of the mortgage balance outstanding. A *weighted average maturity*, or WAM, is found by weighting the remaining number of months to maturity for each mortgage loan in the pool by the amount of the mortgage balance outstanding.

Stripped Mortgage-Backed Securities

A mortgage passthrough security divides the cash flows from the underlying pool of mortgages on a pro rata basis to the security holders. A *stripped mortgage-backed security* is created by altering that distribution of principal and interest from a pro rata distribution to an unequal distribution. In the most common type of stripped mortgage-backed securities all the interest is allocated to one class (called the *interest only* or *IO* class) and all the principal to the other class (called the *principal only* or *PO* class). The IO class receives no principal payments.

Collateralized Mortgage Obligations

An investor in a mortgage passthrough security is exposed to prepayment risk. By redirecting how the cash flows of passthrough securities are paid to different bond classes, securities can be created that have different exposure to prepayment risk. When the cash flows of mortgage-related products are redistributed to different bond classes, the resulting securities are called *collateralized mortgage obligations*. The creation of a CMO cannot eliminate prepayment risk, it can only redistribute prepayment risk among different classes of bondholders.

The basic principle is that redirecting cash flows (interest and principal) to different bond classes, called *tranches*, mitigates different forms of prepayment risk. It is *never* possible to eliminate prepayment risk. If one tranche in a CMO structure has less prepayment risk than the mortgage passthrough securities that are collateral for the structure, then another tranche in the same structure has greater prepayment risk than the collateral.

CMOs are referred to as *paythroughs* or *multi-class passthroughs*. (CMOs are also referred to as *REMICs*.) A security structure in which collateral is carved into different bond classes is not uncommon. There are similar paythrough or multi-class passthrough structures in the asset-backed securities market.

PREPAYMENT CONVENTIONS AND CASH FLOWS

In order to value a mortgage-backed security, it is necessary to project its cash flows. The difficulty is that the cash flows are unknown because of prepayments. The only way to project cash flows is to make some assumption about the prepayment rate over the life of the underlying mortgage pool. The prepayment rate is sometimes referred to as the *speed*. Two conventions have been used as a benchmark for prepayment rates — conditional prepayment rate and Public Securities Association prepayment benchmark.

Conditional Prepayment Rate

One convention for projecting prepayments and the cash flows of a mortgage-backed security assumes that some fraction of the remaining principal in the pool is prepaid each month for the remaining term of the mortgage. The prepayment rate assumed for a pool, called the *conditional prepayment rate* (CPR), is based on the characteristics of the pool (including its historical prepayment experience) and the current and expected future economic environment.

The CPR is an annual prepayment rate. To estimate monthly prepayments, the CPR must be converted into a monthly prepayment rate, commonly referred to as the *single-monthly mortality rate* (SMM). A formula can be used to determine the SMM for a given CPR:

$$SMM = 1 - (1 - CPR)^{1/12}$$

Suppose that the CPR used to estimate prepayments is 6%. The corresponding SMM is:

$$SMM = 1 - (1 - 0.06)^{1/12}$$
$$= 1 - (0.94)^{0.08333} = 0.005143$$

An SMM of $w\%$ means that approximately $w\%$ of the remaining mortgage balance at the beginning of the month, less the scheduled principal payment, will prepay that month. That is,

Prepayment for month t
$= SMM \times$ (Beginning mortgage balance for month t
$-$ Scheduled principal payment for month t)

For example, suppose that an investor owns a passthrough in which the remaining mortgage balance at the beginning of some month is $290 million. Assuming that the SMM is 0.5143% and the scheduled principal payment is $3 million, the estimated prepayment for the month is:

$$0.005143 \times (\$290,000,000 - \$3,000,000) = \$1,476,041$$

PSA Prepayment Benchmark

The Public Securities Association (PSA) prepayment benchmark is expressed as a monthly series of CPRs.[1] The PSA benchmark assumes that prepayment rates are low for newly originated mortgages and then will speed up as the mortgages become seasoned.

---

[1] This benchmark is commonly referred to as a prepayment model, suggesting that it can be used to estimate prepayments. Characterization of this benchmark as a prepayment model is inappropriate. It is simply a market convention describing the expected behavior pattern of prepayments.

The PSA benchmark assumes the following prepayment rates for 30-year mortgages:

(1) a CPR of 0.2% for the first month, increased by 0.2% per year per month for the next 30 months when it reaches 6% per year, and
(2) a 6% CPR for the remaining years

This benchmark is referred to as "100% PSA" or simply "100 PSA." Mathematically, 100 PSA can be expressed as follows:

$$\text{if } t \leq 30 \text{ then CPR} = \frac{6\% \ t}{30}$$

if $t > 30$ then CPR = 6%

where t is the number of months since the mortgage originated.

Slower or faster speeds are then referred to as some percentage of PSA. For example, 50 PSA means one-half the CPR of the PSA benchmark prepayment rate; 150 PSA means 1.5 times the CPR of the PSA benchmark prepayment rate; 300 PSA means three times the CPR of the benchmark prepayment rate. A prepayment rate of 0 PSA means that no prepayments are assumed.

FACTORS AFFECTING PREPAYMENT BEHAVIOR

The factors that affect prepayment behavior are: (1) prevailing mortgage rate, (2) characteristics of the underlying mortgage pool, (3) seasonal factors, and (4) general economic activity.

Prevailing Mortgage Rate

The single most important factor affecting prepayments because of refinancing is the current level of mortgage rates relative to the borrower's contract rate. The more the contract rate exceeds the prevailing mortgage rate, the greater the incentive to refinance the mortgage loan. For refinancing to make economic sense, the interest savings must be greater than the costs associated with refinancing the mortgage. These costs include legal expenses, origination fees, title insurance, and the value of the time associated with obtaining another mortgage loan. Some of these costs — such as title insurance and origination points — will vary proportionately with the amount to be financed. Other costs such as the application fee and legal expenses are typically fixed.

The historical pattern of prepayments and economic theory suggest that it is not only the level of mortgage rates that affects prepayment behavior but also the path that mortgage rates take to get to the current level. To illustrate why, suppose the underlying contract rate for a pool of mortgage loans is 11% and that three years after origination, the prevailing mortgage rate declines to 8%. Let's consider two possible paths of the mortgage rate in getting to the 8% level. In the first path, the mortgage rate declines to 8% at the end of the first year, then rises to 13% at the end of the second year, and then falls to 8% at the end of the third year. In the second path, the mortgage rate rises to 12% at the end of the first year, continues its rise to 13% at the end of the second year, and then falls to 8% at the end of the third year.

If the mortgage rate follows the first path, those who can benefit from refinancing will more than likely take advantage of this opportunity when the mortgage rate drops to 8% in the first year. When the mortgage rate drops again to 8% at the end of the third year, the likelihood is that prepayments because of refinancing will not surge; those who can benefit by taking advantage of the refinancing opportunity will have done so already when the mortgage rate declined the first time. This prepayment behavior is referred to as *refinancing burnout* (or simply, *burnout*).

In contrast, the expected prepayment behavior when the mortgage rate follows the second path is quite different. Prepayment rates are expected to be low in the first two years. When the mortgage rate declines to 8% in the third year, refinancing activity and therefore prepayments are expected to surge. Consequently, burnout is related to the path of mortgage rates. As explained below, this is the primary reason why the binomial model (which uses backward induction) is not used.

Characteristics of the Underlying Mortgage Loans

The following characteristics of the underlying mortgage loans affect prepayments: (1) the contract rate, (2) whether the loans are FHA/VA-guaranteed or conventional, (3) the amount of seasoning, (4) the type of loan, for example, a 30-year level payment mortgage, 5-year balloon mortgage, etc., and (4) the geographical location of the underlying properties.

Seasonality

There is a well-documented seasonal pattern in prepayments. This pattern is related to activity in the primary housing market, with home buying increasing in the spring, and gradually reaching a peak in the late summer. Home buying declines in the fall and winter. Mirroring this activity are the prepayments that result from the turnover of housing as home buyers sell their existing homes and purchase new ones. Prepayments are low in the winter months and begin to rise in the spring, reaching a peak in the summer months. However, probably because of delays in passing through prepayments, the peak may not be observed until early fall.

Macroeconomic Factors

Economic theory would suggest that general economic activity affects prepayment behavior through its effect on housing turnover. The link is as follows: a growing economy results in a rise in personal income and in opportunities for worker migration; this increases family mobility and as a result increases housing turnover. The opposite holds for a weak economy.

PREPAYMENT MODELS

A prepayment model is a statistical model that is used to forecast prepayments. It begins by modeling the statistical relationships among the factors that are expected to affect prepayments. The four factors discussed above explain most of the prepayment activity. These factors are then combined into one model.

Wall Street firms and vendors report their projections for different types of passthroughs in their publications. For example, in its weekly report, *Spread Talk*, Prudential Securities provides 6-month, 1-year, and long-term prepayment projections assuming shifts in interest rates. Information is provided by the type of passthrough and passthrough coupon rate. For example, in its December 15, 1995 *Spread Talk*, a long-term rate of 119 PSA was projected for Ginnie Mae 30-year passthroughs with a coupon rate of 8% (issued in 1992 with a weighted average maturity (WAM) of 25 years and 11 months) if rates are unchanged, and a lower long-term rate of 100 PSA was projected if rates increased by 100 basis points.

In addition to reports to their clients, MBS dealers provide their prepayment projections to sources such as Bloomberg, Reuters, Telerate, and Knight-Ridder.

THE VALUATION METHODOLOGY[2]

For some fixed income securities and derivative instruments, the periodic cash flows are *interest rate path-dependent*. This means that the cash flow received in one period is determined not only by the current interest rate level, but also by the path that interest rates took to get to the current level.

In the case of passthrough securities, prepayments are path-dependent because this month's prepayment rate depends on whether there have been prior opportunities to refinance since the underlying mortgages were originated — the phenomenon we referred to earlier as prepayment burnout. Unlike passthroughs, the decision as to whether a corporate issuer will elect to refund an issue when the current rate is below the issue's coupon rate is not dependent on how rates evolved over time to the current level.

Moreover, in the case of adjustable-rate passthroughs (ARMs), prepayments are not only path-dependent but the periodic coupon rate depends on the history of the reference rate upon which the coupon rate is determined. This is because ARMs have periodic caps and floors as well as a lifetime cap and floor. For example, an ARM whose coupon rate resets annually could have the following restriction on the coupon rate: (1) the rate cannot change by more than 200 basis points each year and (2) the rate cannot be more than 500 basis points from the initial coupon rate.

---

[2] Portions of the material in this section and the one to follow are adapted from Frank J. Fabozzi and Scott F. Richard, "Valuation of CMOs," Chapter 6 in Frank J. Fabozzi (ed.), *CMO Portfolio Management* (Summit, N.J.: Frank J. Fabozzi Associates, 1994).

Pools of passthroughs are used as collateral for the creation of CMOs. Consequently, there are typically two sources of path dependency in a CMO tranche's cash flows. First, the collateral prepayments are path-dependent as discussed above. Second, the cash flow to be received in the current month by a CMO tranche depends on the outstanding balances of the other tranches in the deal. Thus, we need the history of prepayments to calculate these balances.

Conceptually, the valuation of passthroughs using the Monte Carlo model is simple. In practice, however, it is very complex. The simulation involves generating a set of cash flows based on simulated future mortgage refinancing rates, which in turn imply simulated prepayment rates.

Valuation modeling for CMOs is similar to valuation modeling for passthroughs, although the difficulties are amplified because the issuer has sliced and diced both the prepayment risk and the interest rate risk into tranches. The sensitivity of the passthroughs comprising the collateral to these two risks is not transmitted equally to every tranche. Some of the tranches wind up more sensitive to prepayment risk and interest rate risk than the collateral, while some of them are much less sensitive.

The objective is to figure out how the value of the collateral gets transmitted to the CMO tranches. More specifically, the objective is to find out where the value goes and where the risk goes so that one can identify the tranches with low risk and high value: the ones we want to buy. The good news is that this combination usually exists in every deal. The bad news is that in every deal there are usually tranches with low value and high risk.

Using Simulation to Generate
Interest Rate Paths and Cash Flows

The typical model that Wall Street firms and commercial vendors use to generate these random interest rate paths takes as input today's term structure of interest rates and a volatility assumption. The term structure of interest rates is the theoretical spot rate (or zero coupon) curve implied by today's Treasury securities. The volatility assumption determines the dispersion of future interest rates in the simulation. The simulations should be normalized so that the average simulated price of a zero-coupon Treasury bond equals today's actual price.

Each model has its own model of the evolution of future interest rates and its own volatility assumptions. Typically, there are no significant differences in the interest rate models of dealer firms and vendors, although their volatility assumptions can be significantly different.

The random paths of interest rates should be generated from an arbitrage-free model of the future term structure of interest rates. By arbitrage-free it is meant that the model replicates today's term structure of interest rates, an input of the model, and that for all future dates there is no possible arbitrage within the model. We will explain how this is done later.

Exhibit 1: Simulated Paths of 1-Month Future Interest Rates

Month	Interest Rate Path Number						
	1	2	3	...	n	...	N
1	$f_1(1)$	$f_1(2)$	$f_1(3)$	...	$f_1(n)$	...	$f_1(N)$
2	$f_2(1)$	$f_2(2)$	$f_2(3)$	...	$f_2(n)$	...	$f_2(N)$
3	$f_3(1)$	$f_3(2)$	$f_3(3)$	...	$f_3(n)$	...	$f_3(N)$
...	...	...	...	...	...	...	...
t	$f_t(1)$	$f_t(2)$	$f_t(3)$	...	$f_t(n)$	...	$f_t(N)$
...	...	...	...	...	...	...	...
358	$f_{358}(1)$	$f_{358}(2)$	$f_{358}(3)$	...	$f_{358}(n)$	...	$f_{358}(N)$
359	$f_{359}(1)$	$f_{359}(2)$	$f_{359}(3)$	...	$f_{359}(n)$	...	$f_{359}(N)$
360	$f_{360}(1)$	$f_{360}(2)$	$f_{360}(3)$	...	$f_{360}(n)$	...	$f_{360}(N)$

Notation:
$f_t(n)$ = 1-month future interest rate for month t on path n
N = total number of interest rate paths

The simulation works by generating many scenarios of future interest rate paths. In each month of the scenario, a monthly interest rate and a mortgage refinancing rate are generated. The monthly interest rates are used to discount the projected cash flows in the scenario. The mortgage refinancing rate is needed to determine the cash flows because it represents the opportunity cost the mortgagor is facing at that time.

If the refinancing rates are high relative to the mortgagor's original coupon rate (i.e., the rate on the mortgagor's loan), the mortgagor will have less incentive to refinance, or even a positive disincentive (i.e., the homeowner will avoid moving in order to avoid refinancing). If the refinancing rate is low relative to the mortgagor's original coupon rate, the mortgagor has an incentive to refinance.

Prepayments are projected by feeding the refinancing rate and loan characteristics, such as age, into a prepayment model. (A discussion of prepayment modeling is beyond the scope of this book.) Given the projected prepayments, the cash flows along an interest rate path can be determined.

To make this more concrete, consider a newly issued mortgage passthrough security with a maturity of 360 months. Exhibit 1 shows N simulated interest rate path scenarios. Each scenario consists of a path of 360 simulated 1-month future interest rates. Just how many paths should be generated is explained later. Exhibit 2 shows the paths of simulated mortgage refinancing rates corresponding to the scenarios shown in Exhibit 1. Assuming these mortgage refinancing rates, the cash flows for each scenario path are shown in Exhibit 3.

Calculating the Present Value for a Scenario Interest Rate Path

Given the cash flows on an interest rate path, the path's present value can be calculated. The discount rate for determining the present value is the simulated spot rate for each month on the interest rate path plus an appropriate spread. The spot rate on a path can be determined from the simulated future monthly rates. The relationship that holds between the simulated spot rate for month T on path n and the simulated future 1-month rates is:

$$z_T(n) = \{[1 + f_1(n)][1 + f_2(n)]...[1 + f_T(n)]\}^{1/T} - 1$$

where

$z_T(n)$ = simulated spot rate for month T on path n

$f_j(n)$ = simulated future 1-month rate for month j on path n

Exhibit 2: Simulated Paths of Mortgage Refinancing Rates

Month	Interest Rate Path Number						
	1	2	3	...	n	...	N
1	$r_1(1)$	$r_1(2)$	$r_1(3)$	...	$r_1(n)$	...	$r_1(N)$
2	$r_2(1)$	$r_2(2)$	$r_2(3)$	...	$r_2(n)$	...	$r_2(N)$
3	$r_3(1)$	$r_3(2)$	$r_3(3)$	...	$r_3(n)$	...	$r_3(N)$
...	...	...	...	...	...	...	...
t	$r_t(1)$	$r_t(2)$	$r_t(3)$	...	$r_t(n)$	...	$r_t(N)$
...	...	...	...	...	...	...	...
358	$r_{358}(1)$	$r_{358}(2)$	$r_{358}(3)$	...	$r_{358}(n)$	...	$r_{358}(N)$
359	$r_{359}(1)$	$r_{359}(2)$	$r_{359}(3)$	...	$r_{359}(n)$	...	$r_{359}(N)$
360	$r_{360}(1)$	$r_{360}(2)$	$r_{360}(3)$	...	$r_{360}(n)$	...	$r_{360}(N)$

Notation:

$r_t(n)$ = mortgage refinancing rate for month t on path n

N = total number of interest rate paths

Exhibit 3: Simulated Cash Flows on Each of the Interest Rate Paths

Month	Interest Rate Path Number						
	1	2	3	...	n	...	N
1	$C_1(1)$	$C_1(2)$	$C_1(3)$	...	$C_1(n)$	...	$C_1(N)$
2	$C_2(1)$	$C_2(2)$	$C_2(3)$	...	$C_2(n)$	...	$C_2(N)$
3	$C_3(1)$	$C_3(2)$	$C_3(3)$	...	$C_3(n)$	...	$C_3(N)$
...	...	...	...	...	...	...	...
t	$C_t(1)$	$C_t(2)$	$C_t(3)$	...	$C_t(n)$	...	$C_t(N)$
...	...	...	...	...	...	...	...
358	$C_{358}(1)$	$C_{358}(2)$	$C_{358}(3)$	...	$C_{358}(n)$	...	$C_{358}(N)$
359	$C_{359}(1)$	$C_{359}(2)$	$C_{359}(3)$	...	$C_{359}(n)$	...	$C_{359}(N)$
360	$C_{360}(1)$	$C_{360}(2)$	$C_{360}(3)$	...	$C_{360}(n)$	...	$C_{360}(N)$

Notation:

$C_t(n)$ = cash flow for month t on path n

N = total number of interest rate paths

Exhibit 4: Simulated Paths of Monthly Spot Rates

Month	Interest Rate Path Number						
	1	2	3	...	n	...	N
1	$z_1(1)$	$z_1(2)$	$z_1(3)$	...	$z_1(n)$	...	$z_1(N)$
2	$z_2(1)$	$z_2(2)$	$z_2(3)$	...	$z_2(n)$	...	$z_2(N)$
3	$z_3(1)$	$z_3(2)$	$z_3(3)$	...	$z_3(n)$	...	$z_3(N)$
...	...	...	...	...	...	...	...
t	$z_t(1)$	$z_t(2)$	$z_t(3)$	...	$z_t(n)$	...	$z_t(N)$
...	...	...	...	...	...	...	...
358	$z_{358}(1)$	$z_{358}(2)$	$z_{358}(3)$	...	$z_{358}(n)$	...	$z_{358}(N)$
359	$z_{359}(1)$	$z_{359}(2)$	$z_{359}(3)$	...	$z_{359}(n)$	...	$z_{359}(N)$
360	$z_{360}(1)$	$z_{360}(2)$	$z_{360}(3)$	...	$z_{360}(n)$	...	$z_{360}(N)$

Notation:
$z_t(n)$ = spot rate for month t on path n
N = total number of interest rate paths

Consequently, the interest rate path for the simulated future 1-month rates can be converted to the interest rate path for the simulated monthly spot rates as shown in Exhibit 4.

Therefore, the present value of the cash flows for month T on interest rate path n discounted at the simulated spot rate for month T plus some spread is:

$$PV[C_T(n)] = \frac{C_T(n)}{[1 + z_T(n) + K]^T}$$

where

$PV[C_T(n)]$ = present value of cash flows for month T on path n
$C_T(n)$ = cash flow for month T on path n
$z_T(n)$ = spot rate for month T on path n
K = spread

The present value for path n is the sum of the present value of the cash flow for each month on path n. That is,

$$PV[\text{Path}(n)] = PV[C_1(n)] + PV[C_2(n)] + ... + PV[C_{360}(n)]$$

where $PV[\text{Path}(n)]$ is the present value of interest rate path n.

Determining the Theoretical Value

The present value of a given interest rate path can be thought of as the theoretical value of a passthrough if that path was actually realized. The theoretical value of the passthrough can be determined by calculating the average of the theoretical values of all the interest rate paths. That is, the theoretical value is equal to

$$\text{Theoretical value} = \frac{PV[\text{Path}(1)] + PV[\text{Path}(2)] + \dots + PV[\text{Path}(N)]}{N}$$

where N is the number of interest rate paths.

This procedure for valuing a passthrough is also followed for a CMO tranche. The cash flow for each month on each interest rate path is found according to the principal repayment and interest distribution rules of the deal. In order to do this, a CMO structuring model is needed.

Distribution of Path Present Values

The Monte Carlo model is a commonly used management science tool in business. It is employed when the outcome of a business decision depends on the outcome of several random variables. The product of the simulation is the average value and the probability distribution of the possible outcomes.

Unfortunately, the use of Monte Carlo simulation to value fixed income securities has been limited to just the reporting of the average value, which is referred to as the theoretical value of the security. This means that all of the information about the distribution of the path present values is ignored. Yet, this information is quite valuable.

For example, consider a well protected PAC bond. The distribution of the present value for the paths should be concentrated around the theoretical value. That is, the standard deviation should be small. In contrast, for a support tranche, the distribution of the present value for the paths could be wide, or equivalently, the standard deviation could be large.

Therefore, before using the theoretical value for a mortgage-backed security generated from the Monte Carlo model, information about the distribution of the path present values should be obtained.

Option-Adjusted Spread

As explained in previous chapters, the option-adjusted spread is a measure of the yield spread that can be used to convert dollar differences between value and price. In the Monte Carlo model, the OAS is the spread K that when added to all the spot rates on all interest rate paths will make the average present value of the paths equal to the observed market price (plus accrued interest).

Mathematically, OAS is the spread that will satisfy the following condition:

$$\text{Market price} = \frac{PV[\text{Path}(1)] + PV[\text{Path}(2)] + \dots + PV[\text{Path}(N)]}{N}$$

where N is the number of interest rate paths.

Effective Duration and Convexity

In Chapter 4 we explained how to determine the effective duration and effective convexity for any security. These measures can be calculated using the Monte Carlo model as follows. First the bond's OAS is found using the current term structure of interest rates. Next, the initial short-term rate used to generate the interest rate paths in Exhibit 1 is increased by a small number of basis points and new paths of interest rates are generated. Given the new paths, the security is revalued holding the OAS constant. Similarly, the initial short-term rate used to generate the interest rate paths in Exhibit 1 is decreased by a small number of basis points and the security is then revalued holding the OAS constant. The two calculated values are then used in the formula for effective duration and convexity.

Simulated Average Life

The average life of a mortgage-backed security is the weighted average time to receipt of principal payments (scheduled payments and projected prepayments). The formula for the average life is:

$$\frac{1(\text{Principal at time } 1) + 2(\text{Principal at time } 2) + \ldots + T(\text{Principal at time } T)}{12(\text{Total principal received})}$$

where T is the number of months.

The average life reported in a Monte Carlo model is the average of the average lives along the interest rate paths. That is, for each interest rate path, there is an average life. The average of these average lives is the average life reported by the model.

Additional information is conveyed by the distribution of the average life. The greater the range and standard deviation of the average life, the more uncertainty there is about the tranche's average life.

Some Technical Issues

In the binomial model for valuing bonds, the interest rate tree is constructed so that it is arbitrage free. That is, if any on-the-run issue is valued, the value produced by the model is equal to the market price. This means that the tree is calibrated to the market. In contrast, in our discussion of the Monte Carlo model, there is no mechanism that we have described above that will assure the valuation model will produce a value for an on-the-run Treasury security (the benchmark in the case of agency mortgage-backed securities) equal to the market price. In practice, this is accomplished by adding a *drift term* to the short-term rates (Exhibit 1) so that the value produced by the Monte Carlo model for all on-the-run Treasury securities is their market price.[3] A technical explanation of this process is beyond the scope of this chapter.[4]

There is another adjustment made to the interest rate paths. Restrictions on interest rate movements must be built into the model to prevent interest rates from reaching levels that are believed to be unreasonable (e.g., an interest rate of zero or an interest rate of 30%). This is done by incorporating *mean reversion* into

---

[3] This is equivalent to saying that the OAS produced by the model is zero.

[4] For an explanation of how this is done, see Lakhbir S. Hayre and Kenneth Lauterbach, "Stochastic Valuation of Debt Securities," in Frank J. Fabozzi (ed.), *Managing Institutional Assets* (New York: Harper & Row, 1990), pp. 321-364.

the model. By this it is meant that at some point, the interest rate is forced toward some estimated average (mean) value.[5]

Finally, the specification of the relationship between short-term rates and refinancing rates is necessary. Empirical evidence on the relationship is necessary. More specifically, the correlation between the short-term and refinancing rates must be estimated.

Selecting the Number of Interest Rate Paths

Let's now address the question of the number of scenario paths or repetitions, N, needed to value a CMO tranche. A typical analysis might be for 256 to 1,024 interest rate paths. The scenarios generated using the Monte Carlo model look very realistic, and furthermore reproduce today's Treasury curve. By employing this technique, one is effectively saying that Treasuries are fairly priced today and that the objective is to determine whether a specific tranche is rich or cheap relative to Treasuries.

The number of interest rate paths determines how "good" the estimate is, not relative to the truth but relative to the model used. The more paths, the more average spread tends to settle down. It is a statistical sampling problem.

Most models employ some form of *variance reduction* to cut down on the number of sample paths necessary to get a good statistical sample. Variance reduction techniques allows one to obtain price estimates within a tick. By this we mean that if the model is used to generate more scenarios, price estimates from the model will not change by more than a tick. So, for example, if 1,024 paths are used to obtain the estimated price for a tranche, there is little additional information to be had from the model by generating more than that number of paths. (For some very sensitive CMO tranches, more paths may be needed to estimate prices within one tick.)

Several vendor firms have attempted to develop computational procedures that reduce the number of paths required but still provide the accuracy of a full Monte Carlo analysis. The procedure is to use statistical techniques to reduce the number of interest rate paths to similar sets of paths. These paths are called *representative paths*. For example, suppose that 2,000 sample paths are generated. Using a statistical technique known as principal component analysis, these 2,000 sample paths can be collapsed to, say, 16 representative paths. The security is then valued on each of these 16 representative paths. The theoretical value of the security is then the weighted average of the 16 representative paths. The weight for a path is the percentage of that representative path relative to the total sample paths.

Mathematically this is expressed as follows. Let

N	=	number of sample interest rate paths
J	=	number of representative paths
W_j	=	number of sample interest rate paths represented by representative path j divided by the total number of sample interest rate paths
$RPath(j)$	=	representative path j

---

[5] See the appendix to Chapter 3.

Exhibit 5: Diagram of Principal Allocation Structure for FNMA 89-97

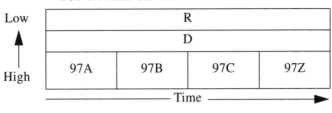

Then the theoretical value is:

Theoretical value
$$= W_1\, PV[RPath(1)] + W_2\, PV[RPath(2)] + ... + W_J\, PV[RPath(J)]$$

ILLUSTRATIONS

In this section we use two deals to show how CMOs can be analyzed using the Monte Carlo model: a plain vanilla structure and a PAC/support structure.

Plain Vanilla Structure

The plain vanilla sequential-pay CMO bond structure in our illustration is FNMA 89-97. A diagram of the principal allocation structure is given in Exhibit 5. The structure includes five tranches, A, B, C, D, and Z, and a residual class. Tranche Z is an accrual bond, and tranche D is an IOette. The focus of our analysis is on tranches A, B, C, and Z.

The top panel of Exhibit 6 shows the OAS and the option cost for the collateral and the five tranches in the CMO structure. The OAS for the collateral is 70 basis points. Since the option cost is 45 basis points, the zero-volatility spread is 115 basis points (70 basis points plus 45 basis points).[6] The weighted-average OAS of all the tranches (including the residual) is equal to the OAS of the collateral.

At the time this analysis was performed, April 27, 1990, the Treasury yield curve was not steep. As we noted in Chapter 2, in such a yield curve environment the zero-volatility spread will not differ significantly from the nominal spread. Thus, for the four tranches shown in Exhibit 6, the zero-volatility spread is 52 for A, 87 for B, 95 for C, and 124 for Z.

Notice that the tranches did not share the OAS equally. The same is true for the option cost. The value tended to go toward the longer bonds, something that occurs in the typical deal. Both the zero-volatility spread and the option cost increase as the maturity increases. The only tranches where there appears to be a

---

[6] Recall from Chapter 5 that the option cost is the difference between the zero-volatility spread and the OAS.

bit of a bargain are B and C. A money manager contemplating the purchase of one of these middle tranches can see that C offers a higher OAS than B and appears to bear less of the risk, as measured by the option cost. The problem a money manager may encounter is that he might not be permitted to extend out as long as the C tranche because of duration, maturity, or average life constraints.

Now let's look at modeling risk. Examination of the sensitivity of the tranches to changes in prepayments and interest rate volatility will help us to understand the interaction of the tranches in the structure and who is bearing the risk.

We begin with prepayments. Specifically, we keep the same interest rate paths as those used to get the OAS in the base case (the top panel of Exhibit 6), but reduce the prepayment rate on each interest rate path to 80% of the projected rate.

As can be seen in the second panel of Exhibit 6, slowing down prepayments does not change the OAS for the collateral and its price at all. This is because the collateral is trading close to par. Tranches created by this collateral do not behave the same way, however. The exhibit reports two results of the sensitivity analysis. First, it indicates the change in the OAS. Second, it indicates the change in the price, holding the OAS constant at the base case.

Exhibit 6: OAS Analysis of FNMA 89-97
Tranches A, B, C, and Z (As of 4/27/90)

Base Case (assumes 12% interest rate volatility)				
		OAS (in basis points)	Option Cost (in basis points)	
Collateral		70	45	
Tranche	A	23	29	
	B	46	41	
	C	59	36	
	Z	74	50	

Prepayments at 80% and 120% of Prepayment Model (assumes 12% interest rate volatility)				
		New OAS (in basis points)		Change in Price per $100 par (holding OAS constant)	
		80%	120%	80%	120%
Collateral		70	71	$0.00	$0.04
Tranche	A	8	40	−0.43	0.48
	B	31	65	−0.86	1.10
	C	53	73	−0.41	0.95
	Z	72	93	−0.28	2.70

Interest Rate Volatility of 8% and 16%				
		New OAS (in basis points)		Change in Price per $100 par (holding OAS constant)	
		8%	16%	8%	16%
Collateral		92	46	$1.03	−$1.01
Tranche	A	38	5	0.42	−0.51
	B	67	21	1.22	−1.45
	C	77	39	1.22	−1.36
	Z	99	50	3.55	−3.41

Source: Goldman, Sachs, & Co.

To see how a money manager can use the information in the second panel, consider tranche A. At 80% of the prepayment speed, the OAS for this tranche declines from 23 basis points to 8 basis points. If the OAS is held constant, the panel indicates that the buyer of tranche A would lose $0.43 per $100 par value.

Notice that for all the tranches reported in Exhibit 6 there is a loss. How could all four tranches lose if prepayments are slowed down and the collateral does not lose value? This is because tranche D and the residual (R), which are not reported in the exhibit, got all the benefit of that slowdown. Notice that tranche Z is actually fairly well protected, so it does not lose much value as a result of the slowdown of prepayments. Tranche A by contrast is severely affected.

Also shown in the second panel of the exhibit is the second part of our experiment that tests the sensitivity of prepayments: the prepayment rate is assumed to be 120% of the base case. Once again, as the collateral is trading at close to par, its price does not move very much, about four cents per $100 of par value. In fact, because the collateral is trading slightly below par, the speeding up of prepayments will make the collateral look better while the OAS increases by only 1 basis point.

Now look at the four tranches. They all benefitted. The results reported in the exhibit indicate that a money manager who is willing to go out to the long end of the curve, such as tranche Z, would realize most of the benefits of that speedup of prepayments. Since the four tranches benefitted and the benefit to the collateral was minor, that means tranche D, the IOette, and the residual were adversely affected. In general, IO types of tranches will be adversely affected by a speedup.

Now let's look at the sensitivity to the interest rate volatility assumption, 12% in the base case. Two experiments are performed: reducing the volatility assumption to 8% and increasing it to 16%. These results are reported in the third panel of Exhibit 6.

Reducing the volatility to 8% increases the dollar price of the collateral by $1 and increases the OAS from 70 in the base case to 92. This $1 increase in the price of the collateral is not equally distributed, however, among the four tranches. Most of the increase in value is realized by the longer tranches. The OAS gain for each of the tranches follows more or less the effective durations of those tranches. This makes sense, because the longer the duration, the greater the risk, and when volatility declines, the reward is greater for the accepted risk.

At the higher level of assumed interest rate volatility of 16%, the collateral is severely affected. The collateral's loss is distributed among the tranches in the expected manner: the longer the duration, the greater the loss. In this case tranche D and the residual are the least affected.

Using the Monte Carlo model, a fair conclusion can be made about this simple plain vanilla structure: what you see is what you get. The only surprise in this structure seems to be tranches B and C. In general, however, a money manager willing to extend duration gets paid for that risk.

PAC/Support Bond Structure

Now let's look at how to apply the methodology to a more complicated CMO structure, FHLMC Series 120. The collateral for this structure is Freddie Mac 9½s. A summary of the deal is provided in Exhibit 7. A diagram of the principal allocation is given in Exhibit 8.

While this deal is more complicated than the previous one, it is simple compared to the deals that have been issued. Nonetheless, it brings out all the key points about application of the Monte Carlo model, specifically, the fact that most deals include cheap bonds, expensive bonds, and fairly priced bonds. The model helps a money manager identify how a tranche should be classified.

There are 14 classes in this structure: nine PAC bonds (including two PAC PO bonds and a PAC IO bond), a TAC support bond, an accrual support bond, a coupon-paying support bond, and a residual bond. From Exhibit 7 it can be seen that tranches B and C are the POs because they have a coupon of 0%. From Exhibit 8 it can be seen that the underlying collateral's interest not allocated to these two PAC POs is allocated to tranche A, which is now a premium PAC with a 16% coupon. Unlike a typical mortgage-backed security backed by premium collateral, prepayments for tranche A will be slower because the underlying collateral is Freddie Mac 9½s, which was not premium collateral at the time the deal was printed. Thus, with PAC A the investor realizes a high coupon rate but a much lower prepayment rate than would be experienced by a high coupon mortgage bond.

Tranches C, D, E, F, G, and H are all longer PACs. Tranche I is a PAC IO.[7] The prepayment protection for the PAC bonds is provided by the support bonds. The three support bonds in this deal are tranches J, K, and Z. Tranche J is the shortest tranche (a TAC bond), and Z (an accrual bond) is the longest.

The top panel of Exhibit 9 shows the base case OAS and the option cost for the collateral and all but the residual and PAC IO classes. The collateral OAS is 72 basis points, and the option cost is 34 basis points. Thus the zero-volatility spread of the collateral to the Treasury spot rate curve is 106 basis points.

The 72 basis points of OAS did not get equally distributed among the tranches — as was the case with the plain vanilla structure. Tranche J, the support TAC, did not realize a good OAS allocation, only 17 basis points, and had an extremely high option cost. Given the prepayment uncertainty associated with this support bond, its OAS would be expected to be higher. The reason for the low OAS is that this tranche was priced at issuance so that its cash flow yield was high. Using the zero-volatility spread as a proxy for the spread over the Treasury yield curve, the 79-basis point spread for tranche J is high given that this appears to be a short-term tranche. Consequently, "yield buyers" probably bid aggressively for this tranche and thereby drove down its OAS, trading off "yield" for OAS. From a total return perspective, however, tranche J should have been avoided. It was an expensive bond. The two longer support bonds did not get treated as badly as tranche J: the OAS for tranches K and Z were 61 basis points and 78 basis points, respectively.

---

[7] Notice that for the PAC IO (the I bond) the coupon rate shown is 857%. Prior to 1992, all classes of a REMIC had to have some principal allocated. In this case, the original balance for the PAC IO class is $100,000.

Exhibit 7: Summary of FHLMC — Multiclass Mortgage Participation Certificates (Guaranteed), Series 120

Total Issue:	$300,000,000	Original Rating:	S&P NR, Moody's NR,
Issue Date:	12/8/89		Fitch NR, D&P NR
Structure Type:	REMIC CMO	Original Settlement Date:	1/30/90
Issuer Class:	Agency	Days Delay:	30
Dated Date:	1/15/90	Payment Frequency:	Monthly; 15th day of month

| | | | | Original Issue Pricing (180% PSA Assumed) | |
Tranche	Original Balance ($)	Coupon (%)	Stated Maturity	Average Life (yr.)	Expected Maturity
120-A(PAC Bond)	37,968,750	16.0	11/15/13	4.0	12/15/95
120-B(PAC Bond)	20,500,000	0.0	2/15/11	3.4	10/15/94
120-C(PAC Bond)	9,031,250	0.0	11/15/13	5.3	12/15/95
120-D(PAC Bond)	12,000,000	9.0	2/15/15	6.3	9/15/96
120-E(PAC Bond)	40,500,000	9.0	5/15/18	7.9	7/15/99
120-F(PAC Bond)	10,000,000	9.0	1/15/19	10.0	8/15/00
120-G(PAC Bond)	6,500,000	9.0	6/16/19	10.9	6/15/01
120-H(PAC Bond)	33,000,000	9.0	2/15/21	15.5	4/15/18
120-I(PAC Bond)	100,000	857.0	2/15/21	7.9	4/15/18
120-J(TAC Bond)	99,600,000	9.5	2/15/21	3.2	10/15/99
120-K	15,700,000	9.5	7/15/15	8.3	7/15/01
120-R	90,000	9.5	2/15/21	8.1	4/15/19
120-S	10,000	9.5	2/15/21	8.1	4/15/19
120-Z	15,000,000	9.5	2/15/21	18.8	4/15/19

Structural Features	
Prepayment Guarantee:	None
Assumed Reinvestment Rate:	0%
Cash Flow Allocation:	Excess cash flow is not anticipated; in the event that there are proceeds remaining after the payments of the bonds, however, the Class 120-R Bonds will receive them. Commencing on the first principal payment date of the Class 120-A Bonds, principal equal to an amount specified in the Prospectus will be applied to the Class 120-A, 120-B, 120-C, 120-D, 120-E, 120-F, 120-G, 120-H, 120-I, and 120-J Bonds. After all other Classes have been retired, any remaining principal will be used to retire the Class 120-J, 120-A, 120-B, 120-C, 120-D, 120-E, 120-F, 120-G, 120-H, and 120-I Bonds.
Redemption Provisions:	Nuisance provision for all Classes: Issuer may redeem the Bonds, in whole but not in part, on any Payment Date when the outstanding principal balance declines to less then 1% of the original amount.
Other:	The PAC range is 90% to 300% PSA for the A-l bonds, and 200% PSA for the Class J Bonds.

Exhibit 8: Principal Allocation Diagram of FHLMC Series 120

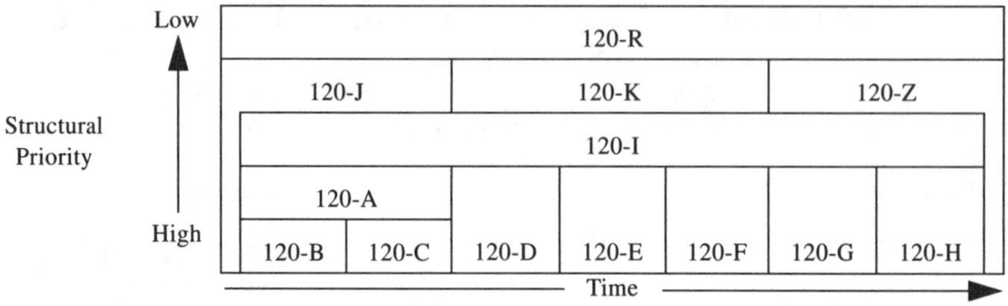

It should be apparent from the results of the base case OAS analysis reported in the top panel of Exhibit 9 where the cheap bonds were in the deal. They were the long PACs, which had a high OAS, a low option cost, and were positively convex. These were well-protected.

Notice that the option costs were negative for tranches B and C, the two PAC POs. The reason is that a PO is itself an option. That is, an investor in a PO is effectively buying an option, and this explains the negative option cost.[8] On a nonPAC PO, such as a super PO, the option cost was even more negative than it was for a PAC PO.

The next two panels in Exhibit 9 show the sensitivity of the OAS and the price (holding OAS constant at the base case) to changes in the prepayment speed (80% and 120% of the base case) and to changes in volatility (8% and 16%). This analysis shows that the change in the prepayment speed did not affect the collateral significantly, while the change in the OAS (holding price constant) and price (holding OAS constant) for each tranche were significant. For example, a slower prepayment speed, which increases the time period over which a PAC PO bondholder can recover the principal, significantly reduced the OAS and price. The opposite effect results if prepayments are faster than the base case.

Tranche A, a high-coupon short PAC bond, benefited from a slowing of prepayments, as the bondholder would receive the higher coupon for a longer time. Faster prepayments represented an adverse scenario. The PAC bonds were quite well-protected. The long PACs actually benefited from a reduced prepayment rate because they would be earning the higher coupon interest longer. So, on an OAS basis, our earlier conclusion that the long PACs were allocated a good part of this deal's value holds up under our first stress test.

A slowdown in prepayments hurt the support tranche J and a speedup benefited this tranche. A somewhat surprising result involves the effect that the change in prepayments had on the accrual bond (the Z-bond). Notice that whether prepayment speeds are slower or faster, the OAS and the price increased. Without the use of a Monte Carlo model, this would not intuitively be obvious.[9]

---

[8] See Chapter 5.

[9] The reason for this is that at the time of this analysis there was a hump in the Treasury spot rate curve.

Exhibit 9: OAS Analysis of FHLMC 120

	Base Case (assumes 12% interest rate volatility)	
	OAS (in basis points)	Option Cost (in basis points)
Collateral	72	34
A (PAC)	52	4
B (PAC PO)	48	−1
C (PAC PO)	64	−7
D (PAC)	67	5
E (PAC)	68	8
F (PAC)	73	9
G (PAC)	75	9
H (PAC)	85	9
J (Support TAC)	17	62
K (Support)	61	58
Z (Support Z)	78	83

	Prepayments at 80% and 120% of Prepayment Model (assumes 12% interest rate volatility)				
	Base Case OAS	New OAS (in basis points)		Change in Price per $100 par (holding OAS constant)	
		80%	120%	80%	120%
Collateral	72	69	77	$0.15	$0.22
A (PAC)	52	65	42	0.43	−0.35
B (PAC PO)	48	17	54	−0.71	0.12
C (PAC PO)	64	14	86	−1.52	0.67
D (PAC)	67	61	62	−0.24	−0.20
E (PAC)	68	65	61	−0.13	−0.37
F (PAC)	73	76	63	0.16	−0.59
G (PAC)	75	80	64	0.33	−0.68
H (PAC)	85	93	75	0.56	−0.69
J (Support TAC)	17	4	56	−0.43	1.34
K (Support)	61	64	75	0.17	0.82
Z (Support Z)	78	85	114	0.75	3.77

	Interest Rate Volatility of 8% and 16%				
	Base Case OAS	New OAS (in basis points)		Change in Price per $100 par (holding OAS constant)	
		8%	16%	8%	16%
Collateral	72	91	51	$0.88	−$0.91
A (PAC)	52	57	43	0.14	−0.31
B (PAC PO)	48	47	51	−0.02	0.07
C (PAC PO)	64	57	75	−0.15	0.35
D (PAC)	67	72	59	0.13	−0.34
E (PAC)	68	74	56	0.21	−0.59
F (PAC)	73	80	60	0.26	−0.80
G (PAC)	75	82	60	0.26	−0.88
H (PAC)	85	92	75	0.27	−0.69
J (Support TAC)	17	47	−17	0.54	−0.31
K (Support)	61	94	26	0.95	−1.98
Z (Support Z)	78	126	28	2.58	−5.30

Source: Goldman, Sachs & Co.

The sensitivity of the collateral and the tranches to changes in volatility are shown in the third panel of Exhibit 9. A lower volatility increased the value of the collateral, while a higher volatility reduced its value. Conversely, lower volatility reduced the value of PO instruments, and higher volatility increased the value. This can be seen for the two PAC IOs, tranches B and C, in Exhibit 9.

The long PACs continued to be fairly well-protected, whether volatility was lower or higher. In the two volatility scenarios they continued to get a good OAS, although not as much as in the base case if volatility was higher (but the OAS still looked like a reasonable value in this scenario). This reinforces our earlier conclusion concerning the investment merit of the long PACs in this deal.

KEY POINTS

1. *The cash flow of a mortgage-backed security consists of net interest (interest after servicing and guarantor fees), regularly scheduled principal payments, and prepayments.*

2. *The convention to generate cash flows is the PSA prepayment benchmark.*

3. *The factors that affect prepayments are (1) the prevailing mortgage rate, (2) characteristics of the underlying mortgage, (3) seasonal factors, and (4) general economic activity.*

4. *It is not only the level of interest rates relative to the contract rates on the underlying mortgage pool that affects prepayments due to refinancing but also the path that interest rates take to get to the current level.*

5. *A path-dependent cash flow is one in which the cash flow received in one period is determined not only by the current interest rate level, but also by the path that interest rates took to get to the current level.*

6. *Because of refinancing burnout, the cash flows for a mortgage-backed security are interest rate path-dependent.*

7. *Payment rules for collateralized mortgage obligations also cause the cash flows for these securities to be interest rate path-dependent.*

8. *The Monte Carlo model is the most flexible of the two valuation models for valuing fixed income securities whose periodic cash flows are interest rate path-dependent.*

9. *The Monte Carlo model involves randomly generating many scenarios of future interest rate paths.*

10. *The interest rate paths are generated based on some volatility assumption for interest rates.*

11. *The random paths of interest rates should be generated from an arbitrage-free model of the future term structure of interest rates.*

12. *The Monte Carlo model applied to mortgage-backed securities involves randomly generating a set of cash flows based on simulated future mortgage refinancing rates.*

13. *The theoretical value of a security on any interest rate path is the present value of the cash flows on that path where the spot rates are those on the corresponding interest rate path.*

14. *The theoretical value of a security is the average of the present values over all the interest rate paths.*

15. *Information about the distribution of the present value for the interest rate paths provides guidance as to the degree of uncertainty associated with the theoretical value.*

16. *In the Monte Carlo model, the option-adjusted spread is the spread that when added to all the spot rates on all interest rate paths will make the average present value of the paths equal to the observed market price (plus accrued interest).*

17. *The Monte Carlo model is calibrated to the market by adding a drift term.*

18. *Mean reversion is included in the model to prevent interest rates from reaching unrealistic rates.*

19. *The effective duration and effective convexity are calculated using the Monte Carlo model by holding the OAS constant and shifting the term structure up and down.*

20. *The average life reported in the Monte Carlo model is the average of the average lives from all the interest rate paths and information about the distribution of the average life is useful.*

21. *The number of interest paths analyzed is determined by a variance reduction rule.*

22. *Vendors have developed procedures to reduce the number of paths needed to value a security.*

23. *When the Monte Carlo method is used to value a mortgage-backed security, a prepayment model is needed to obtain the cash flows on each interest rate path.*

Chapter 9

Valuation of
Asset-Backed Securities

The objectives of this chapter are to:

1. explain the cash flow characteristics of asset-backed securities;

2. explain the difference between an amortizing and nonamortizing asset-backed security;

3. discuss the approaches to valuation that can be used to value asset-backed securities;

4. explain how the valuation approach employed depends on the characteristics of the underlying loans; and,

5. explain the cash flows of the four major types of asset-backed securities: auto-loan backed securities, credit card receivable-backed securities, home-equity loan securities, and manufactured housing-backed securities.

While residential mortgage loans are the largest type of asset that has been securitized, securities backed by other assets (consumer and business loans and receivables) have been securitized. The four largest sectors of the asset-backed securities market in the United States are securities backed by credit card receivables, auto loans, home equity loans, and manufactured housing loans. In this chapter, we look at how to value asset-backed securities.

CASH FLOWS OF ASSET-BACKED SECURITIES

The collateral for an asset-backed security (ABS) can be classified as either amortizing or non-amortizing assets. *Amortizing assets* are loans in which the borrower's periodic payment consists of scheduled principal and interest payments over the life of the loan. The schedule for the repayment of the principal is called the *amortization schedule*. The standard residential mortgage loan falls into this category. Auto loans and certain types of home equity loans (specifically, closed-end home equity loans discussed later in this chapter) are amortizing assets. Any excess payment over the scheduled principal payment is called a *prepayment*. Prepayments can be made to pay off the entire balance or a partial prepayment, called a *curtailment*.

In contrast to amortizing assets, *non-amortizing assets* do not have a schedule for the periodic payments that the borrower must make. Instead, a non-amortizing asset is one in which the borrower must make a minimum periodic payment. If that payment is less than the interest on the outstanding loan balance, the shortfall is added to the outstanding loan balance. If the periodic payment is greater than the interest on the outstanding loan balance, then the difference is applied to the reduction of the outstanding loan balance. There is no schedule of principal payments (i.e., no amortization schedule) for a non-amortizing asset. Consequently, the concept of a prepayment does not apply. Credit card receivables are examples of non-amortizing assets.

For an amortizing asset, projection of the cash flows requires projecting prepayments. One factor that *may* affect prepayments is the prevailing level of interest rates relative to the interest rate on the loan. In projecting prepayments it is critical to determine the extent to which borrowers take advantage of a decline in interest rates below the loan rate in order to refinance the loan.

Modeling defaults for the collateral is critical in estimating the cash flows of an asset-backed security. Proceeds that are recovered in the event of a default of a loan prior to the scheduled principal repayment date of an amortizing asset represents a prepayment. Projecting prepayments for amortizing assets requires an assumption of the default rate and the recovery rate. For a non-amortizing asset, while the concept of a prepayment does not exist, a projection of defaults is still necessary to project how much will be recovered and when.

The analysis of prepayments can be performed on a pool level or a loan level. In *pool-level analysis* it is assumed that all loans comprising the collateral are identical. For an amortizing asset, the amortization schedule is based on the gross weighted average coupon (GWAC) and weighted average maturity (WAC) for that single loan. Pool-level analysis is appropriate where the underlying loans are homogeneous. *Loan-level analysis* involves amortizing each loan (or group of homogeneous loans).

APPROACHES TO ABS VALUATION

In the preceding chapters, we discussed three valuation approaches. The first approach is to value a security by discounting the expected cash flows by the issuer's on-the-run spot rates. If some type of spread measure is sought, the zero-volatility spread is calculated. This is the spread that must be added to either the on-the-run Treasury spot rates or the on-the-run spot rate for the issuer to obtain the market price (plus accrued interest). As demonstrated in Chapter 5, the zero-volatility spread differs from the nominal spread if (1) the yield curve is steep and/or (2) the security is an amortizing asset (i.e., principal is repaid periodically). Because most ABS are amortizing assets, the zero-volatility approach is superior to the nominal spread.

When there is an embedded option in a security, then either the binomial model or Monte Carlo simulation model can be used. When an ABS has an embedded option it is in the form of a call or prepayment option. Whether the binomial or Monte Carlo model should be used depends on whether or not the cash flows are interest rate path-independent or interest rate path-dependent. In the former case, at any point on an interest rate path or node of an interest rate tree, how the interest rate evolved to get to that point is unimportant and will not affect the cash flow at that point. In such cases, the binomial model is employed. This is why the binomial model is used to value agency, corporate, and municipal bonds. In contrast, because of prepayment burnout, the prepayments at a given point on an interest rate path will depend on how the interest rate evolved to get to that point. For interest rate path-dependent securities, the Monte Carlo model is employed. This is why this model is used to value mortgage-backed securities. With either model, an option-adjusted spread (OAS) can be calculated.

The decision of which valuation model to employ is diagramed in Exhibit 1. Which model should be used for ABS? The answer depends on the particular type of ABS. Specifically, while an ABS that has a prepayment or call option whose exercise will depend on the prevailing level of interest rates versus the loan rate paid by the borrower, whether or not in practice that option will be exercised must be assessed empirically. We will give examples below of ABS that have a prepayment option but borrowers have not demonstrated that they take advantage of refinancing when market rates decline below the rate on their loan. Thus, the approach of discounting at the spot rate for the on-the-run issuer or Treasury is employed to obtain the value of the ABS and the zero-volatility spread is used as the spread measure. When there is a prepayment option that borrowers appear to exercise when the prevailing borrowing rate declines below the loan rate, typically the cash flows are interest rate path-dependent. Thus, the Monte Carlo model is used and OAS is used as a spread measure.

Exhibit 1: Selecting a Model for the Valuation of Asset-Backed Securities

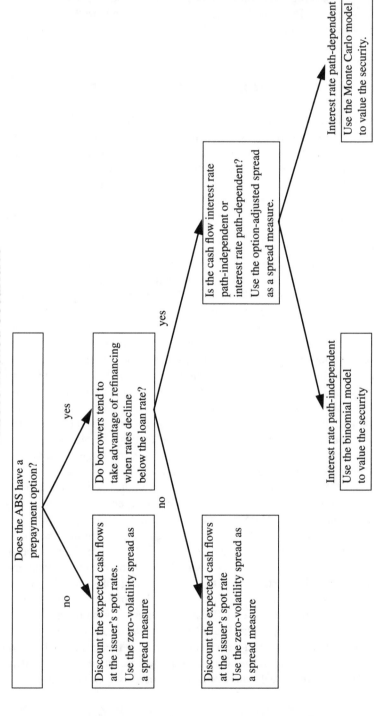

Below we will take a look at the four most popular types of ABS. While there are many more types of ABS, the general principle is the same.

AUTO LOAN-BACKED SECURITIES

The cash flow for auto loan-backed securities consists of regularly scheduled monthly loan payments (interest and scheduled principal repayments) and any prepayments. The monthly interest rate may be fixed or floating. Prepayments for auto loan-backed securities are measured in terms of the *absolute prepayment rate*, denoted *not* by APR but by *ABS* (probably because it was the first prepayment measure used for asset-backed securities). The ABS is the monthly prepayment expressed as a percentage of the original collateral amount. Recall from Chapter 8 that the SMM (monthly CPR) expresses prepayments based on the prior month's balance.

Prepayments result from (1) sales and tradeins requiring full payoff of the loan, (2) repossession and subsequent resale of the automobile, (3) loss or destruction of the vehicle, (4) payoff of the loan with cash to save on the interest cost, and (5) refinancing of the loan at a lower interest cost.

Prepayments due to repossessions and subsequent resale are sensitive to the economic cycle. In recessionary economic periods, prepayments due to this factor increase. While refinancings may be a major reason for prepayments of mortgage loans, they are of minor importance for automobile loans. Moreover, the interest rates for the automobile loans underlying several issues are substantially below market rates if they are offered by manufacturers as part of a sales promotion. Consequently, the appropriate valuation approach is to discount using spot rates. The more complex modeling to recognize the embedded options is not necessary.

CREDIT CARD RECEIVABLE-BACKED SECURITIES

Credit card receivable-backed securities are backed by credit card receivables. Credit cards are originated by banks (e.g., Visa and MasterCard), retailers (e.g., JC Penney and Sears), and travel and entertainment companies (e.g., American Express). The cash flows consist of net interest, principal, and finance charges collected. Interest to security holders is paid periodically (e.g, monthly, quarterly, or semiannually). The interest may be fixed or floating.

In contrast to an auto loan-backed security, the principal repayment of a credit card receivable-backed security is not amortized. Instead, for a specified period of time, referred to as the *lockout period* or *revolving period*, the principal payments made by credit card borrowers comprising the pool are retained by the trustee and reinvested in additional receivables. The lockout period can vary from 18 months to 10 years.

After the lockout period, the principal is no longer reinvested but paid to investors. This period is referred to as the *principal-amortization period*. There are three different amortization structures that have been used in credit card receivable-backed security structures: (1) passthrough structure, (2) controlled-amortization structure, and (3) bullet-payment structure. In a *passthrough structure*, the principal cash flows from the credit card accounts are paid to the security holders on a pro rata basis.[1] In a *controlled-amortization structure*, a scheduled principal amount is established. The scheduled principal amount is sufficiently low so that the obligation can be satisfied even under certain stress scenarios. The investor is paid the lesser of the scheduled principal amount and the pro rata amount. In a *bullet-payment structure*, the investor receives the entire amount in one distribution. Since there is no assurance that the entire amount can be paid in one lump sum, the procedure is for the trustee to place principal monthly into an account that generates sufficient interest to make periodic interest payments and accumulate the principal to be repaid. The time period over which the principal is accumulated is called the *accumulation period*.

There are provisions in credit card receivable-backed securities that requires earlier amortization of the principal if certain events occur. Such provisions, which are referred to as either *early amortization* or *rapid amortization*, are included to safeguard the credit quality of the issue. The only way that the cash flows can be altered is by the triggering of the early amortization provision. Early amortization is invoked if the trust is not able to generate sufficient income to cover the investor coupon and the servicing fee. Other events that may trigger early amortization are the default of the servicer, credit support decline below a specified level, or the issuer violating agreements regarding pooling and servicing.

Since the concept of prepayments does not apply to credit card receivable-backed securities, there is no amortization schedule during the lockout period. Instead, for this sector of the asset-backed securities market, participants look at the *monthly payment rate* (MPR). This measure expresses the monthly payment (which includes interest, finance charges, and any principal) of a credit card receivable portfolio as a percentage of debt outstanding in the previous month. For example, suppose a $500 million credit card receivable portfolio in January realized $50 million of payments in February. The MPR would then be 10% ($50 million divided by $500 million).

Because there are no prepayments, these securities are valued by discounting at spot rates. The spread measure used is the zero-volatility spread.

HOME EQUITY LOAN-BACKED SECURITIES

Home equity loan-backed securities are backed by home equity loans. A *home equity loan* (HEL) is a loan backed by residential property. Typically, the loan is a

---

[1] For a more detailed discussion of these amortization structures, see Robert Karr, Greg Richter, R.J. Shook, and Lirenn Tsai, "Credit-Card Receivables," Chapter 3 in Anand K. Battacharya and Frank J. Fabozzi (eds.), *Asset-Backed Securities* (New Hope, PA: Frank J. Fabozzi Associates, 1997).

second lien on property that has already been pledged to secure a first lien. In some cases, the lien may be a third lien. In recent years, some loans have been first liens.

Home equity loans can be either closed end or open end. The former have been securitized. A *closed-end HEL* is structured the same way as a fully amortizing residential mortgage loan. That is, it has a fixed maturity and the payments are structured to fully amortize the loan by the maturity date.[2] There are both fixed-rate and variable-rate closed-end HELs. Typically, variable-rate loans have a reference rate of 6-month LIBOR and have periodic caps and lifetime caps, just as with adjustable-rate mortgages discussed in Chapter 8. The cash flow of a pool of closed-end HELs is comprised of interest, regularly scheduled principal repayments, and prepayments, just as with mortgage-backed securities. Thus, it is necessary to have a prepayment model and a default model to forecast cash flows. The prepayment speed is measured in terms of a conditional prepayment rate (CPR).

Borrowers are segmented into four general credit quality groups — A, B, C, and D. As will be explained, the borrower's credit is an important indicator as to whether or not the prepayment option will be exercised. While there is no industry-wide definition for classifying a borrower, the following definitions based on the borrower's credit history criteria appear to be what many originators use:[3]

> *A/A– (excellent/good credit quality):* (1) no more than two 30-day delinquencies in the past 12 months and (2) no prior bankruptcies
>
> *B & C (satisfactory/fair credit quality):* (1) no more than four 30-day, two 60-day, and one 90-day delinquencies in the past 12 months and (2) no bankruptcies in the past 2 to 3 years
>
> *D (unsatisfactory/poor credit quality):* (1) more than four 30-day, two 60-day and one 90-day delinquencies in past 12 months and (2) no bankruptcies in past 2 years

The monthly cash flow for a home equity loan-backed security is the same as for mortgage-backed securities. That is, the cash flow consists of (1) net interest, (2) regularly scheduled principal payments, and (3) prepayments. The uncertainty about the cash flows arises from prepayments.

There are differences in the prepayment behavior for home equity loans and traditional residential mortgage loans. In general it is expected that prepayments due to refinancings would be less important for HELs than for traditional residential mortgage loans because typically the average loan size is less for HELs. In general it is

---

[2] With an *open-end HEL* the homeowner is given a credit line and can write checks or use a credit card for up to the amount of the credit line. The amount of the credit line depends on the amount of the equity the borrower has in the property. There is a revolving period over which the homeowner can borrow funds against the line of credit. At the end of the term of the loan, the homeowner either pays off the amount borrowed in one payment or the outstanding balance is amortized.

[3] These definitions are from Joseph C. Hu, "Home Equity Loans (HELs) and HEL-Backed Securities," Chapter 32 in Frank J. Fabozzi (ed.), *The Handbook of Fixed Income Securities* (Burr Ridge, IL: Irwin Professional Publishing, 1997). Hu based his definitions on reports by Fitch, Moody's, and Bear Stearns.

thought that interest rates must fall considerably more for HELs than for traditional residential mortgage loans in order for a borrower to benefit from refinancing.

Wall Street firms involved in the underwriting and market making of home equity loan-backed securities have developed prepayment models for these loans. Several firms have found that the key difference between the prepayment behavior of HELs and traditional residential mortgages is the important role played by the credit characteristics of the borrower.[4]

A study by Bear Stearns strongly suggests that borrower credit quality is the most important determinant of prepayments.[5] The study looked at prepayments for four separate deals. The underlying HELs for each deal had a different level of borrower credit quality (with the credit quality of the loans being classified by the issuer). The four deals whose prepayments were analyzed were FICAL 90-1 (dominated by the highest credit quality borrowers, A++), GE Capital 91-1 (A– borrowers), Fleet Finance 90-1 (B/C borrowers), and Goldome Credit 90-1 (D borrowers). Prepayments were analyzed from the third quarter of 1991 to the third quarter of 1995, a period which encompassed the refinancing wave of 1992 and 1993. The main focus was on how borrower credit quality affected prepayments. The study found that prepayments for the Goldome Credit 90-1 deal (which was comprised of D borrowers) were completely uncorrelated to changes in interest rates. The deal with the highest credit quality borrowers, FICAL 90-1, exhibited prepayments similar to that of mortgage-backed securities in terms of their sensitivity to interest rates. The correlation between prepayments and interest rates for the deal with A– borrowers (Capital 91-1) was less than for FICAL 90-1 but greater than for the deal with B/C borrowers (Fleet Finance 90-1). Consequently, the sensitivity of refinancing to interest rates is reduced the lower the credit quality of the borrower.

Borrower characteristics and the seasoning process must be kept in mind when trying to assess prepayments for a particular deal. In the prospectus of an offering a base case prepayment assumption is made — the initial speed and the amount of time until the collateral is expected to be seasoned. Thus, the prepayment benchmark is issue specific. Investors are now using the concept of a *prospectus prepayment curve* or *PPC*. This is just a multiple of the base case prepayments assumed in the prospectus. For example, in the prospectus for the Contimortgage Home Equity Loan Trust 1996-1, the base case prepayment assumption for the fixed-rate mortgages in the pool is as follows (p. 3-37):

> ... a 100% Prepayment Assumption assumes conditional prepayment rates of 4% per annum of the then outstanding principal balance of the Home Equity Loans in the Fixed Rate Group in

---

[4] Dale Westhoff and Mark Feldman, "Prepayment Modeling and Valuation of Home Equity Loan Securities," Chapter 16 in Frank J. Fabozzi, Chuck Ramsey, Frank Ramirez, and Michael Marz (eds.), *The Handbook of Nonagency Mortgage-Backed Securities* (New Hope, PA: Frank J. Fabozzi Associates, 1997).

[5] Westhoff and Feldman, "Prepayment Modeling and Valuation of Home Equity Loan Securities."

the first month of the life of the mortgage loans and an additional 1.455% (precisely 16/11%) per annum in each month thereafter until the twelfth month. Beginning in the twelfth month and in each month thereafter during the life of the mortgage loans, 100% Prepayment Assumption assumes a conditional prepayment rate of 20% per annum each month.

Therefore, if an investor analyzed the deal based on 200% PPC, this means doubling the CPRs cited in the excerpt and using 12 months for seasoning.

In the Champion Home Equity Loan Trust 1996-1, the base case prepayment assumption is specified in the prospectus as follows (S-28):

The model used with respect to the Fixed Rate Certificates (the "Prepayment Ramp") assumes that the Home Equity Loans in Loan Group One prepay at a rate of 4% CPR in the first month after origination, and an additional 1.5% each month thereafter until the 14th month. Beginning in the 15th month and each month thereafter, the Prepayment Ramp assumes a prepayment rate of 25% CPR.

Thus, 100% PPC is based on the CPRs above assuming seasoning after 14 months.

Given this background for prepayments of HEL securities, we can see that the approach to valuation that is used depends on the credit of the borrowers. For lower credit quality borrowers, it appears that the prepayment option is not important and, as a result, such securities should be valued by discounting the cash flows at the spot rates. The appropriate spread measure is the zero-volatility spread. For securities backed by high credit quality borrowers, a model that recognizes the embedded option must be used. As with traditional residential mortgages, the cash flows are interest rate path-dependent. Thus, the Monte Carlo model should be used. Moreover, the OAS is the appropriate spread measure.

MANUFACTURED HOUSING-BACKED SECURITIES

Manufactured housing-backed securities are backed by loans for manufactured homes. In contrast to site-built homes, manufactured homes are built at a factory and then transported to a manufactured home community or private land. These homes are more popularly referred to as mobile homes. The loan may be either a mortgage loan (for both the land and the mobile home) or a consumer retail installment loan.

Manufactured housing-backed securities are issued by Ginnie Mae and private entities. The former securities are guaranteed by the full faith and credit of the U.S. government. The manufactured home loans that are collateral for the securities issued and guaranteed by Ginnie Mae are loans guaranteed by the Federal Housing Administration (FHA) or Veterans Administration (VA). Loans not backed by the FHA or VA are called conventional loans. Manufactured housing-backed securities that are backed by such loans are called *conventional manufactured housing-backed securities*. These securities are issued by private entities.

The typical loan for a manufactured home is 15 to 20 years. The loan repayment is structured to fully amortize the amount borrowed. Therefore, as with residential mortgage loans and HELs, the cash flows consist of net interest, regularly scheduled principal, and prepayments. As with residential mortgage loans and HELs, prepayments on manufactured housing-backed securities are measured in terms of CPR. However, prepayments are more stable for manufactured housing-backed securities because they are not sensitive to refinancing.

There are several reasons for this.[6] First, the loan balances are typically small so that there is no significant dollar savings from refinancing. Second, the rate of depreciation of mobile homes may be such that in the earlier years depreciation is greater than the amount of the loan paid off. This makes it difficult to refinance the loan. Finally, typically borrowers are of lower credit quality and therefore find it difficult to obtain funds to refinance. Consequently, securities backed by these loans can be valued by discounting at the issuer's spot rates. The spread measure that should be used is the zero-volatility spread.

---

[6] Thomas Zimmerman and Inna Koren, "Manufactured Housing Securities," Chapter 5 in *Asset-Backed Securities*.

KEY POINTS

1. The collateral for an asset-backed security can be either amortizing assets (e.g., auto loans and closed-end home equity loans) or nonamortizing assets (e.g., credit card receivables).

2. For amortizing assets, projection of the cash flows requires projecting prepayments.

3. For nonamortizing assets, the prepayment concept does not apply since there is no schedule of principal repayments.

4. One factor that may affect prepayments is the prevailing level of interest rates relative to the interest rate on the loan.

5. Since a default is a prepayment, prepayment modeling for an asset-backed security backed by amortizing assets requires a model for projecting the amount that will be recovered and when it will be recovered.

6. Cash flow analysis can be performed on a pool level or a loan level.

7. When the prepayment option is present but not likely to be exercised by borrowers, the ABS should be valued by discounting the expected cash flows by the issuer's spot rates and, in calculating spread, the appropriate spread measure is the zero-volatility spread.

8. When the prepayment option is present and is likely to be exercised for refinancing purposes, a valuation model that recognizes the embedded option must be used and the appropriate spread measure is the option-adjusted spread.

9. The valuation model that should be used when the prepayment option is likely to be exercised for refinancing purposes depends on whether or not the cash flows are interest rate path-independent (in which case the binomial model should be used) or interest rate path-dependent (in which case the Monte Carlo model should be used).

10. The cash flows for auto loan-backed securities consist of regularly scheduled monthly loan payments (interest and scheduled principal repayments), and any prepayments.

11. Prepayments on auto loan-backed securities are measured in terms of the absolute prepayment rate (denoted ABS) which measures monthly prepayments relative to the original collateral amount.

12. Prepayments on auto loans are not interest rate sensitive; therefore, the expected cash flows should be valued by discounting at the issuer's spot rates and the zero-volatility spread is the appropriate spread measure.

13. For credit card receivable-backed securities, the cash flows consist of interest (paid monthly, quarterly, or semiannually), principal, and finance charges collected.

14. The principal repayment of a credit card receivable-backed security is not amortized; instead, during the lockout period, the principal payments made by credit card borrowers are retained by the trustee and reinvested in additional receivables and after the lockout period (the principal-amortization period), the principal received by the trustee is no longer reinvested but paid to investors.

15. There are provisions in credit card receivable-backed securities that require early amortization of the principal if certain events occur.

16. Since for credit card receivable-backed securities the concept of prepayments does not apply, participants look at the monthly payment rate (MPR) which expresses the monthly payment (which includes interest, finance charges, and any principal) of a credit card receivable portfolio as a percentage of debt outstanding in the previous month.

17. There are three amortization structures that have been used in credit card receivable-backed security structures: (1) passthrough structure, (2) controlled-amortization structure, and (3) bullet-payment structure.

18. Since for credit card receivable-backed securities the concept of prepayments does not exist, the expected cash flows should be valued by discounting at the issuer's spot rates and the zero-volatility spread is the appropriate spread measure.

19. A home equity loan (HEL) is a loan backed by residential property and the lien is typically a second or third lien on the property.

20. Home equity loan borrowers are segmented into four general credit quality groups, A, B, C, and D, but there is no industry-wide definition for classifying a borrower.

21. The monthly cash flow for a home equity loan-backed security backed by closed-end HELs consists of (1) net interest, (2) regularly scheduled principal payments, and (3) prepayments.

22. In general it is expected that prepayments due to refinancings would be less important for HELs than for traditional residential mortgage loans.

23. Several studies by Wall Street firm have found that the key difference between the prepayment behavior of HELs and traditional residential mortgages is the important role played by the credit characteristics of the borrower.

24. One study strongly suggests that borrower credit quality is the most important determinant of prepayments, with the sensitivity of refinancing to interest rates being greater the higher the borrower's credit quality.

25. *In the prospectus of an offering a base case prepayment assumption is made — the initial speed and the amount of time until the collateral is expected to season.*

26. *A prospectus prepayment curve is a multiple of the base case prepayments assumed in the prospectus.*

27. *Because the prepayment characteristics of HEL-backed securities depend on the credit quality of the borrowers, the valuation model depends on the credit quality of the borrowers.*

28. *For HELs backed by low credit quality borrowers, the security's value is determined by discounting the cash flows at the issuer's spot rates and the zero-volatility spread is the appropriate spread measure.*

29. *For HELs backed by high credit quality borrowers, the security's value is determined by using the Monte Carlo model and the appropriate spread measure is the option-adjusted spread.*

30. *Manufactured housing-backed securities are backed by loans on manufactured homes (i.e., homes built at a factory and then transported to a site).*

31. *A manufactured housing loan's cash flows consist of net interest, regularly scheduled principal, and prepayments.*

32. *Prepayments are more stable for manufactured housing-backed securities because they are not sensitive to refinancing and therefore the expected cash flows should be discounted at the issuer's spot rates.*

Chapter 10

Valuation of Inverse Floaters

The objectives of this chapter are to:

1. explain how an inverse floater is created;

2. set forth a methodology for valuing an inverse floater;

3. explain how a change in the shape of the yield curve affects the value of an inverse floater;

4. show the price volatility characteristics of an inverse floater when interest rates change;

5. explain the relationship between an inverse floater and an interest rate swap; and,

6. explain the different types of inverse floaters created in the collateralized mortgage obligation and municipal bond markets.

Floating-rate securities are securities whose coupon rate is reset at specified dates at some spread to a reference rate. In recent years, inverse floating-rate securities have been introduced to the fixed income market. The coupon rate on an inverse floating-rate security, or simply, *inverse floater*, changes in the direction opposite to that of some reference rate or market rate.

CREATION OF INVERSE FLOATERS

Inverse floaters exist in the corporate bond market, the municipal bond market, and the mortgage-backed securities market. In general, an inverse floater is created from a fixed-rate security. The security from which the inverse floater is created is called the *collateral*. From the collateral two bonds, or *tranches*, are created: a floater and an inverse floater. This is depicted in Exhibit 1.

Conditions that Must Be Satisfied

The two tranches are created such that (1) the total coupon interest paid to the two tranches in each period is less than or equal to the collateral's coupon interest in each period, and (2) the total principal paid in any period to the two tranches is less than or equal to the collateral's total principal in each period. Equivalently, the floater and inverse floaters are structured so that the cash flow from the collateral in each period will be sufficient to satisfy the obligation of the two tranches.

For example, consider a 10-year 7.5% coupon semiannual-pay bond. Suppose $100 million par value of the bond is used as collateral to create a floater with a principal of $50 million and an inverse floater with a principal of $50 million. Suppose that the reference rate is LIBOR and that the coupon rate for the floater and the inverse floater are reset every six months based on the following formula:

Floater coupon: LIBOR + 1%
Inverse floater coupon: 14% – LIBOR

Notice that the total principal of the floater and inverse floater equals the principal of the collateral, $100 million. The weighted average of the coupon rate of the combination of the two tranches is:

$$0.5(\text{LIBOR} + 1\%) + 0.5(14\% - \text{LIBOR}) = 7.5\%$$

Exhibit 1: Creation of an Inverse Floater

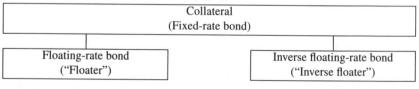

Thus, regardless of the level of LIBOR, the combined coupon rate for the two tranches is the coupon rate of the collateral, 7.5%.

There is one problem with the coupon formulas given above. Suppose that LIBOR exceeds 14%. Then the formula for the inverse floater will give a negative coupon rate. To prevent this from happening a restriction, or *floor*, is placed on the coupon rate for the inverse floater. Typically, the floor is set at zero. Because of the floor, the coupon rate on the floater must be restricted so that the coupon interest paid to the two tranches does not exceed the collateral's coupon interest. In our hypothetical structure, the maximum coupon rate that must be imposed on the floater is 15%. Thus, when a floater and an inverse floater are created from the collateral, a floor is imposed on the inverse and a cap is imposed on the floater.

In our simple structure, we assumed an equal allocation of the par value between the two tranches. This need not happen, and, as explained later in this chapter, in the mortgage-backed securities market typically less than half of the collateral's principal is allocated to the inverse floater.

General Formula for Inverse Floater Coupon

In general, a wide range of allocations of the collateral's principal are possible, permitting an infinite number of possibilities for the formula for the inverse floater. The general formula for the inverse floater is: $K - L \times R$ where R is the reference rate, and K and L are values that can be selected by the creator of the floater and the inverse floater.

Let's interpret the two parameters. K is the maximum coupon rate that the inverse floater can realize; that is, it is the *inverse cap*. This occurs when the reference rate is zero. L is the *coupon leverage*, or simply, *leverage*. It indicates the multiple by which the coupon rate will change for a 100 basis point change in the reference rate. For example, if L is 4, this means that the coupon rate on the inverse floater will change 400 basis points for each 100 basis point change in the reference rate (subject to any restrictions imposed on the coupon rate). Thus, the general formula for the coupon rate of an inverse floater can be expressed as follows:

Inverse Cap − Leverage × Reference Rate

Any cap or floor imposed on the coupon rate for the floater and the inverse floater must be selected so as to maintain the integrity of the combined coupon rate. That is, the combined coupon rate must be less than or equal to the collateral's coupon rate. The relationships among the parameters for the collateral, floater, and inverse floater are shown in Exhibit 2.

The amount of leverage is not determined arbitrarily by the creator of the inverse floater. Rather, it is dictated by client inquiries and/or market demand for other issues that have been recently created.

Exhibit 2: Relationships for Principal and Coupon for Creation of Floater and Inverse Floater Tranches[*]

Parameters for collateral:
Collateral principal
Collateral coupon rate

Parameters for floater tranche:
Floater spread
Floater cap
Floater floor
Current value of reference rate

Parameters for inverse floater tranche:
Coupon leverage
Inverse floater cap
Inverse floater floor

Relationships:

Floater coupon = Current value of reference rate + Floater spread

$$\text{Floater principal} = \frac{\text{Coupon leverage} \times \text{Collateral principal}}{(1 + \text{Coupon leverage})}$$

Inverse principal = Collateral principal – Floater principal

Inverse interest = (Collateral principal × Collateral coupon rate)
−(Floater principal × Floater coupon rate)

$$\text{Floater cap} = \frac{\text{Collateral coupon}}{\text{Floater principal}}$$

$$\text{Inverse floor} = \frac{\text{Inverse interest when floater coupon at cap}}{\text{Inverse principal}}$$

$$\text{Inverse cap} = \frac{\text{Inverse interest when floater coupon at floor}}{\text{Inverse principal}}$$

* Assumes that all of the collateral principal and interest will be distributed to the floater and inverse floater.

VALUING AN INVERSE FLOATER

As emphasized throughout this book, the value of any financial asset is the present value of its expected cash flows. It is difficult to value an inverse floater in these terms because of uncertainty about future values for the reference rate. Fortunately, the valuation of an inverse floater is not complex, as we shall see.

Fundamental Principle

We can express the relationships among the collateral, the floater, and the inverse floater as follows:

Collateral = Floater + Inverse floater

This relationship applies to cash flows as well as valuation. That is, the sum of the value of the floater and the value of the inverse floater must be equal to the value of the collateral from which they are created. If this relationship is violated, arbitrage profits are possible.

An alternative way to express the relationship is:

Value of inverse floater = Value of collateral – Value of floater

This expression states that the value of an inverse floater can be found by valuing the collateral and valuing the floater, then calculating the difference between these two values. In this case, the value of an inverse floater is not found directly, but is instead derived from the value of the collateral and the value of the floater.

The value of the collateral is obtained using the valuation methodologies described in previous chapters. The expected cash flows of the collateral must be discounted at appropriate rates that reflect the inherent risk associated with the collateral. The appropriate discount rate depends on (1) the spot rate curve and (2) the option-adjusted spread of the collateral.

Valuing the Floater

The value of a floater depends on two factors: (1) the spread over the reference rate and (2) the cap on the floater. A floater with a cap can be viewed as a package with an uncapped floater (a floater without a cap) and a cap. That is:

Capped floater = Uncapped floater – Floater cap

The reason for subtracting the value of the cap from the value of an uncapped floater is that the holder of a capped floater has effectively sold a cap.

Assuming that the spread over the reference rate required by the market has not changed since issuance, the uncapped floater should sell at its par value. The value of a capped floater thus can be expressed as follows:

Value of capped floater = Par value – Value of floater cap

If the reference rate plus the spread is far below the floater cap rate, the value of the cap will be close to zero, and the capped floater will trade at par value. However, if the reference rate plus the spread is close to the cap rate or above it, the value of the floater cap will be positive, and the value of a capped floater will be less than its par value.

The question therefore is how to determine the value of the cap embedded in the floater. In Chapter 15 we show how the binomial model can be used to value a cap. What is important to understand here is that there are two key factors that affect the value of a cap: (1) the relationship between the current reference rate plus the spread and the cap rate on the floater and (2) the expected volatility of the reference rate. The farther the reference rate plus the spread is below the floater cap rate, the less the value of the cap. As the reference rate plus the spread approaches the cap rate, the value of the cap increases. With respect to expected volatility of the reference rate, a cap increases in value the greater the expected volatility.

Given that the floater created from the collateral is a capped floater, the value of an inverse floater can be expressed as:

Value of inverse floater = Value of collateral − Value of capped floater

The factors that affect the value of an inverse floater are the factors that affect the value of the collateral and the value of a capped floater.

Leverage and Valuation

It is informative to recast the valuation of inverse floaters by looking at the importance of the leverage that is selected. Suppose that the creator of the floaters and inverse floaters divides the collateral into 100 bonds, 20 inverse floater bonds and 80 floater bonds.[1] This means that the leverage in this structure is 4:1 of floater bonds to inverse floater bonds. Then, the following relationship must hold:

100(Collateral price) = 20(Inverse price) + 80(Floater price)

This can also be expressed as:

20(1 + 4)(Collateral price) = 20(Inverse price) + 20(4)(Floater price)

Dividing both sides by 20, we get:

(1 + 4)(Collateral price) = (Inverse price) + 4(Floater price)

This can be generalized for any leverage L as follows:

(1 + L)(Collateral price) = (Inverse price) + L(Floater price)

---

[1] William R. Leach, "A Portfolio Manager's Perspective of Inverses and Inverse IOs," Chapter 10 in Frank J. Fabozzi (ed.), *CMO Portfolio Management* (Summit, NJ: Frank J. Fabozzi Associates, 1994).

Solving for the inverse price we have:

Inverse price $= (1 + L)$(Collateral price) $- L$(Floater price)

There are two important implications of this price relationship. First, typically it is not difficult to price the floater. The greater difficulty may be in determining the collateral's price. Notice the implication of mispricing the collateral. *The greater the leverage, the greater the impact of mispricing of the inverse floater resulting from mispricing the collateral.* Specifically, every one point mispricing of the collateral results in a $1 + L$ point mispricing of the inverse floater. So with a leverage of 3, a 4 point mispricing of the inverse results for each one point mispricing of the collateral.

The second implication is that the price of the inverse floater is not related to the level of the reference rate as long as the floater cap is not affected. What in fact affects the price performance of an inverse floater is explored next.

PERFORMANCE OF AN INVERSE FLOATER

A common misconception is that the value of an inverse floater should change in a direction opposite from the change in the reference rate. Thus, if the reference rate falls, the value of an inverse floater should rise. This view is incorrect because, as we just explained, the value of an inverse floater is not solely dependent on the reference rate. The reference rate affects the value of the inverse floater only through its effect on the value of the cap of the capped floater, and does not take into consideration the other factors that we have noted will affect the value of an inverse floater.

To see the importance of these relationships for the value of an inverse floater and to make the analysis simple, let's assume that an inverse floater and floater are created from the on-the-run 10-year Treasury issue. While the creation of such securities is not being done at the time of this writing, the basic principles are illustrated and can be extended to more complicated collateral such as corporate bonds, municipal bonds, and collateralized mortgage obligations. The assumptions for the illustration are:

- The reference rate for the floater and inverse floater is the 6-month Treasury bill rate which is currently 6%. (Thus, the reference rate is a short-term rate.)
- The coupon rate for the floater is the 6-month Treasury bill rate flat. That is, there is no spread.
- The cap for the floater is 5%.
- The yield on the 10-year Treasury is 9.5% and the yield on a 9-year Treasury is 9.3%.

Now consider three scenarios one year from now. For each scenario we make an assumption about

(1) the reference rate one year from now,
(2) the expected volatility of the reference rate one year from now, and
(3) the yield on a 9-year Treasury.

We will look at the effect one year from now on the value of the collateral (the original 10-year Treasury) and the value of the capped floater. The difference between these two values is the value of the inverse floater.

Scenario 1: In this scenario, it is assumed that six months from now:

(1) the reference rate declines to 4%,
(2) expected volatility of the 6-month Treasury bill rate declines, and
(3) the yield on a 9-year Treasury increases from its current rate of 9.3% to 11%.

Thus, in Scenario 1, one year from now it is assumed that short-term Treasury rates have declined and intermediate-term rates have increased. This means that the Treasury yield curve has steepened in the short- to intermediate-term range.

Given this scenario, the value of the capped floater will increase for two reasons. First, today the coupon rate on the floater would be 6% in the absence of the floater cap. Because of the floater cap, the coupon rate is 5%. One year from now, the capped floater's value increases because the coupon rate falls below the cap (the new coupon rate is 4%), thereby reducing the value of the cap. Second, expected volatility for the reference rate decreases. Looking at the collateral, its value declines because the yield on the 9-year Treasury rises.

Since the value of an inverse floater is the difference between the value of the collateral (which has decreased) and the value of the capped floater (which has increased), the value of the inverse floater has declined. *Notice that this occurs despite the fact that the reference rate is assumed to decline in this scenario.*

Scenario 2: In this scenario, it is assumed that one year from now:

(1) the reference rate rises to 7%,
(2) expected volatility of the 6-month Treasury bill rate increases, and
(3) the yield on a 9-year Treasury declines from its current rate of 9.3% to 7.6%.

In this scenario it is assumed that short-term rates rise and intermediate-term rates fall. This means that the Treasury yield curve has flattened in the short- to intermediate-term range.

Two factors cause the value of the floater to decrease because the value of the cap increases. First, the reference rate has risen above the cap rate so one year from now the coupon rate is even further below the market rate. Second, the expected volatility has increased.

Now consider the collateral. Its value will increase. Consequently, the value of the inverse floater will increase. *Notice that this occurs even though the reference rate for the inverse floater has increased.*

Scenario 3: In this last scenario, the following is assumed one year from now:

(1) the reference rate declines to 4% (as in Scenario 1),
(2) expected volatility of the reference rate decreases (as in Scenario 1), and
(3) the yield on a 9-year Treasury declines from its current rate of 9.3% to 7.6% (as in Scenario 2).

Under this scenario, the value of the collateral will rise. The value of the inverse floater can either rise or fall, as the collateral has risen in value and the capped floater has risen in value. The net effect depends on the relative change of the collateral and the capped floater.

These illustrations make it clear that the change in the shape of the yield curve is the key factor that affects the performance of an inverse floater. There are two factors that have not been introduced into the analysis yet since we have dealt with a hypothetical inverse floater created from a Treasury issue. The following will affect how non-Treasury collateral and the floater created will affect the value of the inverse floater: (1) how the spread of the floater changes and (2) the option-adjusted spread at which the collateral trades.

Typically, dealers analyze inverse floaters for a potential buyer by modeling the performance under various scenarios. Usually, performance assumptions cover a rise or decline in interest rates of up to 300 basis points. Such analysis can be misleading for several reasons. First, there is no such thing as an "interest rate." Rather there is a structure of interest rates as depicted by the yield curve, and we demonstrated above that changes in the shape of the yield curve can affect the value of an inverse floater. Simply assuming that "interest rates" rise or fall by a particular number of basis points means that all interest rates along the Treasury yield curve change by the same amount (that is, that there is a parallel shift in the Treasury yield curve). Our discussion should make it clear that the value of an inverse floater requires more in-depth analysis than a simple assumption of parallel shifts in the yield curve.

Duration of an Inverse Floater

The duration of an asset is a measure of its price sensitivity to a change in interest rates. Because valuations are additive (that is, the sum of the floater and the inverse floater equals the value of the collateral), durations (properly weighted) are additive as well. Thus, the duration of the inverse floater is related to the duration of the collateral and the duration of the floater.

Assuming that the duration of the floater is close to zero, it can be shown that the duration of an inverse floater is:[2]

Duration of inverse floater

$$= (1 + L)(\text{Duration of collateral}) \times \frac{\text{Collateral price}}{\text{Inverse price}}$$

Thus, the duration of an inverse floater will be a multiple of the duration of the collateral. In the case where the principal from the collateral is split equally between the floater and the inverse floater, L is equal to one and the duration of the inverse floater is two times the duration of the collateral adjusted by the relative prices for the collateral and inverse.

INTERPRETATION OF AN INVERSE FLOATER POSITION

Since the capped floater and inverse floater are created from fixed-rate collateral, the following relationship is true:

Long a fixed-rate collateral = Long a capped floater + Long an inverse floater

Recasting this relationship in terms of an inverse floater, we can write

Long an inverse floater = Long a fixed-rate collateral – Long a capped floater

Or, equivalently,

Long an inverse floater = Long a fixed-rate collateral + Short a capped floater

Thus, the owner of an inverse floater has effectively purchased fixed-rate collateral and shorted a capped floater. But shorting a floater is equivalent to borrowing funds, where the interest cost of the funds is a floating rate where the interest rate is the reference rate plus the spread. Consequently, the owner of an inverse floater has effectively purchased a fixed-rate asset with borrowed funds.

There is another capital market instrument that shares a similar characteristic with an inverse floater, an interest rate swap. One party to an interest rate swap receives a fixed rate and pays a floating rate. With the exception of the cap on the floater, the owner of an inverse floater receives fixed and pays floating. Thus, it should not be surprising that the swap market has also been used to value inverse floaters. The valuation of an interest rate swap is explained in Chapter 14.

---

[2] Leach, "A Portfolio Manager's Perspective of Inverses and Inverse IOs," p. 159.

Exhibit 3: Creation of a CMO Inverse Floater Class

CMO Collateral (Fixed-rate passthroughs and whole loans)

Fixed-rate tranches

A	B	C	D	E (Tranche collateral)	F

Floater	Inverse Floater

CMO INVERSE FLOATER TRANCHES

The largest issuance of inverse floaters has been in the CMO market. In describing CMO inverse floaters we must modify our terminology. In our earlier discussion, we referred to the fixed-rate bond from which the floater and inverse floater were created as the collateral. We referred to the floater and inverse floater as tranches. The term collateral to participants in the CMO market refers to the passthroughs or whole loans from which the CMO was created. The collateral is then carved up to create various tranches. From any fixed-rate tranche, a floater and an inverse floater can be created.

The term "collateral" for the floater and the inverse floater can be misleading in the CMO market. It could mean the collateral for the CMO deal or it could mean the fixed-rate tranche. To avoid confusion, we will refer to the collateral for the entire CMO deal as the *CMO collateral* and the fixed-rate tranche from which the floater and inverse floater are created as the *tranche collateral*.

This is depicted in Exhibit 3. The CMO collateral is shown at the top of the exhibit. From the CMO collateral, six fixed-rate tranches are created, denoted A, B, C, D, E, and F. From fixed-rate tranche E, a floater and an inverse floater are created.

Any type of bond class can be divided into a floater and an inverse floater. That is, a floater and inverse combination can be created from support tranches, sequential-pay tranches, PAC tranches, and TAC tranches. The reference rate has been primarily LIBOR, the Eleventh District Cost of Funds Index (COFI), or the Constant Maturity Treasury.

Inverse floaters with a wide variety of leverages are available in the market. Market participants refer to *low leverage* inverse floaters as those with a leverage between 0.5 and 2.1; *medium leverage* as those with a leverage greater than 2.1 but not exceeding 4.5, and; *high leverage* as those with a leverage greater than 4.5.

Valuing CMO Inverse Floaters

The basic principles that we described earlier about valuing inverse floaters apply to CMO inverse floaters. The added dimension that increases the complexity of the valuation process is the impact of prepayments. Prepayments affect the value of the CMO collateral; in turn, the value of the CMO collateral affects the value of the collateral tranche. Because the tranche collateral's value changes, the value of the inverse floater changes.

Average Life and Duration

The average life of an inverse floater is the same as the average life of the tranche collateral. The average life for the tranche collateral depends on the expected prepayment speed. As we explained earlier, the duration of the inverse floater is a multiple of the duration of the tranche collateral.

Variants in CMO Inverse Structuring

In the CMO market, there are several variants of the inverse floater that have been created. The first is the inverse interest-only (IO) floater. In this structure the inverse floater tranche is further divided into two tranches: a principal only tranche and a tranche that receives only coupon interest. The coupon interest varies inversely with the reference rate.

   The second variant is what is called a *strike bond* or a *two-tiered index bond* (TTIB). In this structure, the inverse floater has a coupon that varies as follows: (1) when the reference rate is above a designated rate, the coupon rate is capped at the designated rate, (2) when the reference rate is below a designated rate, a floor is set for the coupon rate at the designated rate, and (3) when the reference rate is between the cap and floor, the coupon rate has the standard formula for an inverse floater. The reason the bond is called a strike bond is that the designated rates for the cap and the floor are referred to as strike rates.

MUNICIPAL INVERSE FLOATERS

Inverse floaters have been created in the municipal bond market by one of the following transactions:

   (1) a municipal dealer buys in the secondary market a fixed-rate municipal bond, places the bond in a trust, and the trust then issues a floating-rate security and an inverse floating-rate bond; or,

   (2) a new fixed-rate municipal issue is underwritten by an investment banking firm, places it in a trust, and the trust then issues a floating-rate security and an inverse floating-rate bond.

   (3) an investment banking firm underwrites a long-term fixed-rate municipal bond and simultaneously enters into an interest rate swap for a time that is

generally less than the term to maturity of the bond. The investor owns an inverse floater for the term of the swap which then converts to a fixed-rate bond (the underlying) at the end of the swap term.

Note that in the first two transactions, both a floating-rate security and an inverse floating-rate bond are created. In the third transaction, only an inverse floating-rate bond is created.

When a floater is created, the coupon rate on it is reset based on the results of a Dutch auction. The coupon rate on the floater changes in the same direction as market rates. The resulting inverse floater receives the residual interest; that is, the coupon interest is the difference between the coupon interest on the collateral and the coupon rate that has been reset on the floater as a result of the auction. Thus, the coupon rate on the inverse floater changes in the opposite direction of market rates.

The use of the swap market to create an inverse floater eliminates the need for selling the floaters through a Dutch auction. The issuer locks in the cost of the bond at issuance, which is the interest cost of the underlying bond to maturity plus the difference between the fixed payments made and the floating rates received on the underlying swap for the term of the swap. These products are generically called *indexed inverse floaters*. The investor has the option of converting the indexed inverse floater to a fixed-rate bond before the end of the swap term by unwinding the swap. The cost of the conversion is satisfied either up-front or is satisfied by adjusting the fixed rate the investor was to begin receiving at the end of the initial swap term.

Most of the floaters and inverse floaters that have been created in the municipal bond market at the time of this writing have been created by dividing the principal equally between the two classes. That is, if the collateral has a par value of $100 million, the par value for both the floater and inverse floater is $50 million. As explained earlier, this means that the duration of an inverse floater will have roughly twice the duration of the collateral.

Several investment banking firms active in the municipal bond market have developed proprietary products. Merrill Lynch's institutional products are called FLOATS and RITES (Residual Interest Tax Exempt Securities). These products are created using the first two transactions discussed above. Merrill Lynch has an inverse floating-rate bond that it markets to retail investors which it calls TEEMS (Tax Exempt Enhanced Municipal Securities) that is created by means of the third type of transaction. Goldman Sachs' proprietary products are called PARS (Periodic Auction Reset Securities), which are floaters, and INFLOS, which are inverse floaters. Lehman Brothers' proprietary products are called RIBS (Residual Interest Bonds) and SAVRS (Select Auction Variable Rate Securities).

KEY POINTS

1. *Typically, an inverse floater is created from a fixed-rate debt instrument.*

2. *To prevent the coupon rate on a reset date from becoming negative for an inverse floater, there is an interest rate floor.*

3. *Typically the inverse floater's floor is set at zero.*

4. *Because of the floor on the inverse floater, a cap is set on the accompanying floater.*

5. *The leverage of an inverse floater indicates the number of basis points that the coupon rate changes for a given change in the reference rate.*

6. *The value of an inverse floater is determined by the value of the collateral and the corresponding floater.*

7. *The factors that affect the value and performance of an inverse floater are those that affect the value of the collateral from which it is created and the value of the floater.*

8. *The valuation of the collateral becomes critical because mispricing the collateral results in a mispricing of the inverse floater by a factor of 1 plus the leverage.*

9. *The performance of an inverse floater is determined by the change in the shape of the yield curve.*

10. *A decline in the reference rate will not necessarily increase the value of the inverse floater despite the fact that the coupon rate is increased.*

11. *The duration of an inverse floater is a multiple of the duration of the collateral.*

12. *The owner of an inverse floater has effectively purchased a fixed-rate asset and borrowed on a floating-rate basis.*

13. *An inverse floater position is similar in characteristic to a interest rate swap position.*

14. *In the case of a CMO inverse floater, an important factor is the prepayment rate that affects the CMO collateral.*

15. *Municipal inverse floaters can be created from a fixed-rate bond or through an interest rate swap.*

Chapter 11

Valuation of Convertible Securities

The objectives of this chapter are to:

1. describe the basic features of a convertible and exchangeable security;

2. explain the traditional valuation methodology that has been used to value convertible securities;

3. explain the factors that complicate the valuation of convertible securities;

4. describe and illustrate the state-of-the-art option-based valuation methodology for valuing a convertible security; and,

5. demonstrate the risk/return characteristics of a convertible security versus the ownership of the underlying common stock.

A convertible security is a security that can be converted into common stock at the option of the securityholder. These securities include convertible bonds and convertible preferred stock.

BASIC FEATURES OF CONVERTIBLE SECURITIES

The conversion provision of a convertible security grants the securityholder the right to convert the security into a predetermined number of shares of common stock of the issuer. A convertible security is therefore a security with an embedded call option to buy the common stock of the issuer. An *exchangeable security* grants the securityholder the right to exchange the security for the common stock of a firm *other* than the issuer of the security. For example, some Ford Motor Credit convertible bonds are exchangeable for the common stock of the parent company, Ford Motor Company. Throughout this chapter we use the term convertible security to refer to both convertible and exchangeable securities.

In illustrating the calculation of the various concepts described below, we will use the General Signal Corporation (ticker symbol "GSX") 5¾% convertible issue due June 1, 2002. Information about the issue and the stock of this issuer is provided in Exhibit 1.

Exhibit 1: Information About General Signal Corporation Convertible Bond 5¾% Due June 1, 2002 and Common Stock

Convertible bond
Market price (as of 10/7/93): $106.50
Issue proceeds: $100 million
Issue date: 6/1/92
Maturity date: 6/1/02
Non-call until 6/1/95

Call price schedule	
6/1/95	103.59
6/1/96	102.88
6/1/97	102.16
6/1/98	101.44
6/1/99	100.72
6/1/00	100.00
6/1/01	100.00

Coupon rate: 5¾%
Conversion ratio: 25.320 shares of GSX shares per $1,000 par value
Rating: A3/A−

GSX common stock
Expected volatility: 17%
Dividend per share: $0.90 per year
Dividend yield (as of 10/7/93): 2.727%
Stock price: $33

Conversion Ratio

The number of shares of common stock that the securityholder will receive from exercising the call option of a convertible security is called the *conversion ratio*. The conversion privilege may extend for all or only some portion of the security's life, and the stated conversion ratio may change over time. It is always adjusted proportionately for stock splits and stock dividends. For the GSX convertible issue, the conversion ratio is 25.32 shares. This means that for each $1,000 of par value of this issue the securityholder exchanges for GSX common stock, he will receive 25.32 shares.

At the time of issuance of a convertible security, the issuer effectively grants the securityholder the right to purchase the common stock at a price equal to:

$$\frac{\text{Par value of convertible security}}{\text{Conversion ratio}}$$

This price is referred to in the prospectus as the *stated conversion price*. Sometimes the issue price of a convertible security may not be equal to par. In such cases, the stated conversion price at issuance is usually determined by the issue price.

The conversion price for the GSX convertible issue is:

$$\text{Conversion price} = \frac{\$1,000}{25.32} = \$39.49$$

Call Provisions

Almost all convertible issues are callable by the issuer. This is a valuable feature for issuers who deem the current market price of their stock undervalued enough so that selling stock directly would dilute the equity of current stockholders. The firm would prefer to raise funds via a common stock issuance over incurring debt, so it issues a convertible setting the conversion ratio on the basis of a stock price it regards as acceptable. Once the market price reaches the conversion price, the firm will want to see the conversion happen in view of the risk that the stock price may drop in the future. This gives the firm an interest in forcing conversion, even though this is not in the interest of the owners of the security whose price is likely to be adversely affected by the call.

Typically there is a non-call period (i.e., a time period from the time of issuance that the convertible security may not be called). The GSX convertible issue had a non-call period at issuance of three years. There are some issues that have a provisional call feature that allows the issuer to call the issue during the non-call period if the price of the stock reaches a certain price. For example, Whirlpool Corporation zero-coupon convertible bond due 5/14/11 could not be called before 5/14/93 unless the stock price reached $52.35, at which time the issuer had the right to call the issue. In the case of Eastman Kodak zero-coupon convertible bond due 10/15/11, the issuer cannot call the issue before 10/15/93 unless the common stock traded at a price of at least $70.73 for at least 20/30 trading days.

The call price schedule of a convertible security is specified at the time of issuance. Typically, the call price declines over time. The call price schedule for the

GSX convertible issue is shown in Exhibit 1. In the case of a zero-coupon convertible bond, the call price is based on an accreted value. For example, for the Whirlpool Corporation zero-coupon convertible, the call price on 5/14/93 was $28.983 and thereafter accretes daily at 7% per annum compounded semiannually. So, if the issue is called on 5/14/94, the call price would have been $31.047 ($28.983 times 1.035^2).

Putable Provision

A put option grants the bondholder the right to require the issuer to redeem the issue at designated dates for a predetermined price. Some convertible bonds are putable. For example, Eastman Kodak zero-coupon convertible bond due 10/15/11 is putable. The put schedule is as follows: 32.35 if put on 10/15/94; 34.57 if put on 10/15/95; 36.943 if put on 10/15/96; 51.486 if put on 10/15/01; and, 71.753 if put on 10/15/06. The GSX convertible issue is not putable.

Put options can be classified as "hard" puts and "soft" puts. A hard put is one in which the convertible security must be redeemed by the issuer for cash. In the case of a soft put, the issuer has the option to redeem the convertible security for cash, common stock, subordinated notes, or a combination of the three.

TRADITIONAL ANALYSIS
OF CONVERTIBLE SECURITIES

Minimum Value of a Convertible Security

The *conversion value* or *parity value* of a convertible security is the value of the security if it is converted immediately.[1] That is,

Conversion value = Market price of common stock × Conversion ratio

The minimum price of a convertible security is the greater of

1. Its conversion value, or
2. Its value as a security without the conversion option — that is, based on the convertible security's cash flows if not converted (i.e., a plain vanilla security). This value is called its *straight value* or *investment value*. The valuation principles set forth in the previous chapters should be used to determine the straight value.

If the convertible security does not sell for the greater of these two values, arbitrage profits could be realized. For example, suppose the conversion value is greater than the straight value, and the security trades at its straight value. An investor can buy the convertible security at the straight value and convert it.

---

[1] Technically, the standard textbook definition of conversion value given here is theoretically incorrect because as bondholders convert, the price of the stock will decline. The theoretically correct definition for the conversion value is that it is the product of the conversion ratio and the stock price *after* conversion.

By doing so, the investor realizes a gain equal to the difference between the conversion value and the straight value. Suppose, instead, the straight value is greater than the conversion value, and the security trades at its conversion value. By buying the convertible at the conversion value, the investor will realize a higher yield than a comparable straight security.

For the GSX convertible issue, the conversion value on 10/7/93 per $1,000 of par value was equal to:

$$\text{Conversion value} = \$33 \times 25.32 = \$835.56$$

Therefore, the conversion value per $100 of par value was 83.556.

To simplify the analysis of the straight value of the bond, we will discount the cash flows to maturity by the yield on the 10-year on-the-run Treasury at the time, 5.32%, plus a credit spread of 70 basis points that appeared to be appropriate at that time. The straight value using a discount rate of 6.02% and assuming same day settlement for theoretical purposes only is 98.19. Actually, the straight value would be less than this because no recognition was given to the call feature. Since the minimum value of the GSX convertible issue is the greater of the conversion value and the straight value, the minimum value is 98.19.

Market Conversion Price

The price that an investor effectively pays for the common stock if the convertible security is purchased and then converted into the common stock is called the *market conversion price* or *conversion parity price*. It is found as follows:

$$\text{Market conversion price} = \frac{\text{Market price of convertible security}}{\text{Conversion ratio}}$$

The market conversion price is a useful benchmark because once the actual market price of the stock rises above the market conversion price, any further stock price increase is certain to increase the value of the convertible security by at least the same percentage. Therefore, the market conversion price can be viewed as a break-even price.

An investor who purchases a convertible security rather than the underlying stock, pays a premium over the current market price of the stock. This premium per share is equal to the difference between the market conversion price and the current market price of the common stock. That is,

$$\text{Market conversion premium per share}$$
$$= \text{Market conversion price} - \text{Current market price}$$

The market conversion premium per share is usually expressed as a percentage of the current market price as follows:

$$\text{Market conversion premium ratio} = \frac{\text{Market conversion premium per share}}{\text{Market price of common stock}}$$

Why would someone be willing to pay a premium to buy the stock? Recall that the minimum price of a convertible security is the greater of its conversion value or its straight value. Thus, as the common stock price declines, the price of the convertible security will not fall below its straight value. The straight value therefore acts as a floor for the convertible security's price.

Viewed in this context, the market conversion premium per share can be seen as the price of a call option. As explained in Chapter 5, the buyer of a call option limits the downside risk to the option price. In the case of a convertible security, for a premium, the securityholder limits the downside risk to the straight value of the security. The difference between the buyer of a call option and the buyer of a convertible security is that the former knows precisely the dollar amount of the downside risk, while the latter knows only that the most that can be lost is the difference between the convertible security's price and the straight value. The straight value at some future date, however, is unknown; the value will change as market interest rates change or if the issuer's credit quality changes.

The calculation of the market conversion price, market conversion premium per share, and market conversion premium ratio for the GSX convertible issue based on market data as of 10/7/93 is shown below:

$$\text{Market conversion price} = \frac{\$1{,}065}{25.32} = \$42.06$$

$$\text{Market conversion premium per share} = \$42.06 - \$33 = \$9.06$$

$$\text{Market conversion premium ratio} = \frac{\$9.06}{\$33} = 0.275 = 27.5\%$$

Current Income of Convertible Security Versus Common Stock

As an offset to the market conversion premium per share, investing in the convertible security rather than buying the stock directly, generally means that the investor realizes higher current income from the coupon interest paid in the case of a convertible bond (dividends in the case of a convertible preferred) than would be received from common stock dividends based on the number of shares equal to the conversion ratio. Analysts evaluating a convertible security typically compute the time it takes to recover the premium per share by computing the *premium payback period* (which is also known as the *break-even time*). This is computed as follows:

$$\text{Premium payback period} = \frac{\text{Market conversion premium per share}}{\text{Favorable income differential per share}}$$

where the favorable income differential per share is equal to the following for a convertible bond:

$$\frac{\text{Coupon interest} - (\text{Conversion ratio} \times \text{Common stock dividend per share})}{\text{Conversion ratio}}$$

And, for convertible preferred stock:

$$\frac{\text{Preferred dividends} - (\text{Conversion ratio} \times \text{Common stock dividend per share})}{\text{Conversion ratio}}$$

Notice that the premium payback period does *not* take into account the time value of money.

For the GSX convertible issue, the market conversion premium per share is $9.06. The favorable income differential per share is found as follows:

Coupon interest from bond $= 0.0575 \times \$1,000 = \$57.50$

Conversion ratio $\times$ Dividend per share $= 25.32 \times \$0.90 = \$22.79$

Therefore,

$$\text{Favorable income differential per share} = \frac{\$57.50 - \$22.79}{25.32} = \$1.37$$

and

$$\text{Premium payback period} = \frac{\$9.06}{\$1.37} = 6.6 \text{ years}$$

Without considering the time value of money, the investor would recover the market conversion premium per share assuming unchanged dividends in about 6.6 years.

Downside Risk with a Convertible Security

Investors usually use the straight value as a measure of the downside risk of a convertible security, because the price of the convertible security cannot fall below this value. Thus, the straight value acts as the *current* floor for the price of the convertible bond. The downside risk is measured as a percentage of the straight value and computed as follows:

$$\text{Premium over straight value} = \frac{\text{Market price of convertible security}}{\text{Straight value}} - 1$$

The higher the premium over straight value, all other factors constant, the less attractive the convertible security.

Despite its use in practice, this measure of downside risk is flawed because the straight value (the floor) changes as interest rates change. If interest rates rise (fall), the straight value falls (rises) making the floor fall (rise). Therefore, the downside risk changes as interest rates change.

For the GSX convertible issue, since the market price of the convertible security is 106.5 and the straight value is 98.19, the premium over straight value is

$$\text{Premium over straight value} = \frac{\$106.50}{\$98.19} - 1 = 0.085 = 8.5\%$$

The Upside Potential of a Convertible Security

The evaluation of the upside potential of a convertible security depends on the prospects for the underlying common stock. Thus, the techniques for analyzing common stocks discussed in books on equity analysis should be employed.

INVESTMENT CHARACTERISTICS OF A CONVERTIBLE SECURITY

The investment characteristics of a convertible security depend on the common stock price. If the price is low, so that the straight value is considerably higher than the conversion value, the security will trade much like a straight security. The convertible security in such instances is referred to as a *fixed income equivalent* or a *busted convertible*.

When the price of the stock is such that the conversion value is considerably higher than the straight value, then the convertible security will trade as if it were an equity instrument; in this case it is said to be a *common stock equivalent*. In such cases, the market conversion premium per share will be small.

Between these two cases, fixed income equivalent and common stock equivalent, the convertible security trades as a *hybrid security*, having the characteristics of both a fixed income security and a common stock instrument.

AN OPTION-BASED VALUATION APPROACH

In our discussion of convertible securities, we did not address the following questions:

1. What is a fair value for the conversion premium per share?
2. How do we handle convertible securities with call and/or put options?
3. How does a change in interest rates affect the stock price?

Consider first a noncallable/nonputable convertible security. The investor who purchases this security would be effectively entering into two separate transactions: (1) buying a noncallable/nonputable straight security and (2) buying a call option (or warrant) on the stock, where the number of shares that can be purchased with the call option is equal to the conversion ratio.

The question is: What is the fair value for the call option? The fair value depends on the factors discussed in Chapter 5 that affect the price of a call option. While the discussion in that chapter focused on options where the underlying is a fixed income instrument, the principles apply also to options on common stock. One key factor is the expected price volatility of the stock: the higher the expected price volatility, the greater the value of the call option. The theoretical value of a call option can be valued using the Black-Scholes option pricing model. This model is discussed in Chapter 13. As a first approximation to the value of a convertible security, the formula would be:

Convertible security value = Straight value + Value of the call option on the stock

The value of the call option is added to the straight value because the investor has purchased a call option on the stock.

Now let's add in a common feature of a convertible security: the issuer's right to call the security. The issuer can force conversion by calling the security. For example, suppose that the call price is 103 and the conversion value is 107. If the issuer calls the security, the optimal strategy for the investor is to convert the security and receive shares worth \$107.[2] The investor, however, loses any premium over the conversion value that is reflected in the market price. Therefore, the analysis of convertible securities must take into account the value of the issuer's right to call. This depends, in turn, on (1) future interest rate volatility and (2) economic factors that determine whether or not it is optimal for the issuer to call the security. The Black-Scholes option pricing model cannot handle this situation.

To link interest rates and stock prices together (the third question we raise above), statistical analysis of historical movements of these two variables must be estimated and incorporated into the model.

Valuation models based on an option pricing approach have been suggested by several researchers.[3] These models can generally be classified as one-factor or multi-factor models. As we explained in Chapter 3, by factor we mean the stochastic variables that are assumed to drive the value of a convertible security. The obvious candidates for factors are the price movement of the underlying common stock and the movement of interest rates. According to Mihir Bhattacharya and Yu Zhu, the most widely used convertible valuation model has been the one-factor model and the factor is the price movement of the underlying common stock.[4]

Specifically, the valuation model is based on the solution to a partial differential equation. The no arbitrage conditions that the convertible bond price must satisfy is:[5]

---

[2] Actually, the conversion value would be less than \$107 because the per share value after conversion would decline.

[3] See, for example: Michael Brennan and Eduardo Schwartz, "Convertible Bonds: Valuation and Optimal Strategies for Call and Conversion," *Journal of Finance* (December 1977), pp. 1699-1715; Jonathan Ingersoll, "A Contingent-Claims Valuation of Convertible Securities," *Journal of Financial Economics* (May 1977), pp. 289-322; Michael Brennan and Eduardo Schwartz, "Analyzing Convertible Bonds," *Journal of Financial and Quantitative Analysis* (November 1980), pp. 907-929; and, George Constantinides, "Warrant Exercise and Bond Conversion in Competitive Markets," *Journal of Financial Economics* (September 1984), pp. 371-398.

[4] Mihir Bhattacharya and Yu Zhu, "Valuation and Analysis of Convertible Securities," Chapter 42 in Frank J. Fabozzi (ed.), *The Handbook of Fixed Income Securities* (Chicago: Irwin Professional Publishing).

[5] Bhattacharya and Zhu, "Valuation and Analysis of Convertible Securities."

$$\frac{\delta V}{\delta t} + \frac{1}{2}\sigma^2 S^2 \frac{\delta^2 V}{\delta S^2} + rS\frac{\delta V}{\delta S} = rV$$

where

V = value of convertible bond = $V(S,t)$
S = price of the underlying stock
t = time
r = short rate
σ^2 = instantaneous variance of the stock price return

The characteristics of the issue such as the maturity, coupon rate, conversion ratio, call and put provisions, and changing conversion ratios and provisional call features are incorporated into the boundary conditions to solve the partial differential equation.

For the GSX convertible issue, the solution to the partial differential equation as of 10/7/93, assuming that the standard deviation of the stock price return is 17%, is 106.53. This value is equal to the actual market price at the time of 106.5 which suggests that the issue is fairly priced.

The difference between the value of the convertible bond as determined from the valuation model and the straight value (properly adjusted for the call option granted to the issuer and any put option) is the value of the embedded call option for the stock. That is,

Value of the embedded call option for underlying stock

= Theoretical value of convertible bond – Straight value

For the GSX convertible issue, since the theoretical value for the issue is 106.53 and the straight value is 98.19 (recall that this was not adjusted for the issuer's call option), the approximate value of the embedded call option for the underlying stock is 8.34.

The valuation model as applied to the GSX issue indicated that the issue was fairly priced. Exhibit 2 compares the theoretical value of Motorola's Liquid Yield Option Notes (LYONs)[6] to the actual market price of the convertible issue from the issue date (9/7/89) to 3/26/93. During this period, the price of Motorola's stock increased from $28\frac{1}{16}$ to $65\frac{1}{4}$. In January 1991, the market conversion premium ratio reached a high of 44%. The exhibit indicates that the valuation appears to track the market price well.

Because the inputs into the valuation model are not known with certainty, it is important to test the sensitivity of the model. As an example, the Merrill Lynch theoretical valuation model was used to value as of November 20, 1992 the Whirlpool Corporation zero-coupon bond due 5/14/11 (a LYON) assuming the

---

[6] LYON is a Merrill Lynch trademark name for zero-coupon convertible bonds that are both callable and putable.

following as a base case: a common stock price of $43⅝, volatility for the stock price of 25.21%, a constant dividend yield, a yield to maturity of 8.10%, and a yield to put of 6.98%. The theoretical value for the Whirlpool issue for this base case was $33.16.[7] The market price for this issue at the time was $33, so the issue appeared to be cheap relative to its theoretical value.

Tests of the sensitivity of the model to the base case inputs indicated the following for the theoretical value as of November 20, 1992 and also one year later by changing each input:

	Theoretical value (% change)			
	11/20/92		11/20/93	
Base case	$33.16		$33.33	
Stock volatility = 20%	32.67	–1.0%	33.07	0.2%
Stock price up 25%	39.52	19.8%	39.46	19.6%
Stock price down 25%	29.59	–10.3%	30.93	–6.3%
Interest rate down 100 bp	33.47	1.44%	33.66	1.9%
Interest rate up 100 bp	32.89	–0.3%	33.05	0.15%

The results for the stock volatility analysis indicate that if stock price volatility is 20% rather than the 25.21% assumed in the base case, the theoretical value as of November 20, 1992 would be less. This is expected since the value of a call option on a stock is lower the lower the expected stock price volatility. Thus, while the Whirlpool issue would be cheap relative to its market price of $33 if stock price volatility is 25.21%, it is expensive if stock price volatility is 20%.

Exhibit 2: Motorola LYONs: Market Price versus Theoretical Value (9/7/89 — 3/26/93)

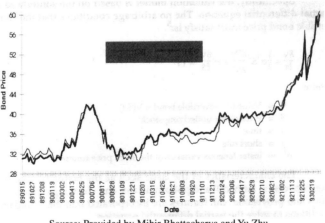

Source: Provided by Mihir Bhattacharya and Yu Zhu.

---

[7] Preston M. Harrington II, Bernie Moriarty, and Hareesh Paranjape, *LYONs Review*, November/December 1992 Quarterly Update, Merrill Lynch, Pierce, Fenner & Smith, Inc., p. 104.

Exhibit 3: Comparison of 1-Year Return for GSX Stock and Convertible Issue for Assumed Changes in Stock Price

Beginning of horizon: 10/7/93
End of horizon: 10/07/94
Price of GSX stock on 10/7/93: $33.00
Assumed volatility of GSX stock return: 17%

Stock price change (%)	GSX stock return (%)	Convertible's theoretical value	Convertible's return (%)
−25	−22.24	100.47	−0.16
−10	−7.24	102.96	2.14
0	2.73	105.27	4.27
10	12.76	108.12	6.90
25	27.76	113.74	12.08

THE RISK/RETURN PROFILE OF A CONVERTIBLE SECURITY

Let's use the GSX convertible issue and the valuation model to look at the risk/return profile by investing in a convertible issue or the underlying common stock.

Suppose on 10/7/93 an investor is considering the purchase of either the common stock of GSX or the 5¾% convertible issue due 6/1/02. The stock can be purchased in the market for $33. By buying the convertible bond, the investor is effectively purchasing the stock for $42.06 (the market conversion price per share). Exhibit 3 shows the total return for both alternatives one year later assuming (1) the stock price does not change, (2) it changes by ±10%, and (3) it changes by ±25%. The convertible's theoretical value is based on the Merrill Lynch valuation model.

If the GSX's stock price is unchanged, the stock position will underperform the convertible position despite the fact that a premium was paid to purchase the stock by acquiring the convertible issue. The reason is that even though the convertible's theoretical value decreased, the income from coupon more than compensates for the capital loss. In the two scenarios where the price of GSX declines, the convertible position outperforms the stock position because the straight value provides a floor for the convertible. In contrast, the stock position outperforms the convertible position in the two cases where the stock rises in price because of the premium paid to acquire the stock via the convertible's acquisition.

One of the critical assumptions in this analysis is that the straight value does not change except for the passage of time. If interest rates rise, the straight value will decline. Even if interest rates do not rise, the perceived creditworthiness of the issuer may deteriorate, causing investors to demand a higher yield. The illustration clearly demonstrates that there are benefits and drawbacks of investing in convertible securities. The disadvantage is the upside potential give-up because a premium per share must be paid. An advantage is the reduction in downside risk (as determined by the straight value).

KEY POINTS

1. *Convertible and exchangeable securities can be converted into shares of common stock.*

2. *The conversion ratio is the number of common stock shares for which a convertible security may be converted.*

3. *Almost all convertible securities are callable and some are putable.*

4. *The conversion value is the value of the convertible bond if it is immediately converted into the common stock.*

5. *The market conversion price is the price that an investor effectively pays for the common stock if the convertible security is purchased and then converted into the common stock.*

6. *The premium paid for the common stock is measured by the market conversion premium per share and market conversion premium ratio.*

7. *The straight value or investment value of a convertible security is its value if there was no conversion feature.*

8. *The minimum value of a convertible security is the greater of the conversion value and the straight value.*

9. *A fixed income equivalent (or a busted convertible) refers to the situation where the straight value is considerably higher than the conversion value so that the security will trade much like a straight security.*

10. *A common stock equivalent refers to the situation where the conversion value is considerably higher than the straight value so that the convertible security trades as if it were an equity instrument.*

11. *A hybrid equivalent refers to the situation where the convertible security trades with characteristics of both a fixed income security and a common stock instrument.*

12. *While the downside risk of a convertible security usually is estimated by calculating the premium over straight value, the limitation of this measure is that the straight value (the floor) changes as interest rates change.*

13. *An advantage of buying the convertible rather than the common stock is the reduction in downside risk.*

14. *The disadvantage of a convertible relative to the straight purchase of the common stock is the upside potential give-up because a premium per share must be paid.*

15. An option-based valuation model is a more appropriate approach to value convertible securities because of the multiple embedded options.

16. There are various option-based valuation models: one-factor and multiple-factor models.

17. The most common convertible bond valuation model is the one-factor model in which the one factor is the stock price return.

18. Incorporated into the boundary conditions to solve the partial differential equation to determine the theoretical value of a convertible bond are the characteristics of the issue such as the maturity, coupon rate, conversion ratio, call and put provisions, and changing conversion ratios and provisional call features.

19. Because the inputs into the valuation model are not known with certainty, it is important to test the sensitivity of the model to changes in these inputs.

20. A critical input of the valuation model is the volatility of the stock's return.

Chapter 12

Valuation of Interest Rate Futures Contracts

The objectives of this chapter are to:

1. describe what a futures contract is;

2. explain the differences between a futures contract and a forward contract;

3. describe basic features of several currently traded interest rate futures contracts;

4. explain for the Treasury bond futures contract what the cheapest-to-deliver issue is and how it is determined;

5. demonstrate how the theoretical price of a futures contract is determined;

6. show how the theoretical price of a Treasury bond futures contract is affected by the delivery options; and,

7. explain the complications in extending the standard arbitrage pricing model to the valuation of several currently traded interest rate futures contracts.

With the advent of interest rate futures, options, swaps, caps, and floors, risk management, in its broadest sense, has assumed a new dimension. It is now possible to alter the interest rate sensitivity of a bond portfolio or an asset/liability position economically and quickly. These *derivative contracts*, so called because they derive their value from an underlying asset, offer market participants risk and return patterns that previously were either unavailable or too costly to create. In this chapter, we focus on the valuation of interest rate futures contracts. The valuation of interest rate options, interest rate swaps, and interest rate caps and floors are explained in the next three chapters. While our focus is on valuation of these contracts, we provide a basic description of each contract. An explanation of the portfolio management applications is not provided in this book.

INTEREST RATE FUTURES CONTRACTS

A *futures contract* is a legal agreement between a buyer (seller) and an established exchange or its clearinghouse in which the buyer (seller) agrees to take (make) delivery of something at a specified price at the end of a designated period of time. The price at which the parties agree to transact in the future is called the *futures price*. The designated date at which the parties must transact is called the *settlement* or *delivery date*.

To illustrate, suppose there is a futures contract traded on an exchange where the something to be bought or sold is bond XYZ, and the settlement is three months from now. Assume further that Bob buys this futures contract, and Sally sells this futures contract, and the price at which they agree to transact in the future is $100. Then $100 is the futures price. At the settlement date, Sally will deliver bond XYZ to Bob. Bob will give Sally $100, the futures price.

Most financial futures contracts have settlement dates in the months of March, June, September, or December. This means that at a predetermined time in the contract settlement month the contract stops trading, and a price is determined by the exchange for settlement of the contract.

When an investor takes a position in the market by buying a futures contract, the investor is said to be in a *long position* or to be *long futures*. If, instead, the investor's opening position is the sale of a futures contract, the investor is said to be in a *short position* or *short futures*.

Role of the Clearinghouse

Associated with every futures exchange is a clearinghouse, which performs several functions. One of these functions is guaranteeing that the two parties to the transaction will perform. When an investor takes a position in the futures market, the clearinghouse takes the opposite position and agrees to satisfy the terms set forth in the contract. Because of the clearinghouse, the investor need not worry about the financial strength and integrity of the party taking the opposite side of the trade. After initial execution of an order, the relationship between the two parties ends. The clearinghouse interposes itself as the buyer for every sale and the seller for every purchase. Thus investors are free to liquidate their positions without involving the other party in the original contract, and without worry that the other party may default. This is the reason why we define a futures contract as an agreement between a party and a clearinghouse associated with an exchange.

Besides its guarantee function, the clearinghouse makes it simple for parties to a futures contract to unwind their positions prior to the settlement date.

Margin Requirements

When a position is first taken in a futures contract, the investor must deposit a minimum dollar amount per contract as specified by the exchange. This amount, which is called *initial margin*, is required as deposit for the contract.[1] The initial margin may be in the form of an interest-bearing security such as a Treasury bill. As the price of the futures contract fluctuates, the value of the investor's equity in the position changes. At the end of each trading day, the exchange determines the settlement price for the futures contract. This price is used to mark-to-market the investor's position, so that any gain or loss from the position is reflected in the investor's equity account.

Maintenance margin is the minimum level (specified by the exchange) to which an investor's equity position may fall as a result of an unfavorable price movement before the investor is required to deposit additional margin. The additional margin deposited is called *variation margin*, and it is an amount necessary to bring the equity in the account back to its initial margin level. Unlike initial margin, variation margin must be in cash, not interest-bearing instruments. Any excess margin in the account may be withdrawn by the investor. If a party to a futures contract who is required to deposit variation margin fails to do so within 24 hours, the futures position is closed out.

Although there are initial and maintenance margin requirements for buying securities on margin, the concept of margin differs for securities and futures. When securities are acquired on margin, the difference between the price of the security and the initial margin is borrowed from the broker. The security purchased serves as collateral for the loan, and the investor pays interest. For futures contracts, the initial margin, in effect, serves as "good faith" money, an indication that the investor will satisfy the obligation of the contract. Normally no money is borrowed by the investor.

FUTURES VERSUS FORWARD CONTRACTS

A *forward contract*, just like a futures contract, is an agreement for the future delivery of the underlying at a specified price at the end of a designated period of time. Futures contracts are standardized agreements as to the delivery date (or month) and quality

---

[1] Individual brokerage firms are free to set margin requirements above the minimum established by the exchange.

of the deliverable, and are traded on organized exchanges. A forward contract differs in that it is usually nonstandardized (that is, the terms of each contract are negotiated individually between buyer and seller), there is no clearinghouse, and secondary markets are often nonexistent or extremely thin. Unlike a futures contract, which is an exchange-traded product, a forward contract is an over-the-counter instrument.

Because there is no clearinghouse which guarantees the performance of a counterparty in a forward contract, the parties to a forward contract are exposed to *counterparty risk*. Counterparty risk is the risk that the other party to the transaction will fail to perform. That is, a party to a forward contract is exposed to credit or default risk.

Although both futures and forward contracts set forth terms of delivery, futures contracts are not intended to be settled by delivery. In fact, generally less than 2% of outstanding contracts are settled by delivery. Forward contracts, in contrast, are intended for delivery.

A futures contract is *marked-to-market* at the end of each trading day, while a forward contract may or may not be marked-to-market. Just how much variation margin may be required by one or both parties of a forward contract depends on the terms negotiated. Therefore, while a futures contract is subject to interim cash flows as additional margin may be required in the case of adverse price movements, or as cash is withdrawn in the case of favorable price movements, variation margin may or may not result from a forward contract.

Other than these differences, most of what we say about futures contracts applies to forward contracts.

CURRENTLY TRADED INTEREST RATE FUTURES CONTRACTS

The more actively traded interest rate futures contracts in the United States are described below. Most major financial markets outside of the United States have futures contracts in which the underlying is a fixed income security issued by the central government.

Treasury Bill Futures

The Treasury bill futures contract, which is traded on the International Monetary Market (IMM) of the Chicago Mercantile Exchange, is based on a 13-week (3-month) Treasury bill with a face value of $1 million. More specifically, the seller of a Treasury bill futures contract agrees to deliver to the buyer at the settlement date a Treasury bill with 13 weeks remaining to maturity and a face value of $1 million. The Treasury bill delivered can be newly issued or seasoned. The futures price is the price at which the Treasury bill will be sold by the short and purchased by the long. For example, a Treasury bill futures contract that settles in 9 months requires that 9 months from now the short deliver to the long $1 million face value of a Treasury bill with 13 weeks remaining to maturity. The Treasury bill could be a newly issued 13-week Treasury bill or a Treasury bill that was issued one year prior to the settlement date and therefore at the settlement date has only 13 weeks remaining to maturity.

Treasury bills are quoted in the cash market in terms of the annualized yield on a bank discount basis, where

$$Y_d = \frac{D}{F} \times \frac{360}{t}$$

where

Y_d = annualized yield on a bank discount basis (expressed as a decimal)
D = dollar discount, which is equal to the difference between the face value and the price of a bill maturing in t days
F = face value
t = number of days remaining to maturity.

The dollar discount (D) is found by:

$$D = Y_d \times F \times \frac{t}{360}$$

In contrast, the Treasury bill futures contract is quoted not directly in terms of yield, but instead on an index basis that is related to the yield on a bank discount basis as follows:

$$\text{Index price} = 100 - (Y_d \times 100)$$

For example, if Y_d is 8%, the index price is

$$100 - (0.08 \times 100) = 92$$

Given the price of the futures contract, the yield on a bank discount basis for the futures contract is determined as follows:

$$Y_d = \frac{100 - \text{Index price}}{100}$$

To see how this works, suppose that the index price for a Treasury bill futures contract is 92.52. The yield on a bank discount basis for this Treasury bill futures contract is:

$$Y_d = \frac{100 - 92.52}{100} = 0.0748 \text{ or } 7.48\%$$

The invoice price that the buyer of $1 million face value of 13-week Treasury bills must pay at settlement is found by first computing the dollar discount, as follows:

$$D = Y_d \times \$1,000,000 \times \frac{t}{360}$$

where t is either 90 or 91 days.

Typically, the number of days to maturity of a 13-week Treasury bill is 91 days. The invoice price is then:

Invoice price $= \$1,000,000 - D$

For example, for the Treasury bill futures contract with an index price of 92.52 (and a yield on a bank discount basis of 7.48%), the dollar discount for the 13-week Treasury bill to be delivered with 91 days to maturity is:

$$D = 0.0748 \times \$1,000,000 \times \frac{91}{360} = \$18,907.78$$

The invoice price is:

Invoice price $= \$1,000,000 - \$18,907.78 = \$981,092.22$

The minimum index price fluctuation or "tick" for this futures contract is 0.01. A change of 0.01 for the minimum index price translates into a change in the yield on a bank discount basis of 1 basis point (0.0001). A 1 basis point change results in a change in the invoice price as follows:

$$0.0001 \times \$1,000,000 \times \frac{t}{360}$$

For a 13-week Treasury bill with 91 days to maturity, the change in the dollar discount is:

$$0.0001 \times \$1,000,000 \times \frac{91}{360} = \$25.28$$

For a 13-week Treasury bill with 90 days to maturity, the change in the dollar discount would be $25. Despite the fact that a 13-week Treasury bill typically has 91 days to maturity, market participants commonly refer to the value of a basis point (or dollar value of an 01) for this futures contract as $25.

Eurodollar CD Futures

Eurodollar certificates of deposit (CDs) are denominated in dollars but represent the liabilities of banks outside the United States. The rate paid on Eurodollar CDs is the London interbank offered rate (LIBOR). The 3-month Eurodollar CD is the underlying instrument for the Eurodollar CD futures contract. The contracts are traded on both the International Monetary Market of the Chicago Mercantile Exchange and the London International Financial Futures Exchange.

As with the Treasury bill futures contract, this contract is for $1 million of face value and is traded on an index price basis. The index price basis in which the contract is quoted is equal to 100 minus the annualized futures LIBOR rate. For example, a Eurodollar CD futures price of 94.00 means a futures 3-month LIBOR rate of 6%.

The minimum price fluctuation (tick) for this contract is 0.01 (or 0.0001 in terms of LIBOR). This means that the price value of a basis point for this contract is $25, found as follows. The simple interest on $1 million for 90 days is equal to:

$$\$1,000,000 \times (\text{LIBOR} \times 90/360)$$

If LIBOR changes by one basis point (0.0001), then:

$$\$1,000,000 \times (0.0001 \times 90/360) = \$25$$

The Eurodollar CD futures contract is a cash settlement contract. That is, the parties settle in cash for the value of a Eurodollar CD based on LIBOR at the settlement date. The Eurodollar CD futures contract is one of the most heavily traded futures contract in the world. It is frequently used to trade the short end of the yield curve, and market participants have found this contract to be the best hedging vehicle for a wide range of hedging situations.

Treasury Bond Futures

The Treasury bond futures contract is traded on the Chicago Board of Trade (CBOT). The underlying instrument for a Treasury bond futures contract is $100,000 par value of a hypothetical 20-year 8% coupon bond. However, no such Treasury bond exists. Instead, the CBOT delivery rules allow one of several Treasury bond issues to be delivered. The choice of which Treasury bond issue to deliver from among those in the pool that may be delivered is given to the seller of the futures contract.

The CBOT has established criteria that a Treasury bond issue must satisfy in order to be acceptable for delivery. Specifically, an issue must have at least 15 years to maturity from the date of delivery if not callable; in the case of callable bonds, the issue must not be callable for at least 15 years from the first day of the delivery month. Exhibit 1 shows the 30 Treasury bond issues that the seller can select from to deliver to the buyer of the June 1997 futures contract.

The futures price is quoted in terms of par value being 100. Quotes are in 32nds of 1%. Thus a quote for a Treasury bond futures contract of 108-23 means 108 and 23/32nds, or 108.71875. So, if a buyer and seller agree on a futures price of 108-23, this means that the buyer agrees to accept delivery of the hypothetical underlying Treasury bond and pay 108.71875% of par value and the seller agrees to accept 108.71875% of par value. Since the par value is $100,000, the futures price that the buyer and seller agree to pay for this hypothetical Treasury bond is $108,718.75.

The minimum price fluctuation for the Treasury bond futures contract is a 32nd of 1%. The dollar value of a 32nd for a $100,000 par value (the par value for the underlying Treasury bond) is $31.25. Thus, the minimum price fluctuation is $31.25 for this contract.

Exhibit 1: Treasury Bond Issues Acceptable for Delivery to Satisfy the June 1997 Futures Contract

Issue		Conversion
Coupon (%)	Maturity	Factor
6.625	2/15/27	0.8451
6.500	11/15/26	0.8312
6.750	8/15/26	0.8598
6.000	2/15/26	0.7767
6.875	8/15/25	0.8750
7.625	2/15/25	0.9585
7.500	11/15/24	0.9447
6.250	8/15/23	0.8097
7.125	2/15/23	0.9054
7.625	11/15/22	0.9594
7.250	8/15/22	0.9194
8.000	11/15/22	0.9998
8.125	8/15/21	1.0132
8.125	5/15/21	1.0130
7.875	2/15/21	0.9868
8.750	8/15/20	1.0783
8.750	5/15/20	1.0778
8.500	2/15/20	1.0518
8.125	8/15/19	1.0128
8.875	2/15/19	1.0891
9.000	11/15/18	1.1012
9.125	5/15/18	1.1128
8.875	8/15/17	1.0866
8.750	5/15/17	1.0736
7.500	11/15/16	0.9511
7.250	5/15/16	0.9276
9.250	2/15/16	1.1196
9.875	11/15/15	1.1781
10.625	8/15/15	1.2482
11.250	2/15/15	1.3033

Conversion Factor and Converted Price

The delivery process for the Treasury bond futures contract makes the contract interesting. At the settlement date, the seller of a futures contract (the short) is required to deliver to the buyer (the long) $100,000 par value of an 8% 20-year Treasury bond. Since no such bond exists, the seller must choose from one of the acceptable deliverable Treasury bonds that the CBOT exchange has specified. Suppose the seller is entitled to deliver $100,000 of a 6% 20-year Treasury bond to settle the futures contract. The value of this bond, of course, is less than the value of an 8% 20-year bond. If the seller delivers the 6% 20-year, this would be unfair to the buyer of the futures contract who contracted to receive $100,000 of an 8% 20-year Treasury bond. Alternatively, suppose the seller delivers $100,000 of a

10% 20-year Treasury bond. The value of a 10% 20-year Treasury bond is greater than that of an 8% 20-year bond, so this would be a disadvantage to the seller.

How can this problem be resolved? To make delivery equitable to both parties, the CBOT introduced *conversion factors* for determining the price of each acceptable deliverable Treasury issue if an issue is delivered to satisfy the Treasury bond futures contract. The conversion factor is determined by the CBOT before a contract with a specific settlement date begins trading. Exhibit 2 shows for each of the acceptable Treasury issues the corresponding conversion factor. The conversion factor is based on the price that a deliverable bond would sell for at the beginning of the delivery month if it were to yield 8%. The conversion factor is constant throughout the trading period of the futures contract.

The product of the settlement price and the conversion factor for a deliverable issue is called the *converted price*. The amount that the buyer must pay the seller when a Treasury bond is delivered is called the *invoice price*. The invoice price is the settlement futures price plus accrued interest. However, as just noted, the seller can deliver one of several acceptable Treasury issues. To make delivery fair to both parties, the invoice price must be adjusted based on the actual Treasury issue delivered. It is the conversion factor that is used to adjust the invoice price. The invoice price is:

Invoice price = Contract size × Futures contract settlement price
× Conversion factor + Accrued interest

Suppose that the June 1997 Treasury bond futures contract settles at 108-16 and that the issue delivered is the 11.25s of 2/15/15. The futures contract settlement price of 108-16 means 108.5% of par value or 1.085 times par value As indicated in Exhibit 1, the conversion factor for this issue is 1.3033. Since the contract size is $100,000, the invoice price the buyer pays the seller is:

$100,000 × 1.085 × 1.3033 + Accrued interest
= $141,408.05 + Accrued interest

If, instead, the 6.625s of 2/15/27 which has a conversion factor of 0.8451 is delivered, the invoice price would be:

$100,000 × 1.085 × 0.8451 + Accrued interest
= $91,693.35 + Accrued interest

Cheapest-to-Deliver Issue

In selecting the issue to be delivered, the short will select from among all the deliverable issues the one that will give the largest rate of return from a *cash and carry trade*. A cash and carry trade is one in which a cash bond that is acceptable for delivery is purchased and simultaneously the Treasury bond futures contract is sold. The bond purchased can be delivered to satisfy the short futures position. Thus, by buying the Treasury bond issue that is acceptable for delivery and selling the futures, an investor has effectively sold the bond at the delivery price (i.e., converted price).

A rate of return can be calculated for this trade. The rate of return is determined by:

1. the price plus accrued interest of the Treasury bond that could be purchased
2. the converted price plus the accrued interest that will be received upon delivery of that Treasury bond issue to satisfy the short futures position
3. the coupon payments that will be received between today and the delivery date
4. the reinvestment income that will be realized on the coupon payments between the time received and the delivery date.

The first three elements are known. The last element, reinvestment income, depends on the rate that can be earned on any interim coupon payments. What is assumed is that this rate is the prevailing term repo rate where the term is the number of days between receipt of the interim coupon payment and the bond delivery.

The annual rate of return on the cash and carry trade is calculated as follows:[2]

$$\text{Annual return} = \frac{\text{Dollar return}}{\text{Purchase Price} + \text{Accrued Interest Paid}} \times \frac{360}{\text{Days}_1}$$

where

Proceeds at settlement date
= Converted price + Accrued interest received + Interim coupon payment + Interest from reinvesting interim coupon payment

Converted price = Futures price × Conversion factor

Interest from reinvesting interim coupon payment
= Interim coupon × [1 + term repo rate × (Days$_2$/360)]

Days$_2$ = Number of days between interim coupon payment and actual delivery date

Days$_1$ = Number of days between settlement date and actual delivery

Dollar return = Proceeds at settlement date − Purchase price − Accrued interest paid

---

[2] The formula can be modified to allow for the fact that the interim coupon payment reduces the amount invested (the denominator of the first term). The modified formula is:

$$\text{Annual return} = \frac{\text{Dollar return}}{\text{Adjusted investment cost}} \times 360$$

where
Adjusted investment cost = Days$_1$(Purchase price + Accrued interest paid) − Days$_2$(Interim coupon payment)

Exhibit 2: Determination of Cheapest-to-Deliver Issue Based on the Implied Repo Rate

Implied repo rate: Rate of return by buying an acceptable Treasury issue, shorting the Treasury bond futures, and delivering the issue at the settlement date.

Buy this issue:	Deliver this issue at futures price:	Calculate return (implied repo rate):
Acceptable Treasury issue #1	Deliver issue #1	Implied repo rate #1
Acceptable Treasury issue #2	Deliver issue #2	Implied repo rate #2
Acceptable Treasury issue #3	Deliver issue #3	Implied repo rate #3
. . .	. . .	. . .
Acceptable Treasury issue #N	Deliver issue #N	Implied repo rate #N

Cheapest-to-deliver issue is the issue that produces the maximum implied repo rate.

The annual rate of return calculated for an acceptable Treasury issue is called the *implied repo rate*. Market participants will seek to maximize the implied repo rate; that is, they will use the acceptable Treasury issue that gives the largest rate of return in the cash and carry trade. The issue that satisfies this criterion is referred to as the *cheapest-to-deliver issue*. This is depicted in Exhibit 2. The cheapest-to-deliver issue plays a key role in the pricing of this futures contract.

Exhibit 3 shows the implied repo rate on March 25, 1997 for each deliverable issue to satisfy the June 1997 futures contract. The highest implied repo rate is 5.25% for the 11.25% 2/15/15 issue. Therefore, it is this issue that is the cheapest-to-deliver issue.

While an issue may be the cheapest to deliver today, changes in factors may cause some other issue to be the cheapest to deliver at a future date. A sensitivity analysis can be performed to determine how a change in yield affects the cheapest to deliver.[3] For the June 1997 futures contract, the 11.25% 2/15/15 issue

---

[3] This information was obtained from a printout provided by the Futures Basis Matic (FB)v7 of the Fixed Income Research Department of Goldman, Sachs & Co. The analysis is as of 3/25/97 based on a futures price of 108-23.

would remain the cheapest to deliver if yields decreased. For a rise in yields, the
cheapest-to-deliver issue would be as follows:

Yield change	Cheapest-to-deliver issue	
+20 basis points	10.625%	8/15/15
+40 basis points	8.875%	8/15/17
+60 basis point	8.875%	2/15/19
+80 basis point	8.125%	8/15/21

Exhibit 3: The Implied Repo Rate on March 25, 1997 for the Treasury Bond Issues Acceptable for Delivery to Satisfy the June 1997 Futures Contract[*]

Issue		Implied
Coupon (%)	Maturity	Repo Rate (%)
6.625	2/15/27	−8.48
6.500	11/15/26	−6.19
6.750	8/15/26	−4.28
6.000	2/15/26	−4.29
6.875	8/15/25	−2.76
7.625	2/15/25	−1.51
7.500	11/15/24	−1.26
6.250	8/15/23	−1.59
7.125	2/15/23	−0.17
7.625	11/15/22	0.52
7.250	8/15/22	0.54
8.000	11/15/22	1.51
8.125	8/15/21	1.81
8.125	5/15/21	1.90
7.875	2/15/21	1.81
8.750	8/15/20	2.61
8.750	5/15/20	2.67
8.500	2/15/20	2.74
8.125	8/15/19	2.76
8.875	2/15/19	3.47
9.000	11/15/19	3.47
9.125	5/15/18	3.66
8.875	8/15/17	4.09
8.750	5/15/17	4.03
7.500	11/15/16	3.36
7.250	5/15/16	3.06
9.250	2/15/16	4.63
9.875	11/15/15	4.83
10.625	8/15/15	5.10
11.250	2/15/15	5.25

* Calculation of the implied repo rate for these issues was provided by the Futures Basis Matic (FB)v7 of
the Fixed Income Research Department of Goldman, Sachs & Co. The analysis is as of 3/25/97 based on a
futures price of 108-23.

Exhibit 4: Delivery Options Granted to the Short (Seller) of a CBOT Treasury Bond Futures Contract

Delivery option	Description
Quality or swap option	Choice of which acceptable Treasury issue to deliver
New auction option	Choice of a newly issued Treasury bond to deliver
Timing option	Choice of when in delivery month to deliver
Wild card option	Choice to deliver after the day's settlement price for the futures contract is determined

Delivery Options

In addition to the choice of which acceptable Treasury issue to deliver — sometimes referred to as the *quality option* or *swap option* — the short position has three more options granted under CBOT delivery guidelines. The first is related to the quality option. If a Treasury bond is auctioned prior to the settlement date, then the short can select this new issue. This option is referred to as the *new auction option*. The second option grants the short the right to decide when in the delivery month delivery actually will take place. This is called the *timing option*. The third option is the right of the short to give notice of intent to deliver up to 8:00 p.m. Chicago time after the closing of the exchange (3:15 p.m. Chicago time) on the date when the futures settlement price has been fixed. This option is referred to as the *wild card option*. The quality option, the new auction option, the timing option, and the wild card option (in sum referred to as the *delivery options*), mean that the long can never be sure which Treasury bond will be delivered or when it will be delivered. The delivery options are summarized in Exhibit 4.

For a short who wants to deliver, the delivery procedure involves three days. The first day is the *position day*. On this day, the short notifies the CBOT that it intends to deliver. The short has until 8:00 p.m. central standard time to do so. The second day is the *notice day*. On this day, the short specifies which particular issue will be delivered. The short has until 2:00 p.m. central standard time to make this declaration. (On the last possible notice day in the delivery month, the short has until 3:00 p.m.) The CBOT then selects the long to whom delivery will be made. This is the longest outstanding long position. The long is then notified by 4:00 p.m. that delivery will be made. The third day is the *delivery day*. By 10:00 a.m. on this day the short must have in its account the Treasury issue that it specified on the notice day and by 1:00 p.m. must deliver that bond to the long that was assigned by the CBOT to accept delivery. The long pays the short the invoice price upon receipt of the bond.

Treasury Note Futures

There are three Treasury note futures contracts: 10-year, 5-year, and 2-year. All three contracts are modeled after the Treasury bond futures contract and are traded on the CBOT. The underlying instrument for the 10-year Treasury note futures contract is $100,000 par value of a hypothetical 10-year 8% Treasury note. There are several acceptable Treasury issues that may be delivered by the short. An issue is acceptable if the maturity is not less than 6.5 years and not greater than 10 years from the first day of the delivery month. The delivery options granted to the short position and the minimum price fluctuation are the same as for the Treasury bond futures contract.

For the 5-year Treasury note futures contract, the underlying is $100,000 par value of a U.S. Treasury note that satisfies the following conditions: (1) an original maturity of not more than five years and three months, (2) a remaining maturity no greater then five years and three months, and (3) a remaining maturity not less than four years and three months. The minimum price fluctuation for this contract is a 64th of 1%. The dollar value of a 64th for a $100,000 par value is $15.625 and is therefore the minimum price fluctuation.

The underlying for the 2-year Treasury note futures contract is $200,000 par value of a U.S. Treasury note with a remaining maturity of not more than two years and not less than one year and nine months. Moreover, the original maturity of the note delivered to satisfy the 2-year futures cannot be more than five years and two months. The minimum price fluctuation for this contract is a 128th of 1%. The dollar value of a 128th for a $200,000 par value is $15.625 and is therefore the minimum price fluctuation.

Bond Buyer's Municipal Bond Index Futures

Traded on the CBOT, the underlying product for the Bond Buyer's Municipal Bond Index Futures contract is a basket, or index, of 40 municipal bonds. The Bond Buyer, publisher of *The Bond Buyer* (a trade publication of the municipal bond industry), serves as the index manager for the contract and prices each bond in the index based on prices received between 1:30 and 2:00 p.m. (central standard time) from five municipal bond brokers. It is necessary to obtain several independent prices from brokers because municipal bonds trade in the over-the-counter market.

Once the prices are received from the five pricing brokers for a given issue, the lowest and the highest prices are dropped. The remaining three prices then are averaged, and the resulting value is referred to as the appraisal value. The appraisal value for each issue then is divided by a conversion factor that equates the bond to an 8% issue. This gives a converted price for each issue. The converted prices then are summed and divided by 40, for an average converted price on the index. The index is revised bimonthly, when newer issues are added, and older issues or issues that no longer meet the criteria for inclusion in the index are dropped. A smoothing coefficient is calculated on the index revision date so that the index will not change merely because of changes in the composition of the index. The average converted dollar price for the index is multiplied by this coefficient to get the index value for a particular date.

As delivery on all 40 bonds in the index is not possible, the contract is a cash settlement contract, with settlement price based on the value of the index on the delivery date. The contract is quoted in points and 32nds of a point. For example, suppose the settlement price for the contract is 93-21. This translates into a price of 93 and 21/32, or 93.65635. The dollar value of a contract is equal to $1,000 times the Bond Buyer Municipal Bond Index. For example, the dollar value based on the settlement price is $93,656.35 (= $1,000 × 93.65635).

VALUATION

One of the primary concerns that most traders and investors have when taking a position in futures contracts is whether the futures price at which they transact will be a "fair" price. Buyers are concerned that the price may be too high, and that they will be picked off by more experienced futures traders waiting to profit from the mistakes of the uninitiated. Sellers worry that the price is artificially low, and that savvy traders may have manipulated the markets so that they can buy at bargain basement prices. Furthermore, prospective participants frequently find no rational explanation for the sometimes violent ups and downs that occur in the futures markets. Theories about efficient markets give little comfort to anyone who knows of or has experienced the sudden losses that can occur in the highly leveraged futures markets.

Fortunately, the futures markets are not as irrational as they may at first seem; if they were, they would not have become so successful. The interest rate futures markets are not perfectly efficient markets, but they probably come about as close as any market. Furthermore, there are both very clear reasons why futures prices are what they are and methods by which traders, investors, and borrowers can and will quickly eliminate any discrepancy between futures prices and their fair levels.

To understand how futures contracts are valued, consider the following example. Suppose that a 12% 20-year bond is selling at par. Also suppose that this bond is the deliverable for a futures contract that settles in three months. If the current 3-month interest rate at which funds can be loaned or borrowed is 8% per year, what should be the price of this futures contract?

Suppose the price of the futures contract is 107. Consider the following strategy:

Sell the futures contract at 107.
Purchase the bond for 100.
Borrow 100 for 3 months at 8% per year.

The borrowed funds are used to purchase the bond, resulting in no initial cash outlay for this strategy. Three months from now, the bond must be delivered to settle the futures contract and the loan must be repaid. These transactions will produce the following cash flows:

From settlement of the futures contract:

Flat price of bond	=	107
Accrued interest (12% for 3 months)	=	3
Total proceeds	=	110

From the loan:

Repayment of principal of loan	=	100
Interest on loan (8% for 3 months)	=	2
Total outlay	=	102

Profit = Total proceeds – Total outlay	=	8

This strategy will guarantee a profit of 8. Moreover, the profit is generated with no initial outlay because the funds used to purchase the bond are borrowed. The profit will be realized *regardless of the futures price at the settlement date*. Obviously, in a well-functioning market, arbitrageurs would buy this bond and sell the futures contract, forcing the futures price down and bidding up this bond's price so as to eliminate this profit.

In contrast, suppose that the futures price is 92 instead of 107. Consider the following strategy:

Buy the futures contract at 92.
Sell (short) the bond for 100.
Invest (lend) 100 for 3 months at 8% per year.

Once again, there is no initial cash outlay. Three months from now this bond will be purchased to settle the long position in the futures contract. That bond will then be used to cover the short position (i.e. to cover the short sale in the cash market). The outcome in three months would be as follows:

From settlement of the futures contract:

Flat price of bond	=	92
Accrued interest (12% for 3 months)	=	3
Total outlay	=	95

From the loan:

Principal received from maturing investment	=	100
Interest earned (8% for 3 months)	=	2
Total proceeds	=	102

Profit = Total proceeds – Total outlay	=	7

The profit of 7 is a pure arbitrage profit. It requires no initial cash outlay and will be realized regardless of the futures price at the settlement date.

There is a futures price that will eliminate the arbitrage profit. There will be no arbitrage if the futures price is 99. Let's look at what would happen if the two previous strategies are followed and the futures price is 99. First, consider the following strategy:

> Sell the futures contract at 99.
> Purchase the bond for 100.
> Borrow 100 for 3 months at 8% per year.

In three months, the outcome would be as follows:

From settlement of the futures contract:		
Flat price of bond	=	99
Accrued interest (12% for 3 months)	=	3
Total proceeds	=	102
From the loan:		
Repayment of principal of loan	=	100
Interest on loan (8% for 3 months)	=	2
Total outlay	=	102
Profit = Total proceeds − Total outlay	=	0

There is no arbitrage profit in this case.

> Next consider the following strategy:

> Buy the futures contract at 99.
> Sell (short) the bond for 100.
> Invest (lend) 100 for 3 months at 8% per year.

The outcome in three months would be as follows:

From settlement of the futures contract:		
Flat price of bond	=	99
Accrued interest (12% for 3 months)	=	3
Total outlay	=	102
From the loan:		
Principal received from maturing investment	=	100
Interest earned (8% for 3 months)	=	2
Total proceeds	=	102
Total proceeds − Total outlay = Profit	=	0

Thus neither strategy results in a profit. Hence the futures price of 99 is the theoretical price, because any higher or lower futures price will permit arbitrage profits.

Theoretical Futures Price Based on Arbitrage Model

Considering the arbitrage arguments just presented, the theoretical futures price can be determined on the basis of the following information:

1. The price of the bond in the cash market.
2. The coupon rate on the bond. In our example, the coupon rate is 12% per year.
3. The interest rate for borrowing and lending until the settlement date. The borrowing and lending rate is referred to as the *financing rate*. In our example, the financing rate is 8% per year.

We will let

r = annualized financing rate (%)

c = annualized current yield, or annual coupon rate divided by the cash market price (%)

P = cash market price

F = futures price

t = time, in years, to the futures delivery date

and then consider the following strategy that is initiated on a coupon date:

Sell the futures contract at F.
Purchase the bond for P.
Borrow P at r until the settlement date.

The outcome at the settlement date is

From settlement of the futures contract:

Flat price of bond	=	F
Accrued interest	=	ctP
Total proceeds	=	$F + ctP$

From the loan:

Repayment of principal of loan	=	P
Interest on loan	=	rtP
Total outlay	=	$P + rtP$

The profit will equal:

Profit = Total proceeds − Total outlay

Profit = $F + ctP - (P + rtP)$

In equilibrium the theoretical futures price occurs where the profit from this strategy is zero. Thus to have equilibrium, the following must hold:

$$0 = F + ctP - (P + rtP)$$

Solving for the theoretical futures price, we have

$$F = P + Pt(r - c) \tag{1}$$

Alternatively, consider the following strategy:

Buy the futures contract at F.
Sell (short) the bond for P.
Invest (lend) P at r until the settlement date.

The outcome at the settlement date would be

From settlement of the futures contract:

Flat price of bond	$=$	F
Accrued interest	$=$	ctP
Total outlay	$=$	$\overline{F + ctP}$

From the loan:

Proceeds received from maturing of investment	$=$	P
Interest earned	$=$	rtP
Total proceeds	$=$	$\overline{P + rtP}$

The profit will equal:

Profit = Total proceeds − Total outlay

Profit = $P + rtP - (F + ctP)$

Setting the profit equal to zero so that there will be no arbitrage profit and solving for the futures price, we obtain the same equation for the futures price as equation (1).

Let's apply equation (1) to our previous example in which

$$r = 0.08$$
$$c = 0.12$$
$$P = 100$$
$$t = 0.25$$

Then the theoretical futures price is

$$F = 100 + 100 \times 0.25(0.08 - 0.12) = 100 - 1 = 99$$

This is the futures price that we found earlier will produce no arbitrage profit.

The theoretical price may be at a premium to the cash market price (higher than the cash market price) or at a discount from the cash market price (lower than the cash market price), depending on $(r - c)$. The term $r - c$ is called the *net financing cost* because it adjusts the financing rate for the coupon interest earned. The net financing cost is more commonly called the *cost of carry*, or simply *carry*. *Positive carry* means that the current yield earned is greater than the financing cost; *negative carry* means that the financing cost exceeds the current yield. The relationships can be expressed as follows:

Carry	Theoretical futures price
Positive ($c>r$)	will sell at a discount to cash price ($F<P$)
Negative ($c<r$)	will sell at a premium to cash price ($F>P$)
Zero ($c=r$)	will be equal to cash price ($F=P$)

In the case of interest rate futures, carry (the relationship between the short-term financing rate and the current yield on the bond) depends on the shape of the yield curve. When the yield curve is upward sloping, the short-term financing rate will be less than the current yield on the bond, resulting in positive carry. The theoretical futures price will then sell at a discount to the cash price for the bond. The opposite will hold true when the yield curve is inverted.

Adjustments to the Theoretical Pricing Model

Several assumptions were made to derive the theoretical futures price using the arbitrage argument. Below we discuss these assumptions and explain the implications for the theoretical futures price.

Interim Cash Flows

No interim cash flows due to variation margin or coupon interest payments were assumed in the model. However, for Treasury futures contracts we know that interim cash flows can occur for both of these reasons. Consider first variation margin. If interest rates rise, the short position in a Treasury futures contract will receive margin as the futures price decreases; the margin can then be reinvested at a higher interest rate. If interest rates fall, there will be variation margin that must be financed by the short position; however, because interest rates have declined, financing will be possible at a lower cost.

Incorporating interim coupon payments into the pricing model is not difficult. However, the value of the coupon payments at the settlement date will depend on the interest rate at which they can be reinvested. The shorter the maturity of the contract and the lower the coupon rate, the less important the reinvestment income is in determining the theoretical futures price.

Difference in Borrowing and Lending Rates

In deriving the theoretical futures price it is assumed that the borrowing and lending rates are equal. Typically, however, the borrowing rate is higher than the lending rate.

We will let

r_B = borrowing rate
r_L = lending rate

Consider the following strategy:

- Sell the futures contract at F.
- Purchase the bond for P.
- Borrow P at r_B until the settlement date.

The futures price that would produce no arbitrage profit is

$$F = P + Pt(r_B - c) \tag{2}$$

Now consider the following strategy:

- Buy the futures contract at F.
- Sell (short) the bond for P.
- Invest (lend) P at r_L until the settlement date.

The futures price that would produce no profit is

$$F = P + Pt(r_L - c) \tag{3}$$

Equations (2) and (3) together provide boundaries for the theoretical futures price. Equation (2) provides the upper boundary and equation (3) the lower boundary. For example, assume that the borrowing rate is 8% per year while the lending rate is 6% per year. Then using equation (2) and the previous example, the upper boundary is

$$F(\text{upper boundary}) = \$100 + \$100 \times 0.25(0.08 - 0.12) = \$99$$

The lower boundary using equation (3) is

$$F(\text{lower boundary}) = \$100 + \$100 \times 0.25(0.06 - 0.12) = \$98.50$$

In calculating these boundaries, we assume no transaction costs are involved in taking the position. In actuality, the transaction costs of entering into and closing the cash position as well as the round-trip transaction costs for the futures contract must be considered and do affect the boundaries for the futures contract.

Uncertainty About Deliverable Issue

Another assumption made to derive equation (1) is that only one instrument is deliverable. But the futures contract on Treasury bonds and Treasury notes are designed to allow the short the choice of delivering one of a number of deliverable issues (the quality or swap option). Because there may be more than one deliverable, as explained earlier market participants track the price of each deliverable bond and determine which bond is the cheapest to deliver. The theoretical futures price will then trade in relation to the cheapest-to-deliver issue.

There is the risk that while an issue may be the cheapest to deliver at the time a position in the futures contract is taken, it may not be the cheapest to deliver after that time. Earlier we explained how the cheapest-to-deliver issue was determined. We saw that for the June 1997 Treasury bond futures contract the cheapest-to-deliver issue was the 11.25% 2/15/15 issue. Moreover, we showed how if yields increase the cheapest-to-deliver issue would change.

A change in the cheapest-to-deliver issue can dramatically alter the theoretical futures price. For this reason, many market participants use more than just the cheapest-to-deliver issue in valuing a Treasury futures contract. Market participants who do take this approach have developed proprietary models for selecting the package of issues from the deliverable pool. For example, Goldman, Sachs uses at a minimum one noncallable and one callable Treasury bond. For the June 1997 Treasury bond futures contract, the issues used for valuing the futures contract on March 25, 1997 were the noncallable 11.25% 2/15/15 (which was the cheapest to deliver) and the callable 8.75% 11/15/03.

Because the quality option is an option granted by the long to the short, the long will want to pay less for the futures contract than indicated by equation (1). Therefore, as a result of the quality option, the theoretical futures price as given by equation (1) must be adjusted as follows:

$$F = P + Pt(r - c) - \text{Value of quality option} \qquad (4)$$

Market participants have employed theoretical models in attempting to estimate the fair value of the quality option.

Delivery Date Is Not Known

In the pricing model based on arbitrage arguments, a known delivery date is assumed. For Treasury bond and note futures contracts, the short has a timing and wild card option, so the long does not know when the securities will be delivered. The effect of the timing and wild card options on the theoretical futures price is the same as with the quality option. These delivery options should result in a theoretical futures price that is lower than the one suggested in equation (1), as shown below:

$$F = P + Pt(r - c) - \text{Value of quality option} \qquad (5)$$
$$- \text{Value of timing option} - \text{Value of wildcard option}$$

or alternatively,

$$F = P + Pt(r - c) - \text{Delivery options} \qquad (6)$$

Market participants attempt to value the delivery option in order to apply equation (6).[4]

---

[4] Alex Kane and Alan Marcus, "Valuation and Optimal Exercise of the Wild Card Option in the Treasury Bond Futures Market," *Journal of Finance* (March 1986), pp. 195-207.

Deliverable is Not a Basket of Securities

The municipal bond index futures contract is a cash settlement contract based on a basket of securities. The difficulty in arbitraging this futures contract is that it is too expensive to buy or sell every bond included in the index. Instead, a portfolio including a smaller number of bonds may be constructed to "track" the index. The arbitrage, however, is no longer risk free because there is tracking risk.

Tax Factors

The model completely ignores tax factors. Tax complications arise in the arbitrage in several ways. First, the tax treatment of the capital gain from a futures contract is different from that of the treatment of the capital gain for a cash market security. Second, consider an investor who finds the municipal bond index futures contract is expensive relative to the cash market. To capitalize on this, the investor would sell the futures contract and buy the underlying bonds. The interest earned by carrying the municipal bonds would be interest free. However, the investor must finance the long position in the municipal bonds by borrowing funds. But, under the current tax law, investors are not entitled to deduct the interest paid to carry a position in municipal bonds. Thus, the interest received is not taxed but the interest paid is not tax deductible. The model must be modified to take this into account.

KEY POINTS

1. *A futures contract is a firm legal agreement between a buyer (seller) and an established exchange or its clearinghouse in which the buyer (seller) agrees to take (make) delivery of something at the futures price at the settlement or delivery date.*

2. *A party to a futures contract must comply with margin requirements (initial, maintenance, and variation margin).*

3. *A forward contract differs from a futures contract in that it is usually nonstandardized (that is, the terms of each contract are negotiated individually between buyer and seller), there is no clearinghouse, and secondary markets are often nonexistent or extremely thin.*

4. *Regardless of how rates move, those who are short futures gain relative to those who are short forwards that are not marked-to-market; those who are long futures lose relative to those who are long forwards that are not marked-to-market.*

5. *Currently traded interest rate futures contracts in the United States include Treasury bill futures, Eurodollar CD futures, Treasury bond and note futures, and the Bond Buyer municipal index futures.*

6. *The theoretical price of a futures contract is equal to the cash or spot price plus the cost of carry.*

7. *The cost of carry is equal to the cost of financing the position less the cash yield on the underlying security.*

8. *The shape of the yield curve affects the cost of carry.*

9. *The simple arbitrage model must be modified to take into consideration the nuances of particular contracts.*

10. *For a Treasury bond futures contract, there are delivery options (the quality option, the timing option, and the wild-card option) granted to the short.*

11. *The quality option or swap option grants the short the right to select which Treasury bond to deliver.*

12. *To make delivery equitable to both parties of a Treasury bond futures contract, the exchange specifies conversion factors for determining the invoice price of each Treasury issue that may be delivered.*

13. *In selecting the issue to be delivered, the short will select from all the deliverable issues the one that is cheapest to deliver.*

14. *The implied repo rate is the rate of return that would be earned by buying an acceptable Treasury issue and delivering it to settle the Treasury bond futures contract.*

15. *The cheapest-to-deliver issue is the issue among all acceptable Treasury issues with the highest implied repo rate; the Treasury bond futures and the futures price will then trade in relation to the cheapest-to-deliver issue.*

16. *The cheapest-to-deliver issue may change, resulting in a dramatic change in the futures price.*

17. *For a Treasury bond futures contract, the delivery options granted to the seller reduce the theoretical futures price below the theoretical futures price suggested by the simple arbitrage model.*

18. *Determining the theoretical value of the municipal bond futures contract is complicated by the fact that it is too expensive to buy or sell every bond included in the index, resulting in tracking error.*

19. *Tax factors must be considered in valuing futures contracts, particularly in the case of municipal bond futures contracts.*

Chapter 13

Valuation of Options on Fixed Income Instruments and Interest Rate Futures

The objectives of this chapter are to:

1. *explain the Black-Scholes model for valuing options on fixed income instruments;*

2. *demonstrate the limitations of applying the Black-Scholes model to price options on fixed income instruments;*

3. *explain the arbitrage-free binomial model for valuing options on fixed income instruments;*

4. *explain the Black model for valuing options on interest rate futures;*

5. *describe the various measures for estimating the sensitivity of the option price to changes in factors affecting the value of an option (delta, gamma, theta, and kappa); and,*

6. *explain how the duration of an option is estimated.*

In this chapter we look at how to value options in which the underlying is a fixed income instrument or an interest rate futures contract. Since we described options in Chapter 5, it is not necessary to review the basic features of options here. We begin with a description of a popular option pricing model used in the equity market and explain its limitations in valuing options on fixed income instruments. We then show how the arbitrage-free binomial model described in Chapter 6 can be applied to value options on fixed income instruments. The Black model for valuing options on interest rate futures is then explained.

BLACK-SCHOLES MODEL FOR VALUING OPTIONS ON FIXED INCOME INSTRUMENTS

The most popular model for the pricing of equity options is the Black-Scholes option pricing model. As we explained in Chapter 10, this model is also used to value the equity component of a convertible bond.

By imposing certain assumptions (to be discussed later) and using arbitrage arguments, the Black-Scholes option pricing model computes the fair (or theoretical) price of a European call option on a non-dividend-paying stock. The formula is:

$$C = SN(d_1) - Xe^{-rt}N(d_2) \qquad (1)$$

where

$$d_1 = \frac{\ln(S/X) + (r + 0.5\sigma^2)t}{\sigma\sqrt{t}} \qquad (2)$$

$$d_2 = d_1 - s\sqrt{t} \qquad (3)$$

$\ln$ = natural logarithm
C = call option price
S = current stock price
X = strike price
r = short-term risk-free interest rate
e = 2.718281828 (natural antilog of 1)
t = time remaining to the expiration date (measured as a fraction of a year)
σ = standard deviation of the stock price
$N(.)$ = the cumulative probability density. The value for $N(.)$ is obtained from a normal distribution function.

Notice that the factors that we said in Chapter 5 influence the price of an option are included in the formula. However, the sixth factor, cash payments (coupon interest in the case of a bond), is not included because the model is for a non-dividend-paying stock. The standard deviation of the stock price must be estimated.

The option price derived from the Black-Scholes option pricing model is "fair" in the sense that if any other price existed, it would be possible to earn riskless arbitrage profits by taking an offsetting position in the underlying stock. That is, if the price of the call option in the market is higher than that derived from the Black-Scholes option pricing model, an investor could sell the call option and buy a certain number of shares in the underlying stock. If the reverse is true, that is, the market price of the call option is less than the "fair" price derived from the model, the investor could buy the call option and sell short a certain number of shares in the underlying stock. This process of hedging by taking a position in the underlying stock allows the investor to lock in the riskless arbitrage profit. The number of shares necessary to hedge the position changes as the factors that affect the option price change, so the hedged position must be changed constantly.

Computing the Price of a Call Option on a Zero-Coupon Bond

Because the basic Black-Scholes formula as given by equation (1) is for a non-cash paying security, let's apply it to a zero-coupon bond with three years to maturity. Assume the following values:

Strike price	= $88.00
Time remaining to expiration	= 2 years
Current price	= $83.96
Expected price volatility	= standard deviation = 10%
Risk-free rate	= 6%

Note the current price is $83.96 which is the present value of the maturity value of $100 discounted at 6% (assuming a flat yield curve).

In terms of the values in the formula:

X = $88.00
t = 2
S = $83.96
σ = 0.10
r = 0.06

Substituting these values into equations (2) and (3):

$$d_1 = \frac{\ln(83.96/88) + [0.06 + 0.5(0.10)^2]2}{0.10\sqrt{2}} = 0.5869$$

$$d_2 = 0.5869 - 0.10\sqrt{2} = 0.4455$$

From a normal distribution table:

$$N(0.5869) = 0.7214$$

and

$$N(0.4455) = 0.6720$$

Then, from equation (1):

$$C = 83.96(0.7214) - 88[e^{-(0.06)(2)}(0.6720)] = \$8.116$$

There is no reason to suspect that this estimated value is unreasonable. However, let's change the problem slightly. Instead of a strike price of $88, let's make the strike price $100.25. Substituting the new strike price into equations (2) and (3):

$$d_1 = \frac{\ln(83.96/100.25) + [0.06 + 0.5(0.10)^2]2}{0.10\sqrt{2}} = -0.3346$$

$$d_2 = -0.3346 - 0.10\sqrt{2} = -0.4761$$

From a normal distribution table:

$$N(-0.3346) = 0.3689$$

and

$$N(-0.4761) = 0.3170$$

Then, from equation (1):

$$C = 83.96(0.3689) - 100.25[e^{-(0.06)(2)}(0.3170)] = \$2.79$$

Thus, the Black-Scholes option pricing model tells us that this call option has a fair value of $2.79. Is there any reason to believe this is unreasonable? Well, consider that this is a call option on a zero-coupon bond that will *never* have a value greater than its maturity value of $100. Consequently, a call option struck at $100.25 must have a value of zero. Yet, the Black-Scholes option pricing model tells us that the value is $2.79! In fact, with a higher volatility assumption, the model would give an even greater value for the call option.

The Limitations of the Model

Why is the Black-Scholes model off by so much in our previous illustration? The answer lies in its underlying assumptions (see Exhibit 1).

Exhibit 1: Limitations in Applying the Black-Scholes Stock-Option Pricing Model to Price Interest Rate Options

Assumptions	Fixed Income Realities
• The price of the underlying has some possibility of rising to any price.	There is a maximum price for a bond and any higher price assumes a negative interest rate is possible.
• Short-term rates remain constant.	Changes in short-term rates cause bond price to change.
• Volatility (variance) of price is constant over the life of the option.	Bond price volatility decreases as the bond approaches maturity.

There are three assumptions underlying the Black-Scholes model that limit its use in pricing options on interest rate instruments. First, the probability distribution for the prices assumed by the Black-Scholes option pricing model permits some probability — no matter how small — that the price can take on any positive value. But in the case of a zero-coupon bond, the price cannot take on a value above $100. In the case of a coupon bond, we know that the price cannot exceed the sum of the coupon payments plus the maturity value. For example, for a 5-year 10% coupon bond with a maturity value of $100, the price cannot be greater than $150 (five coupon payments of $10 plus the maturity value of $100). Thus, unlike stock prices, bond prices have a maximum value. The only way that a bond's price can exceed the maximum value is if negative interest rates are permitted. This is not likely to occur, so any probability distribution for prices assumed by an option pricing model that permits bond prices to be higher than the maximum bond value could generate nonsensical option prices. The Black-Scholes model does allow bond prices to exceed the maximum bond value (or, equivalently, allows negative interest rates). That is one of the reasons why we can get a senseless option price for the 3-month European call option on the 3-year zero-coupon bond.

The second assumption of the Black-Scholes option pricing model is that the short-term interest rate is constant over the life of the option. Yet the price of an interest rate option will change as interest rates change. A change in the short-term interest rate changes the rates along the yield curve. Therefore, to assume that the short-term rate will be constant is inappropriate for interest rate options. The third assumption is that the variance of prices is constant over the life of the option. Recall from Chapter 4 that as a bond moves closer to maturity its price volatility declines. Therefore, the assumption that price variance is constant over the life of the option is inappropriate.

While we have illustrated the problem of using the Black-Scholes model to price interest rate options, we can also show that the binomial option pricing model *based on the price distribution of the underlying bond* suffers from the same problems.

ARBITRAGE-FREE BINOMIAL MODEL

The proper way to value options on interest rate instruments is to use an arbitrage-free model that takes into account the yield curve. These models can incorporate different volatility assumptions along the yield curve. The most popular model employed by dealer firms is the Black-Derman-Toy model.[1]

In Chapter 6, we developed the basic principles for employing this model; we explained how to construct a binomial interest rate tree such that the tree would be arbitrage-free. We used the interest rate tree to value bonds (both

---

[1] Fischer Black, Emanuel Derman, and William Toy, "A One-Factor Model of Interest Rates and Its Application to Treasury Bond Options," *Financial Analysts Journal* (January-February 1990), pp. 24-32.

option-free and bonds with embedded options). But the same tree can be used to value a stand-alone option on a bond.

To illustrate how this is done, let's consider a 2-year European call option on a 6.5% 4-year Treasury bond with a strike price of 100.25. We will assume that the yield for the on-the-run Treasuries is the one in Chapter 6 and that the volatility assumption is 10% per year. Exhibit 9 in Chapter 6 repeated here as Exhibit 2 shows the binomial interest rate tree along with the value of the Treasury bond at each node.

It is a portion of Exhibit 2 that we use to value the call option. Specifically, Exhibit 3 shows the value of our Treasury bond (excluding coupon interest) at each node at the end of year 2. There are three values shown: 97.9249, 100.4184 and 102.5335. Given these three values, the value of a call option struck at 100.25 can be determined at each node. For example, if in two years the price of this Treasury bond is 97.9249, then since the strike price is 100.25, the value of the call option would be zero. In the other two cases, since the price two years from now is greater than the strike price, the value of the call option is the difference between the price of the bond and 100.25.

Exhibit 2: Valuing a Treasury Bond with Four Years to Maturity and a Coupon Rate of 6.5%
(10% Volatility Assumed)

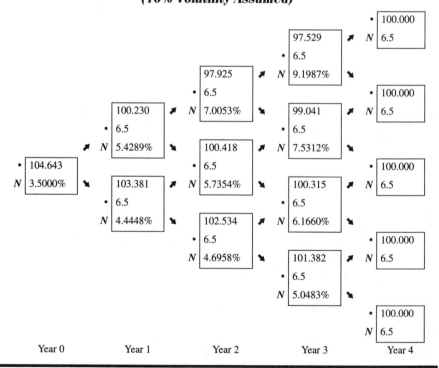

| Year 0 | Year 1 | Year 2 | Year 3 | Year 4 |

Exhibit 3 shows the value of the call option in two years (the option expiration date) for each of the three nodes. Given these values, the binomial interest rate tree is used to find the present value of the call option. The backward induction procedure is used. The discount rates are those from the binomial interest rate tree. For years 0 and 1, this is the second number shown at each node. The first number at each node for year 1 is the average present value found by discounting the call option value at the two nodes to the right using the rate at the node. The value of the option is the first number shown at the root, $0.6056.

The same procedure is used to value a European put option. This is illustrated in Exhibit 4 assuming that the put option has two years to expiration and that the strike price is 100.25. The value of the put option two years from now is shown at each of the three nodes in year 2. The value of this put option is $0.5327.

Put-Call Parity Relationship

There is a relationship between the price of a call option and the price of a put option on the same underlying instrument, with the same strike price and the same expiration date. This relationship is commonly referred to as the *put-call parity relationship*. For European options on coupon bearing bonds, the relationship is:

Put price = Call price + Present value of strike price

+ Present value of coupon payments – Price of underlying bond

To demonstrate that the arbitrage-free binomial model satisfies the put-call parity relationship for European options, let's use the values from our illustration. We just found that:

Call price = 0.6056
Put price = 0.5327

In Chapter 6, we showed that the theoretical price for the 6.5%, 4-year option-free bond is 104.643. Also in Chapter 6, we showed the spot rates for each year. The spot rate for year 2 is 4.2147%. Therefore,

$$\text{Present value of strike price} = \frac{100.25}{(1.042147)^2} = 92.3053$$

The present value of the coupon payments are found by discounting the two coupon payments of 6.5 by the spot rates. As just noted, the spot rate for year 2 is 4.2147%; the spot rate for year 1 is 3.5%. Therefore,

$$\text{Present value of coupon payments} = \frac{6.5}{(1.035)^1} + \frac{6.5}{(1.042147)^2} = 12.265$$

Substituting the values into the right-hand side of the put-call parity relationship for European options we find:

0.6056 + 92.3053 + 12.265 – 104.643 = 0.5329

Exhibit 3: Valuing a European Call Option Using the Arbitrage-Free Binomial Method

Call option:
Expiration: 2 years
Strike price: 100.25
Current price: 104.643
Volatility assumption: 10%

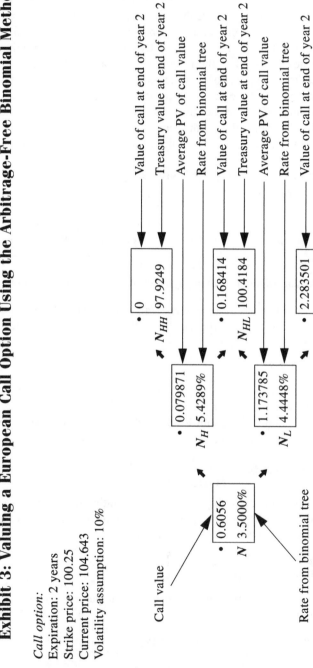

Exhibit 4: Valuing a European Put Option Using the Arbitrage-Free Binomial Method

Put option:
Expiration: 2 years
Strike price: 100.25
Current price: 104.643
Volatility assumption: 10%

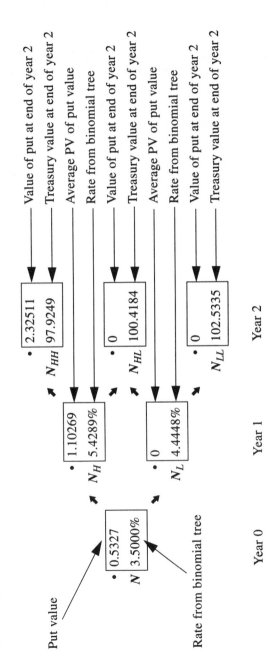

The put value that we found is 0.5327. The discrepancy is due simply to rounding error. Therefore, put-call parity holds.

BLACK MODEL FOR VALUING OPTIONS ON INTEREST RATE FUTURES

The most commonly used model for futures options is the one developed by Black.[2] The model was initially developed for valuing European options on forward contracts. The value of a call and put based on the Black model is:

$$C = e^{-rt} [FN(d_1) - XN(d_2)] \tag{4}$$

$$P = e^{-rt} [XN(-d_2) - FN(-d_1)]$$

where

$$d_1 = \frac{\ln(F/X) + 0.5s^2 t}{s\sqrt{t}} \tag{5}$$

$$d_2 = d_1 - s\sqrt{t} \tag{6}$$

ln = natural logarithm
C = call option price
P = put option price
F = futures price
X = strike price
r = short-term risk-free interest rate
e = 2.718 (natural antilog of 1)
t = time remaining to the expiration date (measured as a fraction of a year)
s = standard deviation of the price
$N(.)$ = the cumulative probability density. The value for $N(.)$ is obtained from a normal distribution function

There are two problems with this model. First, the Black model does not overcome the problems cited earlier for the Black-Scholes model. Failing to recognize the yield curve means that there will not be a consistency between pricing Treasury futures and options on Treasury futures. Second, the Black model was developed for pricing European options on futures contracts. Treasury futures options, however, are American options.

The second problem can be overcome. The Black model was extended by Barone-Adesi and Whaley to American options on futures contracts.[3] This is the

---

[2] Fischer Black, "The Pricing of Commodity Contracts," *Journal of Financial Economics* (March 1976), pp. 161-179.

[3] Giovanni Barone-Adesi and Robert E. Whaley, "Efficient Analytic Approximation of American Option Values," *Journal of Finance* (June 1987), pp. 301-320.

model used by the Chicago Board of Trade to settle the flexible Treasury futures options. However, this model was also developed for equities and is subject to the first problem noted above. Despite its limitations, the Black model is the most popular option pricing model for options on Treasury futures.

SENSITIVITY OF OPTION PRICE TO CHANGE IN FACTORS

In employing options in an investment strategy, a money manager would like to know how sensitive the price of an option is to a change in any one of the factors that affect its price. Here we look at the sensitivity of a call option's price to changes in the price of the underlying bond, the time to expiration, and expected volatility.

The Call Option Price and the Price of the Underlying Bond

Exhibit 4 shows the theoretical price of a call option based on the price of the underlying bond. The horizontal axis is the price of the underlying bond at any point in time. The vertical axis is the call option price. The shape of the curve representing the theoretical price of a call option, given the price of the underlying bond, would be the same regardless of the actual option pricing model used. In particular, the relationship between the price of the underlying bond and the theoretical call option price is convex. Thus, option prices also exhibit convexity.

The line from the origin to the strike price on the horizontal axis in Exhibit 5 is the intrinsic value of the call option when the price of the underlying bond is less than the strike price, since the intrinsic value is zero. The 45-degree line extending from the horizontal axis is the intrinsic value of the call option once the price of the underlying bond exceeds the strike price. The reason is that the intrinsic value of the call option will increase by the same dollar amount as the increase in the price of the underlying bond. For example, if the strike price is $100 and the price of the underlying bond increases from $100 to $101, the intrinsic value will increase by $1. If the price of the bond increases from $101 to $110, the intrinsic value of the option will increase from $1 to $10. Thus, the slope of the line representing the intrinsic value after the strike price is reached is 1.

Since the theoretical call option price is shown by the convex line, the difference between the theoretical call option price and the intrinsic value at any given price for the underlying bond is the time value of the option.

Exhibit 6 shows the theoretical call option price, but with a tangent line drawn at the price of p^*. The tangent line in the figure can be used to estimate what the new option price will be (and therefore what the change in the option price will be) if the price of the underlying bond changes. Because of the convexity of the relationship between the option price and the price of the underlying bond, the tangent line closely approximates the new option price for a small change in the price of the underlying bond. For large changes, however, the tangent line does not provide as good an approximation of the new option price.

Exhibit 5: Theoretical Call Price and Price of Underlying Bond

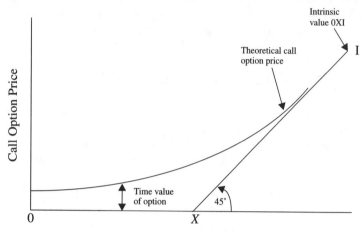

Price of underlying bond

X = Strike price

Exhibit 6: Estimating the Theoretical Option Price with a Tangent Line

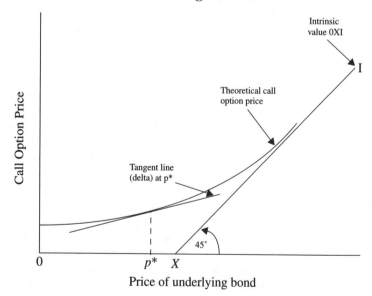

Price of underlying bond

X = Strike price

Exhibit 7: Theoretical Option Price with Three Tangents

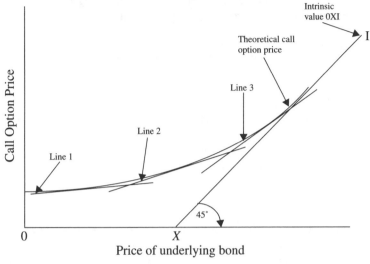

X = Strike Price

The slope of the tangent line shows how the theoretical call option price will change for small changes in the price of the underlying bond. The slope is popularly referred to as the *delta* of the option. Specifically,

$$\text{Delta} = \frac{\text{Change in price of call option}}{\text{Change in price of underlying bond}}$$

For example, a delta of 0.4 means that a $1 change in the price of the underlying bond will change the price of the call option by approximately $0.40.

Exhibit 7 shows the curve of the theoretical call option price with three tangent lines drawn. The steeper the slope of the tangent line, the greater the delta. When an option is deep out of the money (that is, the price of the underlying bond is substantially below the strike price), the tangent line is nearly flat (see Line 1 in Exhibit 7). This means that delta is close to zero. To understand why, consider a call option with a strike price of $100 and two months to expiration. If the price of the underlying bond is $20, its price would not increase by much, if anything, should the price of the underlying bond increase by $1, from $20 to $21.

For a call option that is deep in the money, the delta will be close to one. That is, the call option price will increase almost dollar for dollar with an increase in the price of the underlying bond. In terms of Exhibit 7, the slope of the tangent line approaches the slope of the intrinsic value line after the strike price. As we stated earlier, the slope of that line is 1.

Thus, the delta for a call option varies from zero (for call options deep out of the money) to one (for call options deep in the money). The delta for a call option at the money is approximately 0.5.

The curvature of the convex relationship can also be approximated. This is the rate of change of delta as the price of the underlying bond changes. The measure is commonly referred to a *gamma* and is defined as follows:

$$\text{Gamma} = \frac{\text{Change in delta}}{\text{Change in price of underlying bond}}$$

The Call Option Price and Time to Expiration

All other factors constant, the longer the time to expiration, the greater the option price. Since each day the option moves closer to the expiration date, the time to expiration decreases. The *theta* of an option measures the change in the option price as the time to expiration decreases, or equivalently, it is a measure of *time decay*. Theta is measured as follows:

$$\text{Theta} = \frac{\text{Change in price of option}}{\text{Decrease in time to expiration}}$$

Assuming that the price of the underlying bond does not change (which means that the intrinsic value of the option does not change), theta measures how quickly the time value of the option changes as the option moves towards expiration.

Buyers of options prefer a low theta so that the option price does not decline quickly as it moves toward the expiration date. An option writer benefits from an option that has a high theta.

The Call Option Price and Expected Interest Rate Volatility

All other factors constant, a change in the expected interest rate volatility will change the option price. The *kappa* of an option measures the change in the price of the option for a 1% change in the expected interest rate volatility. That is,

$$\text{Kappa} = \frac{\text{Change in price of option}}{1\% \text{ change in expected interest rate volatility}}$$

Duration of an Option

The duration of an option measures the price sensitivity of the option to interest rate changes. The duration of an option can be shown to be equal to:

$$\begin{array}{c}\text{Duration} \\ \text{of an option}\end{array} = \begin{array}{c}\text{Duration} \\ \text{of underlying instrument}\end{array} \times \text{Delta} \times \frac{\text{Price of underlying instrument}}{\text{Price of option}}$$

As expected, the duration of an option depends on the duration of the underlying bond. It also depends on the price responsiveness of the option to a change in the underlying instrument, as measured by the option's delta. The leverage created by a position in an option comes from the last ratio in the formula. The higher the price of the underlying instrument relative to the price of the option, the greater the leverage (i.e., the more exposure to interest rates for a given dollar investment).

It is the interaction of all three factors that affects the duration of an option. For example, a deep out-of-the-money option offers higher leverage than a deep-in-the-money option, but the delta of the former is less than that of the latter.

Since the delta of a call option is positive, the duration of a call option will be positive. Thus, when interest rates decline, the value of a call option will rise. A put option, however, has a delta that is negative. Thus, duration is negative. Consequently, when interest rates rise, the value of a put option rises.

KEY POINTS

1. The Black-Scholes option pricing model is the most popular model for the pricing of equity options.

2. Three assumptions underlying the Black-Scholes model limit its use in pricing options on fixed income instruments.

3. The Black-Scholes model assumes that (1) the probability distribution for the prices allows for the possibility of negative interest rates, (2) the short-term interest rate is constant over the life of the option, and (3) the variance of prices is constant over the life of the option.

4. The binomial option pricing model based on the price distribution of the underlying fixed income instrument suffers from the same problems as the Black-Scholes model.

5. The arbitrage-free binomial model is the proper model to value options on fixed income instruments.

6. The arbitrage-free binomial model takes into account the yield curve.

7. The most popular model employed by dealer firms is the Black-Derman-Toy model.

8. The most popular model for valuing options on interest rate futures is the Black model.

9. Investors need to know how sensitive an option's value is to changes in the factors that affect the value of an option.

10. The relationship between the theoretical call price and the price of the underlying bond is convex.

11. The delta of an option measures how sensitive the option price is to changes in the price of the underlying bond and the gamma of an option measures the rate of change of delta as the price of the underlying bond changes.

12. The delta for a call option varies from zero (for call options deep out of the money) to one (for call options deep in the money).

13. The theta of an option measures the change in the option price as the time to expiration decreases.

14. The kappa of an option measures the change in the price of the option for a 1% change in expected interest rate volatility.

15. The duration of an option depends on the duration of the underlying bond, the option's delta, and the option's leverage.

Chapter 14

Valuation of Interest Rate Swaps

The objectives of this chapter are to:

1. explain what an interest rate swap is;

2. explain the relationship between an interest rate swap and forward contracts;

3. show the relationship between an interest rate swap and cash market positions;

4. explain how interest rate swap terms are quoted in the market;

5. show how the swap rate is calculated;

6. show how the value of a swap is determined; and,

7. describe the primary determinants of the swap spread.

Participants in financial markets use interest rate swaps to alter the cash flow characteristics of their assets or liabilities, or to capitalize on perceived capital market inefficiencies. We begin with a description of this contract and then explain the general principles for valuing the basic interest rate swap.

INTEREST RATE SWAPS

In an *interest rate swap*, two parties (called *counterparties*) agree to exchange periodic interest payments. The dollar amount of the interest payments exchanged is based on some predetermined dollar principal, which is called the *notional amount*. The dollar amount each counterparty pays to the other is the agreed-upon periodic interest rate times the notional amount. The only dollars that are exchanged between the parties are the interest payments, not the notional amount. In the most common type of swap, one party agrees to pay the other party fixed interest payments at designated dates for the life of the contract. This party is referred to as the *fixed-rate payer*. The other party, who agrees to make interest rate payments that float with some reference rate, is referred to as the *floating-rate payer*.

The reference rates that have been used for the floating rate in an interest rate swap are various money market rates: Treasury bill rate, the London interbank offered rate, commercial paper rate, bankers acceptances rate, certificates of deposit rate, the federal funds rate, and the prime rate. The most common is the London interbank offered rate (LIBOR). LIBOR is the rate at which prime banks offer to pay on Eurodollar deposits available to other prime banks for a given maturity. There is not just one rate but a rate for different maturities. For example, there is a 1-month LIBOR, 3-month LIBOR, and 6-month LIBOR.

To illustrate an interest rate swap, suppose that for the next five years party X agrees to pay party Y 10% per year, while party Y agrees to pay party X 6-month LIBOR (the reference rate). Party X is a fixed-rate payer/floating-rate receiver, while party Y is a floating-rate payer/fixed-rate receiver. Assume that the notional amount is $50 million, and that payments are exchanged every six months for the next five years. This means that every six months, party X (the fixed-rate payer/floating-rate receiver) will pay party Y $2.5 million (10% times $50 million divided by 2). The amount that party Y (the floating-rate payer/fixed-rate receiver) will pay party X will be 6-month LIBOR times $50 million divided by 2. If 6-month LIBOR is 7%, party Y will pay party X $1.75 million (7% times $50 million divided by 2). Note that we divide by two because one-half year's interest is being paid.

Interest rate swaps are over-the-counter instruments. This means that they are not traded on an exchange. An institutional investor wishing to enter into a swap transaction can do so through either a securities firm or a commercial bank that transacts in swaps.[1] These entities can do one of the following. First, they can arrange or broker a swap between two parties that want to enter into an interest rate swap. In this case, the securities firm or commercial bank is acting in a brokerage capacity.

The second way in which a securities firm or commercial bank can get an institutional investor into a swap position is by taking the other side of the swap. This means that the securities firm or the commercial bank is a dealer rather than a broker in the transaction. Acting as a dealer, the securities firm or the commercial bank must hedge its swap position in the same way that it hedges its position in other securities. Also it means that the swap dealer is the counterparty to the transaction.

The risks that the two parties take on when they enter into a swap is that the other party will fail to fulfill its obligations as set forth in the swap agreement. That is, each party faces default risk. The default risk in a swap agreement is called *counterparty risk*. In any agreement between two parties that must perform according to the terms of a contract, counterparty risk is the risk that the other party will default. With futures and exchange-traded options the counterparty risk is the risk that the clearing house established to guarantee performance of the contracts will default. Market participants view this risk as small. In contrast, counterparty risk in a swap can be significant.

Because of counterparty risk, not all securities firms and commercial banks can be swap dealers. Several securities firms have established subsidiaries that are separately capitalized so that they have a high credit rating which permit them to enter into swap transactions as a dealer.

Thus, it is imperative to keep in mind that any party who enters into a swap is subject to counterparty risk.

INTERPRETING A SWAP POSITION

There are two ways that a swap position can be interpreted: (1) a package of forward/futures contracts and (2) a package of cash flows from buying and selling cash market instruments.

Package of Forward Contracts

Consider the hypothetical interest rate swap used earlier to illustrate a swap. Let's look at party X's position. Party X has agreed to pay 10% and receive 6-month LIBOR. More specifically, assuming a $50 million notional amount, X has agreed to buy a commodity called "6-month LIBOR" for $2.5 million. This is effectively a 6-month forward contract where X agrees to pay $2.5 million in exchange for

---

[1] Don't get confused here about the role of commercial banks. A bank can use a swap in its asset/liability management. Or, a bank can transact (buy and sell) swaps to clients to generate fee income. It is in the latter sense that we are discussing the role of a commercial bank in the swap market here.

delivery of 6-month LIBOR. The fixed-rate payer is effectively long a 6-month forward contract on 6-month LIBOR. The floating-rate payer is effectively short a 6-month forward contract on 6-month LIBOR. There is therefore an implicit forward contract corresponding to each exchange date.

Consequently, interest rate swaps can be viewed as a package of more basic interest rate derivative instruments — forwards. The pricing of an interest rate swap will then depend on the price of a package of forward contracts with the same settlement dates in which the underlying for the forward contract is the same reference rate.

While an interest rate swap may be nothing more than a package of forward contracts, it is not a redundant contract for several reasons. First, maturities for forward or futures contracts do not extend out as far as those of an interest rate swap; an interest rate swap with a term of 15 years or longer can be obtained. Second, an interest rate swap is a more transactionally efficient instrument. By this we mean that in one transaction an entity can effectively establish a payoff equivalent to a package of forward contracts. The forward contracts would each have to be negotiated separately. Third, the interest rate swap market has grown in liquidity since its establishment in 1981; interest rate swaps now provide more liquidity than forward contracts, particularly long-dated (i.e., long-term) forward contracts.

Package of Cash Market Instruments

To understand why a swap can also be interpreted as a package of cash market instruments, consider an investor who enters into the transaction below:

- buy $50 million par of a 5-year floating-rate bond that pays 6-month LIBOR every six months

- finance the purchase by borrowing $50 million for five years at a 10% annual interest rate paid every six months.

The cash flows for this transaction are set forth in Exhibit 1. The second column of the exhibit shows the cash flows from purchasing the 5-year floating-rate bond. There is a $50 million cash outlay and then ten cash inflows. The amount of the cash inflows is uncertain because they depend on future LIBOR. The next column shows the cash flows from borrowing $50 million on a fixed-rate basis. The last column shows the net cash flows from the entire transaction. As the last column indicates, there is no initial cash flow (no cash inflow or cash outlay). In all ten 6-month periods, the net position results in a cash inflow of LIBOR and a cash outlay of $2.5 million. This net position, however, is identical to the position of a fixed-rate payer/floating-rate receiver.

It can be seen from the net cash flow in Exhibit 1 that a fixed-rate payer has a cash market position that is equivalent to a long position in a floating-rate bond and a short position in a fixed-rate bond — the short position being the equivalent of borrowing by issuing a fixed-rate bond.

Exhibit 1: Cash Flows for the Purchase of a 5-Year Floating-Rate Bond Financed by Borrowing on a Fixed-Rate Basis

Transaction:
- Purchase for $50 million a 5-year floating-rate bond:
  floating rate = LIBOR, semiannual pay
- Borrow $50 million for five years:
  fixed rate = 10%, semiannual payments

Six Month Period	Cash Flow (In Millions of Dollars) From:		
	Floating-rate Bond*	Borrowing Cost	Net
0	−$50	+$50.0	$0
1	+ (LIBOR$_1$/2) × 50	−2.5	+ (LIBOR$_1$/2) × 50 − 2.5
2	+ (LIBOR$_2$/2) × 50	−2.5	+ (LIBOR$_2$/2) × 50 − 2.5
3	+ (LIBOR$_3$/2) × 50	−2.5	+ (LIBOR$_3$/2) × 50 − 2.5
4	+ (LIBOR$_4$/2) × 50	−2.5	+ (LIBOR$_4$/2) × 50 − 2.5
5	+ (LIBOR$_5$/2) × 50	−2.5	+ (LIBOR$_5$/2) × 50 − 2.5
6	+ (LIBOR$_6$/2) × 50	−2.5	+ (LIBOR$_6$/2) × 50 − 2.5
7	+ (LIBOR$_7$/2) × 50	−2.5	+ (LIBOR$_7$/2) × 50 − 2.5
8	+ (LIBOR$_8$/2) × 50	−2.5	+ (LIBOR$_8$/2) × 50 − 2.5
9	+ (LIBOR$_9$/2) × 50	−2.5	+ (LIBOR$_9$/2) × 50 − 2.5
10	+ (LIBOR$_{10}$/2) × 50 + 50	−52.5	+ (LIBOR$_{10}$/2) × 50 − 2.5

* The subscript for LIBOR indicates the 6-month LIBOR as per the terms of the floating-rate bond at time t.

What about the position of a floating-rate payer? It can be easily demonstrated that the position of a floating-rate payer is equivalent to purchasing a fixed-rate bond and financing that purchase at a floating-rate, where the floating rate is the reference rate for the swap. That is, the position of a floating-rate payer is equivalent to a long position in a fixed-rate bond and a short position in a floating-rate bond.

TERMINOLOGY, CONVENTIONS, AND MARKET QUOTES

Here we review some of the terminology used in the swaps market and explain how swaps are quoted. The date that the counterparties commit to the swap is called the *trade date*. The date that the swap begins accruing interest is called the *effective date*, while the date that the swap stops accruing interest is called the *maturity date*. How often the floating-rate is changed is called the *reset frequency*.

While our illustrations assume that the timing of the cash flows for both the fixed-rate payer and floating-rate payer will be the same, this is rarely the case in a swap. An agreement may call for the fixed-rate payer to make payments annually but the floating-rate payer to make payments more frequently (semiannually or quarterly). Also, the way in which interest accrues on each leg of the transaction differs, because there are several day count conventions in the fixed-income markets.

Exhibit 2: Describing the Counterparties to a Swap

Fixed-rate Payer	Floating-rate Payer
• pays fixed rate in the swap	• pays floating rate in the swap
• receives floating in the swap	• receives fixed in the swap
• is short the bond market	• is long the bond market
• has bought a swap	• has sold a swap
• is long a swap	• is short a swap
• has established the price sensitivities of a longer-term liability and a floating-rate asset	• has established the price sensitivities of a longer-term asset and a floating-rate liability

Source: Robert F. Kopprasch, John Macfarlane, Daniel R. Ross, and Janet Showers, "The Interest Rate Swap Market: Yield Mathematics, Terminology, and Conventions," Chapter 58 in Frank J. Fabozzi and Irving M. Pollack (eds.), *The Handbook of Fixed Income Securities* (Homewood, IL: Dow Jones-Irwin, 1987).

The terminology used to describe the position of a party in the swap markets combines cash market jargon and futures market jargon, given that a swap position can be interpreted as a position in a package of cash market instruments or a package of futures/forward positions. As we have said, the counterparty to an interest rate swap is either a fixed-rate payer or floating-rate payer. Exhibit 2 describes these positions in several ways.

The first two expressions in Exhibit 2 to describe the position of a fixed-rate payer and floating-rate payer are self-explanatory. To understand why the fixed-rate payer is viewed as short the bond market, and the floating-rate payer is viewed as long the bond market, consider what happens when interest rates change. Those who borrow on a fixed-rate basis will benefit if interest rates rise because they have locked in a lower interest rate. But those who have a short bond position will also benefit if interest rates rise. Thus, a fixed-rate payer can be said to be short the bond market. A floating-rate payer benefits if interest rates fall. A long position in a bond also benefits if interest rates fall, so terminology describing a floating-rate payer as long the bond market is not surprising. From our discussion of the interpretation of a swap as a package of cash market instruments, describing a swap in terms of the sensitivities of long and short cash positions follows naturally.

The convention that has evolved for quoting swaps levels is that a swap dealer sets the floating rate equal to the reference rate and then quotes the fixed rate that will apply. To illustrate this convention, consider the following 10-year swap terms available from a dealer:

- *Floating-rate payer:*
    Pay floating rate of 3-month LIBOR quarterly.
    Receive fixed rate of 8.75% semiannually.
- *Fixed-rate payer:*
    Pay fixed rate of 8.85% semiannually
    Receive floating rate of 3-month LIBOR quarterly.

The offer price that the dealer would quote the fixed-rate payer would be to pay 8.85% and receive LIBOR "flat." (The word flat means with no spread.) The bid price that the dealer would quote the floating-rate payer would be to pay LIBOR flat and receive 8.75%. The bid-offer spread is 10 basis points.

The fixed rate is some spread above the Treasury yield curve with the same term to maturity as the swap. In our illustration, suppose that the 10-year Treasury yield is 8.35%. Then the offer price that the dealer would quote to the fixed-rate payer is the 10-year Treasury rate plus 50 basis points versus receiving LIBOR flat. For the floating-rate payer, the bid price quoted would be LIBOR flat versus the 10-year Treasury rate plus 40 basis points. The dealer would quote such a swap as 40-50, meaning that the dealer is willing to enter into a swap to receive LIBOR and pay a fixed rate equal to the 10-year Treasury rate plus 40 basis points; and it would be willing to enter into a swap to pay LIBOR and receive a fixed rate equal to the 10-year Treasury rate plus 50 basis points. The difference between the Treasury rate paid and received is the bid-offer spread.

CALCULATION OF THE SWAP RATE

At the initiation of an interest rate swap, the counterparties are agreeing to exchange future interest rate payments and no upfront payments by either party are made. This means that the swap terms must be such that the present value of the cash flows for the payments to be made by the counterparties must be equal. This is equivalent to saying that the present value of the cash flows of payments to be received by the counterparties must be equal. The equivalence of the cash flows is the principle in calculating the swap rate.

For the fixed-rate side, once a swap rate is determined, the payments of the fixed-rate payer are known. However, the floating-rate payments are not known because they depend on the value of the reference rate at the reset dates. For a LIBOR-based swap, the Eurodollar CD futures contract (discussed in Chapter 12) can be used to establish the forward (or future) rate for 3-month LIBOR. Given the cash flows based on the forward rate for 3-month LIBOR, the swap rate is the interest rate that will make the present value of the payments on the fixed-rate side equal to the payments on the floating-rate side.

The next question is: what interest rate should be used to discount the payments? As explained in Chapter 5, the appropriate rate to discount any cash flow is the theoretical spot rate. Each cash flow should be discounted at a unique discount rate. Where do we get the theoretical spot rates? Recall from Chapter 5 that spot rates can be obtained from forward rates. It is the same 3-month LIBOR forward rates derived from the Eurodollar CD futures contract that can be used to obtain the theoretical spot rates.

Let's illustrate the procedure with an example. Consider the following hypothetical swap:

Swap term: Three years
Notional amount: $100 million
Fixed-rate receiver: Actual/360 day count basis and quarterly payments
Floating-rate receiver: 3-month LIBOR, actual/360 day count basis, quarterly payments, and quarterly reset

Our worktable for calculating the swap rate is Exhibit 3. The first column just lists the quarterly periods. There is a Eurodollar CD futures contract with a settlement date that corresponds to each period. The second column shows the number of days in the period for each Eurodollar CD futures contract. The third column shows the futures price for each contract. We know from Chapter 12 that the future 3-month LIBOR rate is found by subtracting the futures price from 100. This is shown in Column (4) representing the forward rate.[2]

It is from the forward rates that the discount rates that will be used to discount the cash flows (payments) will be calculated. The discount factor (i.e., the present value of $1 based on the spot rate) is found as follows:[3]

$$\frac{\text{Discount factor in the previous period}}{[1 + (\text{forward rate in previous period} \times \text{number of days in period}/360)]}$$

The discount factors are shown in Column (5).

The floating cash flow is found by multiplying the forward rate and the notional amount. However, the forward rate must be adjusted for the number of days in the payment period. The formula to do so is:

$$\frac{\text{Forward rate in previous period} \times \text{number of days in period}}{360} \times \text{notional amount}$$

These values represent the payments by the floating-rate payer and the receipts of the fixed-rate receiver. The values are shown in Column (6). The present value of each of these cash flows is shown in Column (7) using the discount factor shown in Column (5). The present value of the floating cash flow is $14,053,077.

In order for no other payments to be exchanged between the counterparties other than the interest payments, the swap rate must be set such that the present value of the fixed cash flows is equal to the same value, $14,053,077. This can only be found by trial and error. For our hypothetical swap, when a swap rate of 4.987551% is tried, the cash flows are as shown in Column (8). In determining the fixed cash flows, each cash flow must be adjusted for the day count, as follows:

$$\frac{\text{Assumed swap rate} \times \text{number of days in period}}{360} \times \text{notional amount}$$

---

[2] In practice, the forward rate is adjusted for the convexity of the Eurodollar CD futures contract.

[3] The formulas presented below are taken from Chapter 6 of Ravi E. Dattatreya, Raj E.S. Venkatesh, and Vijaya E. Venkatesh, *Interest Rate & Currency Swaps* (Chicago: Probus Publishing, 1994).

Exhibit 3: Determining the Swap Rate

Goal: Determination of swap rate

Three-year swap, notional amount $100 million

Fixed-rate receiver: Actual/360 day count basis, quarterly payments

Floating-rate receiver: 3-month LIBOR, actual/360 day count basis, quarterly payments and reset

Swap rate is the rate that will produce fixed cash flows whose present value will equal the present value of the floating cash flows: in this illustration the swap rate is equal to 4.987551%.

(1)	(2)	(3)	(4)	(5)	(6)	(7)	(8)	(9)
Period	Day Count	Futures Price	Forward Rate	Discount Factor	Floating Cash Flow	PV of Floating CF	Fixed Cash Flow	PV of Fixed CF
1	91		4.05	1.00000				
2	90	95.85	4.15	0.98998	1,012,500	1,002,351	1,246,888	1,234,390
3	91	95.45	4.55	0.97970	1,049,028	1,027,732	1,260,742	1,235,148
4	91	95.28	4.72	0.96856	1,150,139	1,113,978	1,260,742	1,221,104
5	91	95.10	4.90	0.95714	1,193,111	1,141,974	1,260,742	1,206,706
6	94	94.97	5.03	0.94505	1,279,444	1,209,137	1,302,305	1,230,741
7	91	94.85	5.15	0.93318	1,271,472	1,186,516	1,260,742	1,176,503
8	90	94.75	5.25	0.92132	1,287,500	1,186,201	1,246,888	1,148,784
9	91	94.60	5.40	0.90925	1,327,083	1,206,657	1,260,742	1,146,335
10	91	94.50	5.50	0.89701	1,365,000	1,224,419	1,260,742	1,130,899
11	91	94.35	5.65	0.88471	1,390,278	1,229,993	1,260,742	1,115,392
12	93	94.24	5.76	0.87198	1,459,583	1,272,732	1,288,451	1,123,507
13	91	94.10	5.90	0.85947	1,456,000	1,251,387	1,260,742	1,083,569
Total						14,053,077		14,053,078

Explanation of columns:

Column (2): The day count refers to the number of days in the period.

Column (3): The Eurodollar CD futures price.

Column (4): Forward Rate = Futures Rate. The forward rate for LIBOR found from the futures price of the Eurodollar CD futures contract as follows: 100.00 − Futures price

Column (5): The discount factor is found as follows:

$$\frac{\text{Discount factor in the previous period}}{[1 + (\text{forward rate in previous period} \times \text{number of days in period}/360)]}$$

number of days in period is found in Column (2).

Column (6): The floating cash flow is found by multiplying the forward rate and the notional amount, adjusted for the number of days in the payment period. That is:

$$\frac{\text{Forward rate previous period} \times \text{number of days in period}}{360} \times \text{notional amount}$$

Column (7): Present value of floating cash flow, found as follows: Column (5) × Column (6) .

Column (8): This column is found by trial and error, based on a guess of the swap rate. In determining the fixed cash flow, the cash flow must be adjusted for the day count, as follows:

$$\frac{\text{Assumed swap rate} \times \text{number of days in period}}{360} \times \text{notional amount}$$

Column (9): Present value of fixed cash flow, found as follows: Column (5) × Column (7) .

Using the discount factors in Column (5), the present value of the fixed cash flows is equal to $14,053,078. Therefore, the swap rate is 4.987551%, since it is this rate that equates the present value of the floating and fixed cash flows.

Given the swap rate, the swap spread can be determined. For example, since this is a 3-year swap, the 3-year on-the-run Treasury rate would be used as the benchmark. If the yield on that issue is 4.587551%, the swap spread is then 40 basis points.

The calculation of the swap rate for all swaps follows the same principle: equating the present value of the cash flows.[4] Later in this section the economic determinants of the swap spread are discussed.

VALUING AN INTEREST RATE SWAP

Once the swap transaction is completed, changes in market interest rates will change the cash flows of the floating-rate side of the swap. The value of an interest rate swap is the difference between the present value of the cash flows of the two sides of the swap. The 3-month LIBOR forward rates from the current Eurodollar CD futures contracts are used to (1) calculate the floating cash flows and (2) determine the discount factors at which to calculate the present value of the cash flows.

To illustrate this, consider the 3-year swap used to demonstrate how to calculate the swap rate. Suppose that one year later, interest rates change such that Column (3) in Exhibit 4 shows the prevailing futures price for the Eurodollar CD futures contract. Columns (4) and (5) then show the corresponding forward rates and discount factors. Column (6) shows the floating cash flows based on the forward rates in Column (4) and Column (7) shows the present value of the floating cash flows using the discount factors in Column (5). The present value of the floating cash flows is $11,482,103. This means that the floating-rate payer has agreed to make payments with a value of $11,482,103 and the fixed-rate payer will receive cash flows with this value.

Now let's look at the fixed-rate side. The swap rate is fixed over the life of the swap. The fixed cash flows are given in Column (8) and the present values based on the discount factors in Column (5) are shown in Column (9). The present value of the fixed cash flows is $9,498,358. This means that the fixed-rate payer has agreed to make payments with a value of $9,498,358 and the floating-rate payer will be receive cash flows with this value.

From the fixed-rate payer's perspective, floating cash flows with a present value of $11,482,103 are going to be received and fixed cash flows with a present value of $9,498,358 are going to be paid out. The difference between these two present values, $1,983,745, is the value of the swap. It is a positive value for the fixed-rate payer because the present value of what is to be received exceeds the present value of what is to be paid out.

---

[4] For a more detailed explanation of how this is done with more complicated swaps, see Chapter 6 of Dattatreya, Venkatesh, and Venkatesh, *Interest Rate & Currency Swaps*.

Exhibit 4: Determining the Value of a Swap

Goal: Determination of swap value after one year

Two-year swap

Notional amount: $100 million

Fixed-rate receiver: Swap rate 4.987551%, actual/360 day count basis, quarterly payments

Floating-rate receiver: 3-month LIBOR, actual/360 day count basis, quarterly payments and reset

(1) Period	(2) Day Count	(3) Futures Price	(4) Forward Rate	(5) Discount Factor	(6) Floating Cash Flow	(7) PV of Floating CF	(8) Fixed Cash Flow	(9) PV of Fixed CF
1	91		5.25	1.000000				
2	94	94.27	5.73	0.986477	1,370,833	1,352,296	1,302,305	1,284,694
3	91	94.22	5.78	0.972393	1,448,417	1,408,430	1,260,742	1,225,936
4	90	94.00	6.00	0.958542	1,445,000	1,385,093	1,246,888	1,195,194
5	91	93.85	6.15	0.944221	1,516,667	1,432,069	1,260,742	1,190,419
6	91	93.75	6.25	0.929767	1,554,583	1,445,400	1,260,742	1,172,197
7	91	93.54	6.46	0.915307	1,579,861	1,446,057	1,260,742	1,153,965
8	93	93.25	6.75	0.900282	1,668,833	1,502,421	1,288,451	1,159,969
9	91	93.15	6.85	0.885179	1,706,250	1,510,337	1,260,742	1,115,982
Total						11,482,103		9,498,358

PV of floating cash flow $11,482,103

PV of fixed cash flow $9,498,358

Value of swap $1,983,745

From the floating-rate payer's perspective, floating cash flows with a present value of $11,482,103 are going to be paid out and fixed cash flows with a present value of $9,498,358 are going to be received. Once again, the difference between these two present values, $1,983,745, is the value of the swap. It is a negative value for the floating-rate payer because the present value of what is to be received is less than the present value of what is to be paid out.

The same valuation principle applies to more complicated swaps. For example, there are swaps whose notional amount changes in a predetermined way over the life of the swap. These include amortizing swaps, accreting swaps, and roller coaster swaps. Once the cash flows are specified, the present value is calculated as described above.

DURATION OF AN INTEREST RATE SWAP

As with any fixed-income contract, the value of a swap will change as interest rates change. Dollar duration is a measure of the interest rate sensitivity of a fixed-income contract. From the perspective of the party who pays floating and receives fixed, the interest rate swap position can be viewed as follows:

Long a fixed-rate bond + Short a floating-rate bond

This means that the dollar duration of an interest rate swap from the perspective of a floating-rate payer is simply the difference between the dollar duration of the two bond positions that make up the swap. That is,

Dollar duration of a swap = Dollar duration of a fixed-rate bond
− Dollar duration of a floating-rate bond

Most of the dollar price sensitivity of a swap due to interest rate changes will result from the dollar duration of the fixed-rate bond because the dollar duration of the floating-rate bond will be small. The closer the swap is to the date that the coupon rate is to be reset, the smaller the dollar duration of a floating-rate bond.

PRIMARY DETERMINANTS OF SWAP SPREADS

Earlier we provided two interpretations of a swap: (1) a package of futures/forward contracts and (2) a package of cash market instruments. The swap spread is determined by the same factors that influence the spread over Treasuries on financial instruments (futures/forward contracts or cash) that produce a similar return or funding profile. As we explain below, the key determinant of the swap spread for swaps with maturities of five years or less is the cost of hedging in the Eurodollar CD futures market. For longer maturity swaps, the key determinant of the swap spread is the credit spreads in the corporate bond market.

Given that a swap is a package of futures/forward contracts, the swap spread can be determined by looking for futures/forward contracts with the same risk/return profile. A Eurodollar CD futures contract is a swap where a fixed dollar payment (i.e., the futures price) is exchanged for 3-month LIBOR. There are available Eurodollar CD futures contracts that have maturities every three months for five years. A market participant can create a synthetic fixed-rate security or a fixed-rate funding vehicle of up to five years by taking a position in a strip of Eurodollar CD futures contracts (i.e., a position in every 3-month Eurodollar CD up to the desired maturity date).

For example, consider a financial institution that has fixed-rate assets and floating-rate liabilities. Both the assets and liabilities have a maturity of three years. The interest rate on the liabilities resets every three months based on 3-month LIBOR. This financial institution can hedge this mismatched asset/liability position by buying a 3-year strip of Eurodollar CD futures contracts. By doing so, the financial institution is receiving LIBOR over the 3-year period and paying a fixed dollar amount (i.e., the futures price). The financial institution is now hedged because the assets are fixed rate, and the strip of long Eurodollar CDs futures synthetically creates a fixed-rate funding arrangement. From the fixed dollar amount over the three years, an effective fixed rate that the financial institution pays can be calculated. Alternatively, the financial institution can synthetically create a fixed-rate funding arrangement by entering into a 3-year swap in which it pays fixed and receives 3-month LIBOR. The financial institution will use the vehicle that gives the lowest cost of hedging the mismatched position. This will drive the synthetic fixed rate in the swap market to that available by hedging in the Eurodollar CD futures market.

For swaps with maturities longer than five years, the spread is determined primarily by the credit spreads in the corporate bond market. Since a swap can be interpreted as a package of long and short positions in a fixed-rate bond and a floating-rate bond, it is the credit spreads in those two market sectors that will be the key determinant of the swap spread. Boundary conditions for swap spreads based on prices for fixed-rate and floating-rate corporate bonds can be determined.[5] Several technical factors, such as the relative supply of fixed-rate and floating-rate corporate bonds and the cost to dealers of hedging their inventory position of swaps, influence where between the boundaries the actual swap spread will be.[6]

---

[5] These boundary conditions are derived in the appendix to Ellen Evans and Gioia Parente Bales, "What Drives Interest Rate Swap Spreads?" Chapter 13 in Carl R. Beidleman (ed.), *Interest Rate Swaps* (Homewood, IL: Richard D. Irwin, 1991).

[6] For a discussion of these other factors, see Evans and Bales, "What Drives Interest Rate Swap Spreads," pp. 293-301.

KEY POINTS

1. *An interest rate swap is an agreement specifying that the parties exchange interest payments at designated times.*

2. *In a typical swap, one party will make fixed-rate payments, and the other will make floating-rate payments, with payments based on the notional amount.*

3. *A swap position can be interpreted as either a package of forward/futures contracts or a package of cash flows from buying and selling cash market instruments.*

4. *The swap rate is determined by finding the rate that will make the present value of the cash flows of both sides of the swap equal.*

5. *In a LIBOR-based swap, the cash flows for the floating-rate side are determined from the Eurodollar CD futures contract.*

6. *The discount rates used to calculate the present value of the cash flows in a swap are the spot rates.*

7. *The value of an existing swap is equal to the difference in the present value of the two payments.*

8. *The dollar duration of a swap from the perspective of a floating-rate payer is just the difference between the dollar duration of the fixed-rate bond and dollar duration of the floating-rate bond that comprise the swap.*

9. *Most of the interest rate sensitivity of a swap will result from the duration of the fixed-rate bond since the duration of the floating-rate bond will be small.*

10. *The swap spread is determined by the same factors that influence the spread over Treasuries on financial instruments that produce a similar return or funding profile.*

11. *The key determinant of the swap spread for swaps with maturities of five years or less is the cost of hedging in the Eurodollar CD futures market.*

12. *For longer maturity swaps, the key determinant of the swap spread is the credit spreads in the corporate bond market.*

Chapter 15

Valuation of Interest Rate Caps and Floors

The objectives of this chapter are to:

1. what an interest cap is;

2. what an interest rate floor is;

3. the risk and return features of caps and floors;

4. how to value a cap and a floor using the binomial model; and,

5. why a cap and a floor are packages of options.

In this chapter, we look at our last derivative instruments — interest rate caps and floors. These instruments are referred to as *interest rate agreements*. We will see that caps and floors are nothing more than packages of options. Consequently, the binomial model employed to value interest rate options can be used to value these derivative instruments.

INTEREST RATE AGREEMENTS

An *interest rate cap* and *floor* are agreements between two parties whereby one party, for an upfront premium, agrees to compensate the other if a designated rate, called the *reference rate*, is different from a predetermined level. The party that benefits if the reference rate differs from a predetermined level is called the buyer and the party that must make the payment is called the seller. The predetermined interest rate level is called the *strike rate*. An interest rate cap specifies that the seller agrees to pay the buyer if the reference rate exceeds the strike rate. An interest rate floor specifies that the seller agrees to pay the buyer if the reference rate is below the strike rate.

The terms of an interest rate agreement include (1) the reference rate; (2) the strike rate that sets the cap or floor; (3) the length of the agreement; (4) the frequency of reset; and, (5) the notional amount. If a cap or a floor are in the money at a reset date, the payment by the seller is typically made in arrears.

The payoff for the cap buyer at a reset date if the value of the reference rate exceeds the cap rate on that date is as follows:

Notional amount × (Value of reference rate – Cap rate)
× (Number of days in settlement period / Number of days in year)

For the floor buyer, the payoff at a reset date is as follows if the value of the reference rate at the reset date is less than the floor rate:

Notional amount × (Floor rate – Value of reference rate)
× (Number of days in settlement period / Number of days in year)

For example, consider the following interest rate cap:

reference rate	= 3-month LIBOR
strike rate	= 8%
term	= 1 year
frequency of reset	= 4 per year (every 3 months)
notional amount	= $10 million

The payoff for the cap buyer is as follows:

If 3-month LIBOR exceeds 8%, then:[1]

$$[\$10 \text{ million} \times (\text{LIBOR} - 8\%)] \times 91/360$$

If 3-month LIBOR is less than or equal to 8%, then the payoff is zero.

Assume the following rates for 3-month LIBOR:

	Date	3-month LIBOR
Day of trade	—	8%
1st reset date	Feb. 1	10%
2nd reset date	May 1	7%
3rd reset date	Aug. 1	11%

On the first reset date, the payoff to the cap buyer is:

$$[\$10 \text{ million} \times (10\% - 8\%)] \times 91/360 = \$50,556$$

The cap buyer receives this payment on May 1. On the second reset date, there is no payment made by the cap seller since 3-month LIBOR is less than 8%. On the third reset date, the payoff to the cap buyer is:

$$[\$10 \text{ million} \times (11\% - 8\%)] \times 91/360 = \$75,833$$

This payment is received on November 1.

Suppose that instead of an interest rate cap, the agreement is an interest rate floor. The payoff for the floor buyer is:

If 3-month LIBOR is less than 8%, then:

$$[\$10 \text{ million} \times (8\% - \text{LIBOR})] \times 91/360$$

If 3-month LIBOR is greater than or equal to 8%, then the payoff is zero.

Assuming the scenarios for 3-month LIBOR are the same as above to illustrate the payoff of a cap, then for the first reset and third reset dates, the floor buyer does not receive a payment from the floor seller. On the second reset date, the floor buyer receives the following from the floor seller on August 1:

$$[\$10 \text{ million} \times (8\% - 7\%)] \times 91/360 = \$25,278$$

Interest rate caps and floors can be combined to create an interest rate collar. This is done by buying an interest rate cap and selling an interest rate floor. Some commercial banks and investment banking firms now write options on interest rate caps and floors for customers. Options on caps are called *captions*; options on floors are called *flotions*.

---

[1] In practice, instead of 91 in the payoff formula, the number of days in the settlement period is used.

RISK AND RETURN CHARACTERISTICS

In an interest rate cap and floor, the buyer pays an upfront fee, which represents the maximum amount that the buyer can lose and the maximum amount that the seller of the agreement can gain. The only party that is required to perform is the seller of the interest rate agreement. The buyer of an interest rate cap benefits if the reference rate rises above the strike rate because the seller must compensate the buyer. The buyer of an interest rate floor benefits if the reference rate falls below the strike rate because the seller must compensate the buyer.

How can we better understand interest rate caps and interest rate floors? In essence these contracts are equivalent to a package of interest rate options. As with a swap, a complex contract can be seen to be a package of basic contracts — options in the case of caps and floors.

The question is what type of package of options is a cap and a floor. It depends on whether the underlying is a rate or a fixed income instrument. If the underlying is considered a fixed income instrument, its value changes inversely with interest rates. Therefore:

> • *for a call option on a fixed income instrument:*
> (1) interest rates increase → fixed income instrument's price decreases
>   → call option value decreases
> and
> (2) interest rates decrease → fixed income instrument's price increases
>   → call option value increases
>
> • *for a put option on a fixed income instrument*
> (1) interest rates increase → fixed income instrument's price decreases
>   → put option value increases
> and
> (2) interest rates decrease → fixed income instrument's price increases
>   → put option value decreases

To summarize:

Value of:	When interest rates increase	decrease
long call	decrease	increase
short call	increase	decrease
long put	increase	decrease
short put	decrease	increase

For a cap and floor, the situation is as follows

Value of:	When interest rates	
	increase	decrease
short cap	decrease	increase
long cap	increase	decrease
short floor	increase	decrease
long floor	decrease	increase

Therefore, buying a cap (long cap) is equivalent to buying a package of puts on a fixed income instrument and buying a floor (long floor) is equivalent to buying a package of calls on a fixed income instrument.

On the other hand, if the underlying is viewed as an option on an interest rate, then buying a cap (long cap) is equivalent to buying a package of calls on interest rates. Buying a floor (long floor) is equivalent to buying a package of puts on interest rates.

Valuing a Cap

The binomial model discussed in previous chapters can be used to value a cap and a floor. Remember that a cap is nothing more than a package of options. More specifically, a cap is a package of European options on interest rates. Thus, to value a cap, the value of each period's cap is found and all the period caps are then summed. The same can be done for a floor.

To illustrate how this is done, we will once again use the binomial tree given in Exhibit 8 of Chapter 6. Consider first a 5.2% 3-year cap with a notional amount of $10 million. The reference rate is the 1-year rate in the binomial tree. The payoff for the cap is annual.

Exhibit 1 shows how this cap is valued by valuing the cap for each year individually. The value for the cap for any year, say year X, is found as follows. First, calculate the payoff in year X at each node as either:

(1) zero if the 1-year rate at the node is less than or equal to 5.2%, or

(2) the notional amount of $10 million times the difference between the 1-year rate at the node and 5.2% if the 1-year rate at the node is greater than 5.2%.

Mathematically, this is expressed as follows:

$$\$10,000,000 \times \text{Maximum } [(\text{Rate at node} - 5.2\%), 0]$$

Then, the backward induction method is used to determine the value of the year X cap.

For example, consider the year 3 cap. At the top node in year 3 of panel C in Exhibit 1, the 1-year rate is 9.1990%. Since the 1-year rate at this node exceeds 5.2%, the payoff in year 3 is:

$$\$10,000,000 \times (9.1990\% - 5.2\%) = \$399,212$$

Exhibit 1: Valuation of a 3-Year 5.2% Cap (10% Volatility Assumed) By Valuing Each Year's Cap

Assumptions
Cap rate: 5.2%
Notional amount: $10,000,000
Payment frequency: Annual

Panel A: The Value of the Year 1 Cap

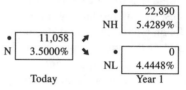

Value of Year 1 cap = $11,058

Panel B: The Value of the Year 2 Cap

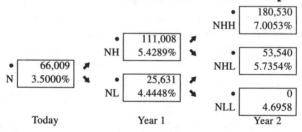

Value of Year 2 cap = $66,009

Panel C: The Value of the Year 3 Cap

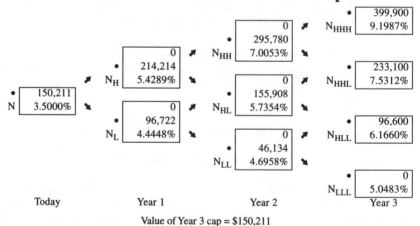

Value of Year 3 cap = $150,211

Summary: Value of 3-Year Cap = $150,211 + $66,009 + $11,058 = $227,278
Note on calculations: Payoff in last box of each exhibit is

$$\$10,000,000 \times \text{Maximum}[(\text{Rate at node} - 5.2\%),0]$$

Exhibit 2: Valuation of a 3-Year 5.2% Cap
(10% Volatility Assumed)

Assumptions
Cap rate: 5.2%
Notional amount: $10,000,000
Payment frequency: Annual

	•	399,900
	N_{HHH}	9.1987%

	180,530 ↗
•	476,310
N_{HH}	7.0053% ↘

•	22,890 ↗
348,113	
N_H	5.4289% ↘

	•	233,100
	N_{HHL}	7.5312%

	53,540 ↗
•	209,448
N_{HL}	5.7354% ↘

•	227,278
N	3.5000% ↘

	0 ↗
•	122,353
N_L	4.4448% ↘

	•	96,600
	N_{HLL}	6.1660%

	0 ↗
•	46,134
N_{LL}	4.6958% ↘

	•	0
	N_{LLL}	5.0483%

Today	Year 1	Year 2	Year 3

Using the backward induction method, the value of the year 3 cap is $150,211. Following the same procedure, the value of the year 2 cap is $66,009, and the value of the year 1 cap is $11,058. The value of the cap is then the sum of the cap for each of the three years. Thus, the value of the cap is $227,278, found by adding $150,211, $66,009, and $11,058.

An alternative procedure is to calculate the value of the cap as follows:

Step 1: For each year, determine the payoff of the cap at each node based on the reference rate at the node. Mathematically, the payoff is:

Notional amount × Maximum [(Rate at node − cap rate), 0]

Step 2: At each node one period prior to the maturity of the cap, the value of the cap at a node is found as follows:

$$\frac{\text{Average of the value at two nodes in next period}}{1 + \text{Rate at node}} + \text{Value found in Step 1}$$

Step 3: Use the backward induction method to determine the value of the cap in year 0.

This is illustrated in Exhibit 2. Notice that the value of the 3-year cap is $227,278, the same value as found earlier.

Exhibit 3: Valuation of a 3-Year 4.8% Floor (10% Volatility Assumed)

Assumptions
Floor rate: 4.8%
Notional amount: $10,000,000
Payment frequency: Annual

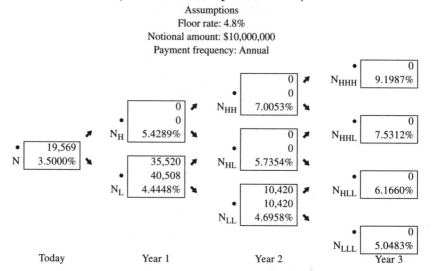

| Today | Year 1 | Year 2 | Year 3 |

VALUING A FLOOR

The value of a floor can be found using the same three-step procedure. However, in Step 1, the payoff is:

Notional amount × Maximum [(Floor rate – Rate at node), 0]

Exhibit 3 illustrates the calculation of a 3-year floor with a strike rate of 4.8% and a $10 million notional amount. The value of the floor is $19,569.

KEY POINTS

1. An interest rate cap is an agreement whereby the seller agrees to pay the buyer if the reference rate exceeds the strike rate.

2. An interest rate floor is an agreement whereby the seller agrees to pay the buyer if the reference rate is below the strike rate.

3. The terms of a cap and floor set forth the reference rate, the strike rate, the length of the agreement, the frequency of reset, and the notional amount.

4. An interest rate collar can be created by buying an interest rate cap and selling an interest rate floor.

5. In an interest rate cap and floor, the buyer pays an upfront fee, which represents the maximum amount that the buyer can lose and the maximum amount that the seller of the agreement can gain.

6. Buying a cap is equivalent to buying a package of puts on a fixed income security and buying a floor is equivalent to buying a package of calls on a fixed income security.

7. If an option is viewed as one in which the underlying is an interest rate, then buying a cap is equivalent to buying a package of calls on interest rates and buying a floor is equivalent to buying a package of puts on interest rates.

8. The binomial model can be used to value a cap or a floor by valuing the cap or floor for each period and then summing these values, or by combining values at each node.

Chapter 16

Estimating Yield Volatility

The objectives of this chapter are to:

1. explain what the standard deviation is and why it is used as a measure of volatility;

2. show how the daily standard deviation is affected by the number of observations and the time period used;

3. explain the different ways in which the daily standard deviation can be annualized;

4. describe the different approaches for forecasting volatility; and,

5. explain what implied volatility is.

An important input required in a valuation model is the expected interest rate volatility. We have seen how in the binomial model this parameter is required to generate the binomial interest rate tree. In the Monte Carlo model we have seen how this parameter is required to generate the interest rate paths. In statistical analysis, the standard deviation is a measure of the variation of a random variable around its mean or expected value. Consequently, market participants use the standard deviation as a measure of volatility. In this chapter we will look at how the standard deviation of interest rates is estimated and methods for forecasting interest rate volatility.

HISTORICAL VOLATILITY

The variance of a random variable using historical data is calculated using the following formula:

$$\text{Variance} = \sum_{t=1}^{T} \frac{(X_t - \bar{X})^2}{T-1} \tag{1}$$

and then

$$\text{Standard deviation} = \sqrt{\text{Variance}}$$

where

X_t = observation t on variable X
$\bar{X}$ = the sample mean for variable X
T = the number of observations in the sample

Our focus is on yield volatility. More specifically, we are interested in the percentage change in daily yields. So, X_t will denote the percentage change in yield from day t and the prior day, $t-1$. If we let y_t denote the yield on day t and y_{t-1} denote the yield on day $t-1$, then X_t which is the natural logarithm of percentage change in yield between two days, can be expressed as:

$$X_t = 100[\text{Ln}(y_t/y_{t-1})]$$

For example, on 10/18/95 the Treasury 30-year zero rate was 6.555% and on 10/19/95 it was 6.593%. Therefore, the natural logarithm of X for 10/19/95 was:

$$X = 100[\text{Ln}(6.593/6.555)] = 0.57804$$

To illustrate how to calculate a daily standard deviation from historical data, consider the data in Exhibit 1 which show the yield on Treasury 30-year zeros from 10/8/95 to 11/12/95 in the third column. From the 26 observations, 25 days of percentage yield changes are calculated in the fourth column. The fifth column shows the square of the deviations of the observations from the mean. The bottom of Exhibit 1 shows the calculation of the daily mean for the 25 observations, the variance, and the standard deviation. The daily standard deviation is 0.6360493%.

The daily standard deviation will vary depending on the 25 days selected. For example, the daily yields from 8/20/95 to 9/24/95 were used to generate 25 daily percentage yield changes. The computed daily standard deviation was 0.8452714%.

Exhibit 1: Calculation of Daily Standard Deviation Based on 25 Daily Observations for 30-Year Treasury Zeros (October 9, 1995 to November 12, 1995)

t	Date	y_t	$X_t = 100[Ln(y_t/y_{t-1})]$	$(X_t - \bar{X})^2$
0	08-Oct-95	6.694		
1	09-Oct-95	6.699	0.06720	0.02599
2	10-Oct-95	6.710	0.16407	0.06660
3	11-Oct-95	6.675	-0.52297	0.18401
4	12-Oct-95	6.555	-1.81411	2.95875
5	15-Oct-95	6.583	0.42625	0.27066
6	16-Oct-95	6.569	-0.21290	0.01413
7	17-Oct-95	6.583	0.21290	0.09419
8	18-Oct-95	6.555	-0.42625	0.11038
9	19-Oct-95	6.593	0.57804	0.45164
10	22-Oct-95	6.620	0.40869	0.25270
11	23-Oct-95	6.568	-0.78860	0.48246
12	24-Oct-95	6.575	0.10652	0.04021
13	25-Oct-95	6.646	1.07406	1.36438
14	26-Oct-95	6.607	-0.58855	0.24457
15	29-Oct-95	6.612	0.07565	0.02878
16	30-Oct-95	6.575	-0.56116	0.21823
17	31-Oct-95	6.552	-0.35042	0.06575
18	01-Nov-95	6.515	-0.56631	0.22307
19	02-Nov-95	6.533	0.27590	0.13684
20	05-Nov-95	6.543	0.15295	0.06099
21	06-Nov-95	6.559	0.24424	0.11441
22	07-Nov-95	6.500	-0.90360	0.65543
23	08-Nov-95	6.546	0.70520	0.63873
24	09-Nov-95	6.589	0.65474	0.56063
25	12-Nov-95	6.539	-0.76173	0.44586
	Total		-2.35020	9.7094094

Sample mean $= \bar{X} = \dfrac{-2.35020}{25} = -0.09401\%$

Variance $= \dfrac{9.7094094}{25 - 1} = 0.4045587$

Std $= \sqrt{0.4045587} = 0.6360493\%$

Exhibit 2: Comparison of Daily and Annual Volatility for a Different Number of Observations (Ending Date November 12, 1995) for Various Treasury Zeros and 3-Month LIBOR

Number of observations	Daily standard deviation (%)	Annualized standard deviation (%)		
		250 days	260 days	365 days
Treasury 30-Year Zero				
683	0.4901505	7.75	7.90	9.36
60	0.6282858	9.93	10.13	12.00
25	0.6360493	10.06	10.26	12.15
10	0.6242041	9.87	10.06	11.93
Treasury 10-Year Zero				
683	0.7497844	11.86	12.09	14.32
60	0.7408469	11.71	11.95	14.15
25	0.7091771	11.21	11.44	13.55
10	0.7458877	11.79	12.03	14.25
Treasury 5-Year Zero				
683	1.0413025	16.46	16.79	19.89
60	0.8267317	13.07	13.33	15.79
25	0.7224093	11.42	11.65	13.80
10	0.8345784	13.20	13.46	15.94
3-Month LIBOR				
683	0.7495924	11.85	12.09	14.32
60	0.2993957	4.73	4.83	5.72
25	0.1465032	2.32	2.36	2.80
10	0.2366242	3.74	3.82	4.52

The selection of the number of observations can have a significant effect on the calculated daily standard deviation. This can be seen in Exhibit 2 which shows the daily standard deviation for the Treasury 30-year zero, Treasury 10-year zero, Treasury 5-year zero, and 3-month LIBOR for 60 days, 25 days, 10 days, and 683 days ending 11/12/95.

Annualizing the Standard Deviation

The daily standard deviation can be annualized by multiplying it by the square root of the number of days in a year.[1] That is,

$$\text{Daily standard deviation} \times \sqrt{\text{Number of days in a year}}$$

---

[1] For any probability distribution, it is important to assess whether the value of a random variable in one period is affected by the value that the random variable took on in a prior period. Casting this in terms of yield changes, it is important to know whether the yield today is affected by the yield in a prior period. The term *serial correlation* is used to describe the correlation between the yield in different periods. Annualizing the daily yield by multiplying the daily standard deviation by the square root of the number of days in a year assumes that serial correlation is not significant.

Exhibit 3: Comparison of Daily Standard Deviation Calculated for Two 25-Day Periods

Dates		Daily standard deviation(%)	Annualized standard deviation(%)		
From	To		250 days	260 days	365 days
Treasury 30-Year Zero					
10/8/95	11/12/95	0.6360493	10.06	10.26	12.15
8/20/95	9/24/95	0.8452714	13.36	13.63	16.15
Treasury 10-Year Zero					
10/8/95	11/12/95	0.7091771	11.21	11.44	13.55
8/20/95	9/24/95	0.9044855	14.30	14.58	17.28
Treasury 5-Year Zero					
10/8/95	11/12/95	0.7224093	11.42	11.65	13.80
8/20/95	9/24/95	0.8145416	12.88	13.13	15.56
3-Month LIBOR					
10/8/95	11/12/95	0.1465032	2.32	2.36	2.80
8/20/95	9/24/95	0.2523040	3.99	4.07	4.82

Market practice varies with respect to the number of days in the year that should be used in the annualizing formula above. Typically, either 250 days, 260 days, or 365 days are used.

Thus, in calculating an annual standard deviation, the investor must decide on:

1. the number of daily observations to use
2. the number of days in the year to use to annualize the daily standard deviation.

Exhibit 2 shows the difference in the annual standard deviation for the daily standard deviation based on the different number of observations and using 250 days, 260 days, and 365 days to annualize. Exhibit 3 compares the 25-day annual standard deviation for two different time periods for the 30-year zero, 10-year zero, 5-year zero, and 3-month LIBOR.

Interpreting the Standard Deviation

What does it mean if the annual standard deviation for the 30-year zero is 12%. It means that if the prevailing yield is 8%, then the annual standard deviation is 96 basis points (12% times 8%).

Assuming that the yield volatility is approximately normally distributed, we can use this probability distribution to construct an interval or range for what the future yield will be. For example, we know that for a normal distribution there is a 68.3% probability that the yield will be between one standard deviation below and above the expected value. The expected value is the prevailing yield. If the annual standard deviation is 96 basis points and prevailing yield is 8%, then there is a 68.3% probability that the yield next year will be between 7.04% (8% minus 96 basis points) and 8.96% (8% plus 96 basis points). For three standard deviations below and above the prevailing yield, there is a 99.7% probability that the yield next year will be in this interval. Using the numbers above, three standard deviations is 288 basis points (3 times 96 basis points). The interval is then 5.12% (8% minus 288 basis points) and 10.88% (8% plus 288 basis points).

The interval or range constructed is called a *confidence interval*. Our first interval of 7.04%-8.96% is a 68.3% confidence interval. Our second interval of 5.12%-10.88% is a 99.7% confidence interval. A confidence interval with any probability can be constructed using a normal probability distribution table.

HISTORICAL VERSUS IMPLIED VOLATILITY

Market participants estimate yield volatility in one of two ways. The first way is by estimating historical yield volatility. This is the method that we have thus far described in this chapter. The resulting volatility is called *historical volatility*. The second way is to estimate yield volatility based on the observed prices of interest rate options or caps. Yield volatility calculated using this approach is called *implied volatility*.

The implied volatility is based on some option pricing model. One of the inputs to any option pricing model in which the underlying is a Treasury security or Treasury futures contract is expected yield volatility. If the observed price of an option is assumed to be the fair price and the option pricing model is assumed to be the model that would generate that fair price, then the implied yield volatility is the yield volatility that when used as an input into the option pricing model would produce the observed option price.

There are several problems with using implied volatility. First, it is assumed the option pricing model is correct. Second, option pricing models typically assume that volatility is constant over the life of the option. Therefore, interpreting an implied volatility becomes difficult.

FORECASTING YIELD VOLATILITY[2]

As can be seen, the yield volatility as measured by the standard deviation can vary based on the time period selected and the number of observations. Now we turn to the issue of forecasting yield volatility. There are several methods. Before

---

[2] For a more extensive and rigorous discussion of forecasting yield volatility, see Frank J. Fabozzi and Wai Lee, "Forecasting Yield Volatility," in Frank J. Fabozzi (ed.) *Perspectives on Interest Rate Risk Management for Money Managers and Traders* (New Hope, PA: Frank J. Fabozzi Associates, 1997).

describing these methods, let's address the question of what mean should be used in the calculation of the forecasted standard deviation.

Suppose at the end of 10/24/95 an investor is interested in a forecast for volatility using the 10 most recent days of trading and updating that forecast at the end of each trading day. What mean value should be used?

The investor can calculate a 10-day moving average of the daily percentage yield change. Exhibit 1 shows the daily percentage change in yield for the Treasury 30-year zero from 10/9/95 to 11/12/95. To calculate a moving average of the daily percentage yield change on 10/24/95, the trader would use the 10 trading days from 10/11/95 to 10/24/95. At the end of 10/25/95, the trader will calculate the 10-day average by using the percentage yield change on 10/25/95 and would exclude the percentage yield change on 10/11/95. That is, the trader will use the 10 trading days from 10/12/95 to 10/25/95.

Exhibit 4 shows the 10-day moving average calculated from 10/24/95 to 11/12/95. Notice the considerable variation over this period. The 10-day moving average ranges from −0.20324% to 0.07902%. For the period from 4/15/93 to 11/12/95, the 10-day moving average ranged from −0.61705% to 0.60298%.

Rather than using a moving average, it is more appropriate to use an expectation of the average. It has been argued that it would be more appropriate to use a mean value of zero.[3] In that case, the variance as given by equation (1) simplifies to:

$$\text{Variance} = \sum_{t=1}^{T} \frac{X_t^2}{T-1} \tag{2}$$

Now let's look at the various methods for forecasting daily volatility.

Exhibit 4: 10-Day Moving Daily Average for Treasury 30-Year Zero

10-Trading Days Ending	Daily Average (%)
24-Oct-95	−0.20324
25-Oct-95	−0.04354
26-Oct-95	0.07902
29-Oct-95	0.04396
30-Oct-95	0.00913
31-Oct-95	−0.04720
1-Nov-95	−0.06121
2-Nov-95	−0.09142
5-Nov-95	−0.11700
6-Nov-95	−0.01371
7-Nov-95	−0.11472
8-Nov-95	−0.15161
9-Nov-95	−0.02728
12-Nov-95	−0.11102

[3] Jacques Longerstacey and Peter Zangari, *Five Questions about RiskMetrics*[TM], JP Morgan Research Publication, 1995.

Exhibit 5: Moving Daily Standard Deviation Based on 10-Days of Observations Assuming a Mean of Zero and Equal Weighting

10-Trading Days Ending	Daily Standard Deviation (%)
24-Oct-95	0.75667
25-Oct-95	0.81874
26-Oct-95	0.58579
29-Oct-95	0.56886
30-Oct-95	0.59461
31-Oct-95	0.60180
1-Nov-95	0.61450
2-Nov-95	0.59072
5-Nov-95	0.57705
6-Nov-95	0.52011
7-Nov-95	0.59998
8-Nov-95	0.53577
9-Nov-95	0.54424
12-Nov-95	0.60003

Equally-Weighted Average Method

The daily standard deviation given by equation (2) assigns an equal weight to all observations. So, if an investor is calculating volatility based on the most recent 10 days of trading, each day is given a weight of 10%. For example, suppose that an investor is interested in the daily volatility of the Treasury 30-year zero yield and decides to use the 10 most recent trading days. Exhibit 5 reports the 10-day volatility for various days using the data in Exhibit 1 and the formula for the variance given by equation (2). For the period 4/15/93 to 11/12/95, the 10-day volatility ranged from 0.16370% to 1.33006%.

Weighted Average Method

To give greater importance to more recent information, observations further in the past should be given less weight. This can be done by revising the variance as given by equation (2) as follows:

$$\text{Variance} = \sum_{t=1}^{T} \frac{W_t X_t^2}{T-1} \tag{3}$$

where W_t is the weight assigned to observation t such that the sum of the weights is equal to 1 (i.e., $\sum W_t = 1$) and the further the observation from today, the lower the weight.

The weights should be assigned so that the forecasted volatility reacts faster to a recent major market movement and declines gradually as we move away from any major market movement. One approach is to use an *exponential moving average*.[4] The formula for the weight W_t in an exponential moving average is:

$$W_t = (1 - \beta)\beta^t$$

where β is a value between 0 and 1. The observations are arrayed so that the closest observation is $t = 1$, the second closest is $t = 2$, etc.

For example, if ß is 0.90, then the weight for the closest observation ($t = 1$) is:

$$W_1 = (1 - 0.90)(0.90)^1 = 0.09$$

For $t = 5$ and β equal to 0.90, the weight is:

$$W_5 = (1 - 0.90)(0.90)^5 = 0.05905.$$

The parameter ß is measuring how quickly the information contained in past observations is "decaying" and hence is referred to as the "decay factor." The smaller the ß, the faster the decay. What decay factor to use depends on how fast the mean value for the random variable X changes over time. A random variable whose mean value changes slowly over time will have a decay factor close to 1. A discussion of how the decay factor should be selected is beyond the scope of this book.[5]

ARCH Method and Variants

A times series characteristic of financial assets suggests that a period of high volatility is followed by a period of high volatility. Furthermore, a period of relative stability in returns appears to be followed by a period that can be characterized in the same way. This suggests that volatility today may depend upon recent prior volatility. This can be modeled and used to forecast volatility.

The statistical model used to estimate this time series property of volatility is called an *auto*regressive *c*onditional *h*eteroscedasticity or ARCH model.[6] The term "conditional" means that the value of the variance depends on or is conditional on the value of the random variable. The term heteroscedasticity means that the variance is not equal for all values of the random variable.

The simplest ARCH model is

$$\sigma_t^2 = a + b(X_{t-1} - \bar{X})^2 \qquad (4)$$

---

[4] This approach is suggested by JP Morgan *RiskMetrics*[TM].

[5] A technical description is provided in *RiskMetrics*[TM]—*Technical Document*, pp. 77-79.

[6] See Robert F. Engle, "Autoregressive Conditional Heteroskedasticity with Estimates of Variance of U.K. Inflation," *Econometrica* 50 (1982), pp. 987-1008.

where

$$\sigma_t^2 \quad = \quad \text{variance on day } t$$

$$X_{t-1} - \overline{X} \quad = \quad \text{deviation from the mean on day } t-1$$

and a and b are parameters.

The parameters a and b must be estimated statistically. The statistical technique of regression analysis is used to estimate the parameters.

Equation (4) states that the estimate of the variance on day t depends on how much the observation on day $t-1$ deviates from the mean. Thus, the variance on day t is "conditional" on the deviation from day $t-1$. The reason for squaring the deviation is that it is the magnitude, not the direction of the deviation, that is important for forecasting volatility.[7] By using the deviation on day $t-1$, recent information (as measured by the deviation) is being considered when forecasting volatility.

The ARCH model can be generalized in two ways. First, information for days prior to $t-1$ can be included into the model by using the squared deviations for several prior days. For example, suppose that four prior days are used. Then equation (4) can be generalized to:

$$\sigma_t^2 = a + b_1(X_{t-1} - \overline{X})^2 + b_2(X_{t-2} - \overline{X})^2$$

$$+ b_3(X_{t-3} - \overline{X})^2 + b_4(X_{t-4} - \overline{X})^2 \tag{5}$$

where a, b_1, b_2, b_3, and b_4 are parameters to be estimated statistically.

A second way to generalize the ARCH model is to include not only squared deviations from prior days as a random variable that the variance is conditional on but also the estimated variance for prior days. For example, the following equation generalizes equation (4) for the case where the variance at time t is conditional on the deviation squared at time $t-1$ and the variance at time $t-1$:

$$\sigma_t^2 = a + b(X_{t-1} - \overline{X})^2 + c\sigma_{t-1}^2 \tag{6}$$

where a, b, and c are parameters to be estimated statistically.

Suppose that the variance at time t is assumed to be conditional on four prior periods of squared deviations and three prior variances, then equation (4) can be generalized as follows:

$$\sigma_t^2 = a + b_1(X_{t-1} - \overline{X})^2 + b_2(X_{t-2} - \overline{X})^2 + b_3(X_{t-3} - \overline{X})^2$$

$$+ b_4(X_{t-4} - \overline{X})^2 + c_1\sigma_{t-1}^2 + c_2\sigma_{t-2}^2 + c_3\sigma_{t-3}^2 \tag{7}$$

where the parameters to be estimated are a, the b_i's ($i=1,2,3,4$), and c_j's ($j=1,2,3$).

---

[7] The variance for the unconditional variance (i.e., a variance that does not depend on the prior day's deviation) is $\sigma_t^2 = a/(1-b)$.

Equations (5), (6), and (7) are referred to as *generalized* ARCH or GARCH models. GARCH models are conventionally denoted as follows: GARCH(i,j) where i indicates the number of prior squared deviations included in the model and j the number of prior variances in the model. Equations (5), (6), and (7) would be denoted GARCH(4,0), GARCH(1,1), and GARCH(4,3), respectively.

There have been further extensions of ARCH models but these extensions are beyond the scope of this chapter.[8]

---

[8] For an overview of these extensions as well as the GARCH models, see Robert F. Engle, "Statistical Models for Financial Volatility," *Financial Analysts Journal* (January-February 1993), pp. 72-78.

KEY POINTS

1. *Variance is a measure of the dispersion of a random variable around its expected value or mean.*

2. *The standard deviation is the square root of the variance and is a commonly used measure of volatility.*

3. *Yield volatility can be estimated from daily yield observations.*

4. *The observation used in the calculation of the standard deviation is the natural logarithm of the percentage change in yield between two days.*

5. *The selection of the number of observations and the time period can have a significant effect on the calculated daily standard deviation.*

6. *A daily standard deviation is annualized by multiplying it by the square root of the number of days in a year.*

7. *Typically, either 250 days, 260 days, or 365 days are used to annualize the daily standard deviation.*

8. *Implied volatility can also be used to estimate yield volatility based on some option pricing model.*

9. *In forecasting volatility, it is more appropriate to use an expectation of zero for the mean value.*

10. *The simplest method for forecasting volatility is weighting all observations equally.*

11. *A forecasted volatility can be obtained by assigning greater weight to more recent observations.*

12. *Autoregressive conditional heteroscedasticity (ARCH) models can be used to capture the times series characteristic of yield volatility in which a period of high volatility is followed by a period of high volatility and a period of relative stability is followed by a period that can be characterized in the same way.*

INDEX